Catching Big Fish
on Light Fly Tackle

Catching Big Fish on Light Fly Tackle

Tom Wendelburg

with
Jeff Mayers

THE UNIVERSITY OF WISCONSIN PRESS

The University of Wisconsin Press
2537 Daniels Street
Madison, Wisconsin 53718

3 Henrietta Street
London WC2E 8LU, England

1   3   5   4   2

Printed in the United States of America

Library of Congress Cataloging-in-Publication Data
Wendelburg, Tom.
Catching big fish on light fly tackle / Tom Wendelburg;
edited by Jeff Mayers.
286 pp.   cm.
Includes index.
ISBN 0-299-17100-0 (cloth)
ISBN 0-299-17104-3 (paper)
1. Fly fishing.   I. Mayers, Jeff, 1959–   II. Title.
SH456 .W372   2001
799.1′24—dc21   00-010618

Contents

Illustrations   vii

Foreword   xi

Acknowledgments   xv

Introduction   3

Light-Tackle Philosophy

Going Light   15
The Mighty Mini-Rod   22
Advanced 2-Weight Tactics for Larger Trout   29

Favorite Fish

Same Trout Again!   37
Small Wets for Big Bass   44
Match the Hatch for Bluegills   50
Skamania: Late Summer's Glory   57

Surface Tactics

Bountiful Spring Creeks   67
Low-Water Camouflage   76
Fly-Fishing the Wind   90
Fishing the Edges Dry   94
Terrestrial Strategies   110

Grasshoppers Only   116
Fish Soft: Hair Bugs and Drys for Top-Water Bass   123

Underwater Tactics

Nymphing under the Hatch   135
Sight Nymphing   141
Short-Line Nymphing   146
Nymphing during the Slack Hours   151
Light-Tackle Streamers   159
Drop the Bomb Accurately for Larger Steelhead and Salmon   169

Favorite Flies

Early-Morning Eye Opener   185
Mayfly Emergers   194
The Duns of Autumn   201
Small Stream Caddis Bonanza   209
More on Caddis Drys—the No-Hackle   225
The Unknown Fly That Turns On Trout   231
Midges: Tiny Dynamite for Trout   237
Wire Nymphs   246
The Deadly Hare's Ear Scud   251
The All-Marabou Leech   255

Previous Publication Credits   263

Topical Index   265

Illustrations

Tom's hairwing dry stone fly, a forerunner of the Stimulator pattern   10

A Rock Creek brown, taken on a dry deer-hair stone fly   17

Playing a trout caught with a tightly looped cast under a branch   20

Playing a large brown on a 5-foot bamboo mini-rod   26

Easing in a big brown with a graphite 2-weight rod   30

A trophy brown caught on a 2-weight rod with a floating fly on
     6X tippet   32

Gently releasing a rainbow back to its home   38

A chameleon wet fly, #8, in the jaw of a hefty bass   48

A bluegill tilting up for a late-season flying ant   55

A Skamania steelhead taken on 6-weight tackle and a #6 chartreuse
     Woolly Bugger   58

A brown released to its 57-degree spring creek environs after a
     spirited fight   70

Releasing a Loch Leven strain of brown, caught on a Wisconsin
     spring creek   73

A brown in very low water fooled with light tackle   78

Light-tackle angling rewarded with a leaping brown   85

Easing in a large rainbow on a wind-rippled Montana spring creek   92

Admiring a 30-inch brown, taken on a 2-weight rod with 6X tippet
     and a small dry fly   96

A leaping brown taken with a good presentation under branches   98

A No-Hackle Hairwing dry fly   101

A 2-weight enthusiast coaxing a Wisconsin trout away from
     the undercut   102

A diagram of possible fly presentations to a streambank edge   103

A diagram of a negative curve cast with S curves   107

A diagram of a positive curve cast opposite the streamflow   108

A 21-inch Wisconsin brown taken with a #22 flying red ant   111
A cricket-beetle pattern   114
A bullethead grasshopper imitation   117
A brown taken with a realistic hopper imitation   120
An airborne largemouth bass with a bullethead long-tailed slider
   hooked in its jaw   124
Favorite bass fly patterns: long bullethead slider, spun-hair soft bug,
   light moth, hair and marabou bluegill, and mouse   128
A big bass taken on ultralight tackle   130
A trout dining on emergent forms of insects deeper in stream,
   despite hatches on the surface   136
A nymph presented downstream   139
A buddy serving as a spotter to help the fly-fisher place an
   accurate cast   144
A brown caught on 6X tippet, a nymph, floating line, and a little
   strike indicator   149
A lunker trout caught while lurking to feed on morsels other than
   aquatic insects   152
A Girdle Bug   153
A brown enticed by an All-Marabou Leech on a 2-weight outfit   160
A king salmon taken on a Lake Michigan tributary with a
   4–5-weight outfit   170
A steelhead taken with a 4-weight rod and 2X tippet   173
Playing a brown during a morning fall of *Tricorythodes*
   mayfly spinners   188
Natural *Tricorythodes* mayfly spinner showing clear wings after
   shedding skins   191
A *Tricorythodes* hen-wing spinner, #24   192
A rainbow fooled by a small *Baetis* emerger pattern   195
A nymph tied with a bit of light wire in the abdomen simulating the
   emergent natural's ascending posture adrift near the surface   196
Two low-winged emergent mayfly duns   199
A leaping trout on a glorious autumn day in the West   202
A #22 gray *Pseudocloeon* dun in the jaw of a big brown   205
An anatomical diagram of an emergence of caddis flies   212
Emergent caddis pupae in the surface region during a hatch   213
A caddis emerger   215
A trout caught while lurking for hatched caddis flies around
   overhanging foliage   221
A trout vaulting for caddises fluttering over the water   223
A no-hackle caddis imitation   226
A split-wing no-hackle caddis imitation   226

A golden stone fly next to its hairwing imitation   233
A brown caught with a midge on 7X tippet, from a snowy bank on
    the Firehole River   243
Small but deadly wire nymphs   247
The Hare's Ear Scud   252
The All-Marabou Leech   256

Foreword

Over the years, I've been fortunate to fish with most of the big names in the world of fly-fishing. Many of these celebrities are good writers and some are good anglers, but only a handful excel with both the pen and the rod. Tom Wendelburg is one of a rare breed that is not only an excellent writer but also a great fisherman. In fact, when it comes to short rods and light tackle, he's the best I've ever seen.

I first ran into Tom back in the early 1970s during a heavy pale morning dun hatch on Armstrong Spring Creek in Montana. That day, I was testing a new version of the Pale Morning Dun no-hackles that Carl Richards and I had developed for our book *Selective Trout*. I felt the pattern might be even more deadly with the addition of a slight tinge of lemon yellow to the duck-quill wing, and it was. The trout were all over it. As long as I made a good presentation, there were no refusals. With all of the excitement, I became oblivious of anything else going on around me. But after awhile, I noticed a guy on the far bank, taking pictures of the action.

We introduced ourselves at long distance—he on the bank with his camera and I in the midst of dozens of rising trout. It has to be a matter of life and death for me to leave a good hatch, so when the activity finally subsided I trudged out of the creek and we shook hands. It didn't take long for me to discover this guy was *really* into the sport. Not a bad photographer either. He had what looked to be a rather inexpensive, beaten up camera, and he used his clip-on sunglasses for polarization. One of the shots he took that day put me on the cover of *Fly Fisherman* magazine.

I've fished with Tom many times since that first encounter, mostly in Michigan and on the spring creeks of Montana, and I'm continually amazed at his streamside abilities, especially with the featherweight equipment he uses. Being a light-tackle proponent myself, I can appreciate his fondness for 5-foot rods and 2-weight lines. One of my favorite rods is a Russ Peak three-piece 5-footer I load with a 3-weight line. I've even used it to catch snook in the backcountry of Florida's Gulf Coast.

If you want to use the short rod effectively, it certainly pays to be a good caster. It takes a little extra effort to get more distance, throw loops that don't tail, and cast curves that are under control. The good news is, you automatically get tighter loops, more accuracy, and a more delicate presentation with the 5- and 6-footers. With the short rod, it's also much easier to keep your fly line from "piercing" the trout's window. This is an incredibly important factor for good small-stream presentation and one of the many elements Tom has figured out better than anyone else.

Observation is one of Tom's greatest attributes. He puts the rod down—most anglers have trouble doing this—and carefully scrutinizes everything going on around him. He checks the stream bottom, intermediate currents, surface edges, the stream bank, trees, bushes, the sky—the entire streamside environment. He uses a fine mesh seine to collect both aquatic and terrestrial critters. He also is very adept at spotting fish, a skill that takes lots of practice to acquire.

Speaking of practice, another reason Tom is such a great fisherman is that he spends endless hours on the stream in every kind of weather and in search of just about any swimming quarry, from trout to carp. I love to chase carp, especially when they're rising selectively to small flies in clear water. In fact, over the past few years, I've been fly-fishing for old "rubber lips" with short 1- and 2-weight rods—just like Tom. What a kick!

Tom also is a great innovator when it comes to developing artificial flies. His mayfly and caddis patterns, most of which are tied no-hackle style, are not only deadly but also easy to tie. He has the unique ability to develop patterns that imitate an insect's key features—the ones most important in gulling a smart, old trout into thinking an artificial is the real thing.

His two most famous patterns are the Hare's Ear Scud and the All-Marabou Leech, and they are dandies! I've used both for many years with outstanding results. The Leech, with its incredible built-in action, has bailed me out of many difficult situations, especially on the spring creeks of Montana and the gin-clear rivers of New Zealand's South Island. His Scud, with its amazing lifelike texture, can be used to imitate almost any subsurface creature when tied in the right size and color. I use both routinely as searching patterns to pound up fish in seemingly dead water.

Most of the fly-fishing books I've read in recent years are simply a rehash of concepts originally developed a long time ago. Very few offer fresh ideas or new techniques. *Catching Big Fish on Light Fly Tackle*, on the other hand, is jam-packed with Tom's unique expertise. There are numerous reasons that he's so talented as a writer and an angler, but probably the two most important are his versatility and his passion. He's very open-minded and not afraid to try new ideas. And he has devoted his life to the sport. We're indebted to him for it.

DOUG SWISHER

Acknowledgments

Many of the people who have played an important part in my angling and writing over the years are mentioned in the coming pages. To elaborate in detail on their contributions and associations would bring up memories too numerous and angling topics too far afield from the theme of this book. Nevertheless, let me acknowledge a few key figures.

I must note my heartfelt regard for the work *Selective Trout* and its coauthors, Doug Swisher and Carl Richards. If it weren't for their work, in my opinion fly-fishing as we know and enjoy the sport today would not have evolved through intelligent approaches to catching trout. I have been fortunate to ply the waters and the keyboard both back in a time before the no-hackle dry fly was developed and also after this concept in fly design was popularized by Doug and Carl. Sometimes the differences are instant, as noted in episodes in this book. *Selective Trout* is more than a reference book and a guide to hatches; it's also a frame of reference that anglers can use to mesh with other concepts in coming up with a successful "taking" pattern. Doug and Carl provided a way for the rest of us to nurture our own angling philosophies. Using fly patterns from a work such as *Selective Trout* will lead you to a better understanding of taking patterns for heavy hatch, sparse hatch, and nonhatch situations.

Two other colleagues are instrumental in providing written words that have led to acceptance of this manuscript by the University of

Wisconsin Press. An editorial relationship with Howard West, recently retired projects manager for Scientific Anglers/3M Company, began 30 years ago when he called and asked if I would write for the Scientific Anglers publications published by Aqua-Field. In effect, Howard provided me with a venue in which I could express advanced angling tactics, often at length, and a large part of this book features selected material I did over decades. Ezra "Sam" Diman, retired associate director of the UW Press, also contributed kind words about my credentials that helped convince a scholarly rooted university press to accept my manuscript.

I had been working on the outline and the idea for the book in recent years, but it took my friend Jeff Mayers, an astute journalist and light-tackle angler, to convince me to show him something in words that he could assist in shaping for the Press. Jeff has been the key in getting the project into the hands of the publisher and has helped in so many ways I don't know what title he should have. The Press settled on "with Jeff Mayers."

Two top-notch illustrators have contributed their artwork. Maurice Mahler put the professional touches on my rough sketches and also provided some of his exquisite originals of trout and insects. Richard Fendrick turned my scrawl-like drawings into renditions of fish "on the feed," which are so realistic they make me feel as if I'm watching the real thing. The photographs were taken either by myself or by fellow anglers as a courtesy.

Though he is gone, an editor I worked with from the beginning and for nearly 20 years probably had more of an influence on me than anyone else in the business. Pete Barrett was outdoor editor for Fawcett Publications and then executive editor for *Field & Stream* until he was appointed fishing editor in the mid-1980s. Sure, he liked my articles on fly-fishing and even accepted light-tackle twists that I worked in whenever I thought I could get away with it. But his magazines sold to a general readership, and he always urged me to "keep it basic." There aren't many of the host of articles I did for Pete in this book. However, the "basics" I wrote about then take many forms and are always present in a how-to angling work. He was prone to accept my early article including rubber-legged flies, for he had seen one in the jaw of an Alaskan rainbow. And he was happy to have my piece on golden stone flies ("The Unknown Fly That Turns On Trout") for *Fawcett's Fishing Journal* in 1976. Both broke some ground on little-known subjects for a national readership in *True's* annual fishing magazines. Later pieces I did for him for *Field & Stream* on various aspects of trouting are part of the lore expressed in this book—just tuned to light tackle. I could talk trout fishing with Pete; he knew well the intricacies of the sport, but I doubt he expressed all that he could have, even in his own excellent articles. He was simply, always, thinking of the reader.

Finally, I would like to dedicate this book to John Mueller, an angler whose spirit I shared in our pursuit of fish, and to others like him.

Catching Big Fish
on Light Fly Tackle

Introduction

Jeff Mayers

TOM WENDELBURG has never met a fish he hasn't tried to catch. If it swims, chances are that Wendelburg has tried to catch it on light-weight fly tackle—and has usually succeeded.

Once, on a saltwater excursion, he got bored with catching Pacific bonita one at a time. He went to one of his tried-and-true freshwater trout techniques, a tandem rig for streamers, and caught them two at a time. At a time when most Montana anglers pursued other sports during the hard winters, Tom pioneered winter dry-fly fishing for trout on the Bitterroot River, sometimes casting in the midst of a snowstorm. When streams weren't open to winter trout fishing, Tom would exploit a legal loophole and stress his light bamboo rod in the off-season by casting weighted streamers ostensibly for Montana whitefish; instead, he'd catch trout and release them. Tom's always thinking of new and different ways to catch big fish on light fly tackle.

Tom got his professional start guiding and writing in Montana and then came back to his native Wisconsin. Along the way, he became a leader in using light tackle for big fish. And when I say "light tackle," I mean short, featherweight rods and tiny reels that together weigh no more than a whiffle-ball bat. "Tom Wendelburg has caught more large trout on a 2-weight fly rod than any fisherman we know of," the *Orvis News* proclaimed in 1991.

Tom also has helped preserve blue-ribbon waters through his detailed conservation writings, made important contributions to the

3

tying of world-class freshwater fly patterns, and helped develop fly-fishing techniques seen as commonplace today.

You may not know Wendelburg, but he has attained a reputation among leading fishing authorities who have fished with him or read his work. Read this collection of his work, and you'll know why he's recognized as one of the best. *Scientific Anglers Fly Fishing Quarterly* in the summer of 1990 said Tom's writing "combines scholarly knowledge with insights gained through many years of angling experience." Tom's writing encompasses fishing, of course, but it also has an important conservationist streak.

Early in the fight against clear-cut timbering, Wendelburg clearly articulated the dangers it posed to Montana's famous Rock Creek, east of Missoula, in an editorial for *Fly Fisherman* magazine. In October of 1970, Tom called for a moratorium on logging in the Rock Creek watershed. "Excellent production of natural trout and insects depends on water quality and undisturbed habitat. Altering Rock Creek's pure water would bring 'unseen' change and rupture the delicate biological chain of life in a stream. Productivity would decline, and another of the dwindling blue-ribbon streams would trickle down the drain," Wendelburg wrote. "If man must 'manage' Rock Creek, dollars from timber sales defended as 'multiple use management' should not have priority."

"It took 21 years to get that moratorium," reported *Fly Fisherman* editor John Randolph in a May 1994 column, recalling Tom's article, "but in 1991 the U.S. Forest Service suspended cuts in the drainage until further study can determine their probable effects on the watershed."

Long before "tailwater fisheries" became widely documented, Tom broke new ground in outlining for a general readership the benefits and problems imposed by changeable water flows due to dam releases and irrigation diversions in "The Up and Down Beaverhead" (*Field & Stream*, January 1971). "I was gauging my fishing by river flow—cubic feet per second—even back then because I noticed that trout and hatches would react differently according to the water flows," Wendelburg says. "Nowadays projected flows for many rivers are available on your computer."

In the days before trout fishing guidebooks proliferated, Tom contributed to one called *88 Top Trout Streams of the West*, compiled by Duncan Campbell. For that 1974 book, Wendelburg wrote pieces on three of his favorite Montana streams, Rock Creek, the Clark Fork River, and the then-little-known Beaverhead River, capturing the guidebook style so prevalent today.

Tom became a prolific contributor to *Fly Fisherman* magazine and other publications. *Fly Fisherman*, in its silver anniversary issue of December 1993, listed Tom as one of its most important contributors. Tom's name appeared in the company of some of the sport's great angler writers: Nick Lyons, Lefty Kreh, Tom McNally, Art Flick, Charlie Fox, Jim Chaprallis, Ernie Schwiebert, Larry Green, Gary LaFontaine, and Eric Leiser.

In that same issue, Randolph credited Don Zahner, the founder and initial editor of *Fly Fisherman* magazine, with starting a national magazine when fly-fishing was neither popular nor widespread. Wendelburg remembers fishing with Zahner on the Au Sable and other Michigan trout rivers. A photo he took of Tom fishing with a 5-foot fly rod appeared on the magazine's cover. "Don was the first to simply understand me," Wendelburg says. "He once wrote in his 'Anglish Spoken Here' column that I was happy only when I was fishing."

Long before trout bumming became a lifestyle choice, Tom became a top angler without the luxury of a steady stream of income and, since the mid-1980s, without a car. He persevered over such obstacles because of a single-minded obsession—fishing.

Tom thinks about fishing almost every waking moment. For Tom, fishing is the beginning, the middle, and the end. The ends and the means. The inside and the outside. The real and the unreal. I don't know about his dream patterns, but they no doubt involve a fish—it could be any fish—rising to one of his exquisitely tied fly patterns, then flexing his 2-weight rod to a near breaking point; after that, he cradles the fish, releases it, makes another long left-handed cast—all with a Marlboro cigarette dangling from his lips. Tom is a highly intelligent man possessed by some inner force that has made him some kind of fishing machine. Tom needs to fish like a fish needs to swim.

Who else would have fished during the moon landing? When other anglers stopped to listen in camp to man's first landing on the moon in July 1969, Tom was oblivious to it all—fishing the stone fly hatch on a Montana river.

But this obsession doesn't fully describe one of the best anglers anywhere, a true American character who lives in Middleton, Wisconsin, a western suburb of the capital city of Madison. To some, he brags about every detail in every fishing exploit; but Tom insists, "I'm just trying to share the good fortune that's out there. The secrets of catching fish are just waiting and not all that enigmatic." To others, he's genuinely funny, possessing a raucous cackle that bursts from his round bearded face and echoes up and down the stream. "Is it that loud?" he jokes. "It's not resounding enough to spook the trout."

Tom once analyzed his laugh for me. "It developed as an instant expression or amazement with an important moment on the stream. It could be the smallest thing—a large trout suddenly leaping for a rare, low-flying bug or the instant I hook up to a trout's splashing rise to my dry fly. The laugh is more original than just 'Wow!' or 'I got him!' Look, at times I remain stealthily silent for long periods of time. But even talking to trout is fun," Wendelburg adds. "Just the other night, while lining up my cast in air, I spoke to a rising fish. 'I can hear you feeding, but I don't know *exactly* where you are.' In a moment, my dry alighted on the right spot, and the big brown's walloping take silenced all other feeding. That trout laughed for me."

Others have analyzed Tom. "He may be infamous, but he's also famous," wrote the late Wisconsin outdoor writer George Vukelich in his magazine portrait of Wendelburg, "Trout Bum: His Talents Are Awesome—Just Ask Him."

Wendelburg, when Vukelich was alive, would jokingly say, "He mostly got it right." But Tom thinks the "trout bum thing" is distracting. He notes that he's been a high school athlete, a teacher, a coach. "There's much, much more to my mainstream life that the typically successful adult would appreciate, but fly-fishing, particularly for brown trout, has won out handily," he says.

For sure, there's evidence to support the "trout bum" label: sleeping along streams in his vehicles—sometimes for an entire season; midnight calls to arrange a fishing trip; and waiting in a cheap motel for the check from the magazine publisher while punching out the next article on a manual typewriter. But "trout bum" misses the complexity of Tom's character and two basic points.

Point one: Tom doesn't view fishing as bumming. To Tom, it's work—his life's work. On one of our many trips to southwestern Wisconsin's spring creek region, a trout heaven and one of Wendelburg's favorite haunts, he confessed: "All I ever wanted to do was fish."

Point two: Tom fishes for any fish that will take a fly—not just trout. He has an "advanced degree" in fish biology and fishing without the formal training—a scholarly training gained through countless observations of fish, extensive interviews with fisheries specialists, and associations with some of fly-fishing's most famous names.

He fished with his hero Joe Brooks (more on that later). Another time, on a trip to Huntsville, Alabama, for the Bassmasters Classic as a press angler (on one day he won the cash prize for largest bass), he met Lee Wulff. Wulff, hired to photograph the event from the air, saw Tom at dinner and the two shared fly-fishing techniques amid the spin-fishing atmosphere. "I felt honored that this greatest of pioneers in light-tackle angling for big fish had wanted to share a mutual understanding, the quest for yet larger fish on yet lighter gear," Tom recalls.

Tom's relationship with Dan Bailey and his famous Livingston, Montana, fly shop ran deeper. Tom credits Bailey, his catalog, and his shop's personnel with providing insights that accounted for much of Tom's early fly-fishing successes. Tom once used a #10 Bailey Muddler Minnow to catch a trout over 4 pounds on 6X tippet from a stream near Livingston; it landed Tom on Dan Bailey's old "Wall of Fame."

"During our friendship Dan gave me a wealth of insights on the 'whys' of successful fly patterns, and he was as unpretentious as he was right," Tom recalls. "I wrote the last of the national articles on Dan and his famous fly shop ('The Flies That Won the West' for *Fly Fisherman* in 1976, spring special issue). Helen, Dan's wife, told me he liked it better than any of the others. Dan thought he had been 'overdone,' in his own word, by writers throughout the years." Since Dan passed away in 1982, his son John has continued the tradition, operating the shop that will always be known simply as Bailey's.

Tom says Dan once told him, "All I wanted to do was fish." Adds Tom, "Those words may have impressed me more than I knew they would." When Tom isn't fishing, he's guiding someone to fish or writing about catching fish or tying flies that will catch fish or thinking about one of the above. He remembers every fishing episode like professional athletes remember playoff games, key game situations, and crucial plays and shots.

Those of us who fish with Tom learn something on every angling excursion. Tom frequently catches fish when nobody else is catching any. And when we do catch fish, he catches more than any of us. Oh, he may exaggerate on occasion, but only when the excitement gets the best of him. But I know he outfishes everyone. I've watched.

I watched him hook a truly great inland trout, a 30-inch brown, on a southwestern Wisconsin spring creek. I snapped a photo as he held it against the quickly fading summer light (p. 96). The episode leads off Tom's "Fishing the Edges Dry," contained in this anthology. Such expertise with the dry fly also has brought him recognition in several books. Among them is Vlad Evanoff's *500 Fishing Experts*, featuring Tom as one of the top trout fly anglers in the country. His overall expertise is featured in three recent books: Ross Mueller's *Upper Midwest Trout Flies; Flyfishing Midwestern Spring Creeks;* and a book I coauthored called *Exploring Wisconsin Trout Streams*.

Tom was born on July 17, 1943, in Milwaukee, and caught the fishing bug at the Washington Park lagoon near his house. At age five, he caught his first fish—a 3½-inch bluegill on a cane pole with a string and a worm. He progressed to bait casting. Then he came upon a 9-foot telescoping tubular steel fly rod. He found a cracked, all-silk fly line and attached a leader to some flies he had tied with a little fly-tying kit. He used that outfit to tease panfish, bass and crappie. By age 10, he had discovered the joys of taking fish on flies he had dreamed up at his vise.

A schoolmate and neighbor, Preston Strunk, introduced him to trout fishing, taking Tom to a family cabin near the North Branch of the Pike River in far northeastern Wisconsin. Tom caught his very first trout at age 13 on a dry fly, an old pattern called the Gray-Hackle Yellow.

In high school, the senior term paper he remembers is the one he did on fish hatcheries and fish biology. He graduated from Brookfield Central High School and advanced to college at the University of Wisconsin–Madison. Tom majored in journalism and often approached his instructors to let him write on some aspect of fishing. One instructor, Elliot Maraniss, then the assistant city editor of the *Capital Times*, introduced him to noted fisheries biologist Ray White, who was then with the Wisconsin Conservation Department. White guided Tom's initial efforts to a stream west of Madison called Black Earth Creek. Tom's first piece on the sewage problems threatening trout there not only worked for journalism class but got published in the *Capital Times*, too. "The $15 I got really hooked me on the rewards of writing for pay, a sentiment I have to this day," he says. That newspaper article later became part of "The Saving of Black Earth Creek," an article published in the Midwest regional section of *Outdoor Life* in June 1972 after the upgrading of sewage facilities on the creek. Black Earth since has become Wendelburg's primary home waters.

In 1965, days after graduation with a journalism degree from the University of Wisconsin, Tom went west, drawn to a place where trout was king. He worked as a reporter for the *Idaho State Journal* in Pocatello and fished between deadlines.

Then he was invited back to his high school to teach journalism and English. He came back to Wisconsin and stayed four years, guiding in Montana during the summers. Later he attended graduate school, where he was a teaching assistant at the University of Montana in Missoula. He subsequently secured significant teaching stints, including what then was the magazine writing course at the University of Montana. But an academic career and his marriage eventually succumbed to the lure of the fishing world.

One of his first guiding stints was at the Elk Horn Ranch on

Tom's version of the Acroneuria *(golden-bodied) stone fly, adapted from Dan Bailey's Bucktail Caddis, featured a wider hackle base for better floatation on Montana's turbulent Rock Creek. Tom also tied a neat, solid fluttering-winged silhouette. Tom took this photo in the late 1960s. This pattern—his favorite and most productive stone fly—was a forerunner of the similar Stimulator pattern.*

Rock Creek. That's where, in 1968, he met one of his boyhood heroes, Joe Brooks, who had just been named fishing editor for *Outdoor Life* magazine. He got a call one day, requesting that he fish with Brooks on Rock Creek. Tom accompanied his idol. "I was awed," says Tom, recalling that he used his hairwing stone fly, a forerunner of today's Stimulator pattern, to catch the largest trout while fishing the same pool with Joe. Tom credits encouraging words from Brooks for giving him the inspiration to write. "Write for the national magazines," Joe advised him.

And write Tom did. During one Rock Creek outing with a 5-foot mini-rod, Tom impressed Campbell, the editor of the guidebook and an editor for the *Flyfisher*, the magazine of the Federation of Fly Fishermen. He was assigned his first piece, and "Montana's Rock Creek" appeared in the 1969 winter issue of the federation's magazine. Over the years, from Montana and then Wisconsin, more than 100 articles came tumbling out, appearing in most of the big outdoor writing venues. He wrote not only about fishing but also about conserving the places where game fish swim. Among these important conservation pieces is "Can We Save Rock Creek?" published by *Outdoor Life* in February 1971. His numerous writings helped inspire environmental legislation and broader environmental awareness in Wisconsin and Montana.

Tom traveled, fished, wrote, and took photos in top fishing spots. That's how he met Doug Swisher one day on Armstrong Spring Creek, near Livingston, Montana. You can read about some of their friendly fishing adventures in "The Duns of Autumn" and "Early-Morning Eye Opener," contained in this collection.

Tom's treasures have stood the test of time. One of the early pieces in this collection, "The Mighty Mini-Rod" (expanded from *Fly Fisherman*, October 1970), is a prime example. Tom writes of his early experimentation with a 5-foot bamboo rod in situations normally reserved for heavier tackle. The piece is as full of insight today as it was when written, and Tom still fishes with the same rod.

His writing is packed full of useful information, no matter what your quarry. Each piece stands on its own, especially after Tom updated certain ones with added information. Strip away the layers, savor a few chapters at a time, and you'll take away something to make you a better angler.

Tom's writing displays his passion for fish and the sport of catching them. Tom is an educator and an environmentalist, and that shows through. This book parallels many of Tom's well-attended seminars and speaking engagements. "The environment and the fish are paramount, and fly-fishers should do their part to keep it that way," he says. "I think of the basics this way: A native, large trout rises to feed in the shade of a bush on insects dependent even more so than the hardy brown on excellent water quality. What are the chances of this scenario continuing through generations of trout?"

Read on for more of Tom's unique fishing wisdom.

Light-Tackle Philosophy

Going Light

M Y ANGLING HISTORY is one of seeking the "light-tackle advantage." Even early on in my 35-year fly-fishing career, I was "thinking light" as a way to improve my sport. While light tackle is a vague idea, for our purposes let's say it'll be a rod, fly line, leader, and tippet lighter than commonly recommended for the quarry at hand. For example, a 2-weight rod and 6X or 7X tippet for spring creek trout fishing and a 4-weight rod and 2X or 3X tippet for river steelhead fishing would be considered light-tackle approaches. Rest assured that modern technology makes "going light" more practical than ever. Whether with bamboo or graphite, going light gives anglers the thrill of catching a bigger fish on lighter tackle, a way to increase the simple enjoyment intrinsic in fly casting, and a method to provide a more effective presentation.

When I first fished the West, using an economical 7½-foot fiberglass rod with a quality 7-weight fly line, I found that a light leader tippet is often one's initiation to better fishing. My first job following graduation from my home-state University of Wisconsin in 1965 was as a reporter for the *Idaho State Journal* in Pocatello (that isn't the only move I've made solely with fly-fishing in mind). That summer, on a staff fishing outing, I netted an 18-inch cutthroat during my first day on a western stream. Later during a dry-fly fishing trip on the South Fork of the Snake, a vast river near

15

Ririe, my angling host and boss, Lyle Olson, was surprised over my success with a mere 5X tippet.

Light tackle really becomes appealing to the serious angler when angling situations are most difficult. A big part of this book analyzes angling situations commonly found on bountiful spring creeks and along low-water streams and rivers. These situations are repetitive over time, occurring enticingly again and again; they're representative, too, of fish behavior and location. They are as recognizable as a learned, careful reading of the stream habitat. And they help anglers understand what larger trout are looking for.

Only a year after my initial sojourn in Idaho, I fished the sprawling, shallow, gliding reaches of the Henry's Fork, sometimes with a 5-foot, 1½-ounce bamboo mini-rod, for dry-fly fun. While spending my summers guiding at a ranch on Montana's Rock Creek, near Missoula, a 7½-foot bamboo Orvis Battenkill fished like a gem on the creek's frequently rough and swift blue-ribbon waters, where trout feed with a watchful eye. As you'll read in the "Mighty Mini-Rod" chapter, my wee 5-footer had its moments, especially on Rock Creek's hidden side channels.

In following years, big strong trout in the low waters of Montana's Beaverhead River gave me thrills on a 4-weight, 7-foot 2-inch glass rod. Once, while admiring a brown that had just taken me several pools downstream in a hurry, I fleetingly thought my light tackle had given me some advantage; after all, hadn't it delivered a Caddis dry flawlessly to a quartet of fine browns in as many casts?

My penchant for a light rod and line boils down to a few concepts. This light-tackle advantage can also be more than the challenge of catching fish on water that would seem best approached with heftier gear; it can be a real advantage including delicacy and sensitivity in presentation plus a mechanical edge in fighting a fish. A short rod, for instance, gives the angler direct control of the fish, a concept that might be used in choosing a 5–7-foot rod for plying a creek for trout or for fish as large as king salmon. On my first salmon outing on a smallish creek some years ago, I chose a resilient 7½-footer and a 5-weight line. In confines familiar to me I took fish

Against the backdrop of Montana's Sapphire Mountains, I heft a Rock Creek brown, taken on a dry deer-hair stone fly.

unfamiliar to me, with a best catch of 40 inches on a 2X tippet. Now I use a similar outfit on some salmon-steelhead outings.

Since Tom Rosenbauer of Orvis Company sent me one of the then-new 2-weight graphite rods to try in the 1980s, my angling has taken on renewed meaning, especially on gently flowing spring creek waters for trout. To me, it's the ultimate fishing rod for enjoyment and results. A 2-weight rod tests an angler's skills, yet offers versatility in the use of all types of flies, from the little ones the rod was intended for to larger, sleeker patterns. For years, I believe I was the sole 2-weight devotee on a large, sedate valley meadow stream in southern Wisconsin. I since have a number of converts who ply streams with feather-light rods, including my friend and collaborator on this book, Jeff Mayers.

Another is Rich Hansen. He is as fine a student of the "trouting" game as I have known. A few seasons ago, he compared our fishing results and decided, on reflection, that his light tackle was not light enough. Subsequently, we've shared many Wisconsin spring creeks with our 2-weights. Key is my system of a 3–4-foot, tapered, braided leader butt knotted to tapering monofilament sections. With this tackle, he's become an excellent angler, catching trout to 24 inches.

Another convert, especially to my use of a 2-weight even in nighttime hatches of the large *Hexagenia* mayflies, is Steve Born. Jeff and Steve coauthored the aforementioned book *Exploring Wisconsin Trout Streams* with two other fishing friends; Born is a professor of water resource management at the University of Wisconsin and a national leader of Trout Unlimited.

Part of the light-tackle advantage is that fish of all kinds can seem big when caught using featherweight tools. Large bluegills assume a status otherwise reserved for game fish; beefy bass achieve big-game status; a spirited 12-inch hatchery-reared rainbow might zip line off the reel like a hulking trout.

Even carp take on the excitement of fishing for lake-run salmonids. I occasionally sight nymph for carp in a local lagoon. One spring, a carp took me into my backing and forced me to follow him around the perimeter. I finally waded in and captured the trophy, which may have been a record for a carp caught on a 2-weight with 6X tippet, if records for such things are even kept.

Rating a rod for the fishing at hand is expressed in arbitrary terms: length, action, and weight. The customary words associated with rod action—*fast, medium,* and *slow*—don't adequately explain a unique combination of rod length, taper, and parameters of construction. These characteristics differ from manufacturer to manufacturer and depend upon your sense of feel when the rod is flexed in your hand or cast with a line. I also consider a rod by the strength of tippet needed to break it when fighting a fish. I rated a favorite 4–5-weight rod for a tippet no stronger than 2X; sure enough, the rod splintered with 1X against a sizable Atlantic salmon.

Think about rod length, too. For example, a short 5–7-footer may be right for the angler wading a foliage-hemmed creek, while a longer rod may be more practical for the angler fishing from the bank and making back casts that need to clear tall grasses. My friend Bob Pierce once waded a creek for a native 6½-pound brown using his pet 7-foot, 3-weight rod and 5X tippet. That same day I fished my longer 2-weight rod and 6X tippet from bankside on another stream in the area and took a brace of rainbows in the same class size.

Rod weight differs according to material and other factors. Graphite rods can be made lighter but often have a stiffer backbone than a rod made from fiberglass or bamboo. No rod material, however, enables you to achieve as delicate a presentation as bamboo does.

Some of the most productive small-fly fishing I've known on gently flowing to mirror-smooth waters has been accomplished with a slow-action, parabolic bamboo rod rated for 4-weight line. This outfit has hooked big fish along the edges of the lower Bitterroot in Montana, but its bailiwick is a spring creek during low-water conditions and hatches. The 6½-footer has enabled me to deliver the fly as lightly as a falling feather to trout in difficult, narrow, foliage-framed crannies under the canopy as well as on open meadowed reaches of spring creeks.

Note my wet waders. After kneeling for a low angle to slide the short rod's tightly looped cast under a branch, I stand to play a splashing trout.

During one trip I ventured to try it on the Beaverhead and took a larger brown. But a rambunctious 12-inch rainbow broke the tip. Hastily repaired and now 3 inches shorter, its delicacy has remained intact. Switching to this rod made notable differences in presentations for difficult trout that fed freely to multiple hatches on a nearby spring creek. Though refurbished with a new tip, the little rod has remained in its case in recent years but for a few days. My first catch, a 24-inch brown on 6X tippet, brings back recollections from the years when I used it extensively. Despite the trend to graphite, every angler should experience the feel and fine presentation of bamboo.

I like a small reel that balances a light rod—a reel such as a Hardy. Since most rods will cast two or even three weights of lines, toting an extra reel spool is a handy way to adapt to conditions and personal preferences. A line one weight lighter than recommended for the rod makes for smooth, longer casts, while a line one weight heavier flexes the rod correctly on shorter casts. The reel should carry enough nonstretch backing line for the conditions.

Choosing the best tackle for your angling may come down to trying something lighter than you've been using on your favorite waters. You could take advice from me, but it's ultimately up to you to define what is the right tackle for you and your angling. Discover that enjoyment and increased success. Light-tackle adventures await.

The Mighty Mini-Rod

"SOME DAY," Wally Marks chided, "a big bass will splinter your pea-shooter fly rod into bamboo match sticks!"

A fish smacked the popping bug, and I felt the heavy pounding of that bass zigzagging away. The reel drag scratched out line, and the fragile rod bowed to the butt. I held my breath, afraid the rod would crack as Wally had predicted. But a minute later I netted a scrappy 8-inch bluegill.

"Wally," I said, "these lunkers are dynamite on my mini-rod." The 5-foot, 1½-ounce bamboo fly rod took hundreds of "big-game" bluegills from lakes before I toted it on a trout stream.

The tiny rod false cast line under the low tree limbs, and its light 4-weight, weight-forward line presented a dry fly upstream without a splash. On that wooded stream, one road lane wide, the mini-rod snapped short casts under brush. It arrowed the fly onto pockets I hadn't been able to fish with a longer rod. As those bluegills had, 10-inch brookies arced the rod into an inverted U. "Small streams with pan-sized trout—that's mini-rod water," I thought.

But the next summer I experimented further on the vast, shallowly gliding Henry's Fork of the Snake River in Idaho. Wading thigh deep, I cast the light line onto flat water like a thread on glass, raising cautious rainbows to take a #14 dry fly. When 2-pounders jumped on my line, I knew a mini-rod would catch fish where I could wade within 40 feet of a trout on the prowl for small flies.

Then my mini-rod graduated to fast water. Even after spring

runoff, western Montana's Rock Creek near Missoula runs swiftly along a mountain valley. Overcoming an inclination to leave the mini-rod in its case, I rigged it up with a Royal Wulff and caught about 50 rainbows and browns up to 17 inches. That day hooked me on the little rod. Through the low-water season it took hundreds of trout on #12–28 dry flies and #4–10 Muddler Minnows. I learned to work up line speed that cast out the bulky-headed Muddlers, which are shaped roughly like an airfoil to knife the air.

Those experiences over three years made a sham of myths that a mini-rod is a mere "toy" reflecting today's trend to light tackle. Now I'm confident uncasing my mini-rod on any size stream when short casts with small flies on 4–7X tippets are the menu for spooky trout in low summer and fall waters.

But at the time I bought the rod, I believed it was too fragile for any fish larger than the palm of my hand. I thought it couldn't be effective on wider trout streams. Today those myths probably scare away many light-tackle buffs from fishing a mini-rod. In past years writers like Lee Wulff popularized the midge 6-foot, 2-ounce rods. Anglers now fish them from small streams for brookies to big rivers for Atlantic salmon. More feather flingers might use mini-rods in the 5-foot, less-than-2-ounce range if they believed such small rods are practical fishing tools like 6-foot rods. After my exhibition with bluegills mentioned at the outset, my longtime friend Wally, an engineer by trade, became enamored of a mini-rod. Thereafter, he wielded a 5½-foot fly rod and light line on Wisconsin creeks, from brookie sanctuaries in the northwoods region to spring creeks of the Badger State's southerly meadows.

You need exact timing to cast a light fly line with a short rod; one myth is that this takes super skill. By keeping the casting wrist rigid and bending the elbow as the fulcrum, your forearm becomes an extension of the rod. As you false cast, this extra "rod length" gives you more leverage than the old style of casting with the wrist and keeping the elbow stiff. A proper grip is essential. The thumb (or forefinger) of the rod hand pointed toward the tip on top of the rod handle lines up the forearm with the rod.

In making the final forward cast, develop a fluid motion. First drive your rod shoulder into a cast, then pivot at the elbow, and finally snap the wrist downward so the rod points to the 10 o'clock position.

I cast without tiring for hours with my featherweight outfit, anchored with a single-action reel only 2½ inches in diameter. In response to skepticism that a little rod "won't cast worth a damn," it's not redundant to point out that a mini-rod executes basic casts, including roll casts and slack-line casts, with precision. I've even scored with the bow-and-arrow cast on desk-wide, brushy brooks for cutthroats. On longer casts, 18-inch browns clobbered a darting Muddler as viciously, I bet, as that big bass Wally feared might splinter my rod.

When you set a hook into a fish, a mini-rod snaps into a U. The short rod uses up its elasticity almost at once to absorb a shock like a striking or lunging trout. So you must react more quickly than with a longer rod in order to give line to a runaway fish and avoid snapped 6X tippets.

But another myth is that it takes all day to bring in a trout on a mini-rod. I've played out 2-pounders hooked on the same water in about equal time with my mini-rod and my 7½-foot bamboo rod. In heavy or snag-filled water, though, a light mini-rod lacks backbone to turn a big, streaking trout.

Using a mini-rod is about the only way to fly-fish many "up tight" streams. On a 15-foot-wide channel of Rock Creek one summer, brown trout were sipping in spruce moths. The water was limpid, and drooping tree branches and thick bankside foliage were a hazard to a cast.

The short rod worked false casts well-under overhead limbs and between bushes behind me, and the light line presented a #14 hairwing moth upstream without scratching the surface. A brownie stuck its head out from under a log, stabbed at the fly, and ducked back under the cover. A second later the 15-incher stiffened out of the water on the other side. Ping! The 6X tippet snapped. Then the brownie jumped in a farewell salute.

I arrowed a new moth onto a foot-wide corridor just upstream between another log and the bank, by sidearming the line under brush. A brown took the fly, and I pressured this smaller one, about a pound, out to open water.

I breathed more easily as I eyed a long pool upstream. Standing at the tail, I worked out 30 feet of line under the trees tented over the channel. The first cast put the fly down lightly, but it floated slowly back to me. On my second cast to that spot, the fly disappeared in a swirl.

"A big daddy for 6X," I said. I gave the heavy brown a completely slack line as it zipped away upstream. With no pressure on, the fish put on its brakes, then tried to rub the hook out on the rocky bottom. It sulked. Then the brownie tried to sneak past me downstream, so I waded over to herd it back upstream. We played that game back and forth across the channel. It tired, and I coaxed it in. I scooped up with my net, but the brownie ducked through my legs. I stepped back over the line and netted the 2½-pounder. The moral of that comedy act: Give a slack line to a leader-busting-sized trout hooked on a light tippet in open water, and the fish will tire itself out.

That afternoon the little rod landed more than a dozen other browns, including eight from 13 to 15 inches. On that small stream, a longer rod would have snagged the fly on foliage; a heavier line may have splashed and put down feeding trout.

A 9-foot leader is okay on low water for wary trout because the small-diameter line point of 4-weight line cuts down splash. On broken water I often shorten the leader to 7 feet. The leader should be balanced and tapered to the lightest tippet that will roll out the fly naturally. I suggest you learn to tie tapered leaders so you can make on-the-stream modifications with 4–7X tippets and #12–28 dry flies.

Following are mini-rod experiences, some excerpted from my article "Fine Points of Fishing the Short Fly Rod for Trout and Panfish" (*Fishing World*, November–December 1978).

Doug Swisher and I waded a placid Au Sable River in Michigan. Our 5-foot rods and light lines painted casts lightly to trout on open water as well as beneath foliage and fallen trees. Doug mentioned that a short rod naturally increases accuracy, simply because the rod

I play a large brown on a 5-foot bamboo mini-rod.

tip is closer to the angler's eye. While driving the rod tip to the target, a short rod forms a tighter loop.

A fast-action rod is versatile and highly efficient in presenting a high-speed cast for accuracy and forming a narrow loop so the line and leader unfurl through minimal space for a pinpoint presentation. A tight loop also delivers a fly under low overhead cover. The important factor in forming a tight loop is that the rod tip travels in a straight line during the front cast. Thus the angler can cast a narrow loop with a limber rod, which has a slow casting cycle. And for the ultimate in delicacy, I, along with many other anglers, appreciate a willowy bamboo rod.

A simple key to casting with a short rod is to maintain a light but firm grip on the handle. A cork-wringing grip can result in excessively snappy wrist action that ripples a cast with loss in line control. With the relaxed grip, when going for a little extra casting distance, a short rod is a simple machine with the capability to cast a balancing line. When a deep bend is put in the rod, the control of a short stick is obvious even with smaller fish. Bluegills fan behind a bush over a stream. Once hooked, those vigorous fish dart quickly for the cover, and a 7-foot light rod seems a bit "flip-floppy" while I play them. When I fish a 5-foot rod, the shorter stick gives me better control. In this instance there's little practical difference, though the angler notices slight aspects in tackle performance with a short rod and light line.

The plane of a short rod can be adjusted quickly to counter a fish's actions. When a fish submarines into cover, I quickly lower the rod to give it near slack; then simply angling the rod lower toward open water coaxes it in the right direction. Often surprisingly little or no bend in the rod guides a fish into the clear. Once a 4-pound brown snagged the 6X tippet on a lone little submerged twig. I instantly gave it complete slack in the sluggish current and announced to my partner, "Watch this. There's a chance even with a fish this size." With the pressure off, in protracted seconds that seemed an eternity, the motionless trout eventually swam slowly, freeing the tippet. The fight continued, and I was able to ease this one in by allowing it to swim against little pressure that barely bowed the rod tip. I was using a 7-foot rod, but with any rod that might be considered short or light for the angling, you need quick reactions to transmit alterations through the line and to the hooked fish.

A trout had run out all my line, and its bellying weight in the current soon parted the tippet. I returned again with lighter tackle. Hooking a fish in the same spot, I instantly raised the shorter rod to a high and horizontal position as the trout sped away. A rod in this position keeps as much line as possible off the water and reduces stress on the tippet. The beauty leaped, surged in fast runs, and often changed directions, taking line off the reel, but my little rod tired it in good time, and I was able to admire a 3-pounder in hand.

Here's one more trick. I often shorten a fly line to provide space for more backing on the small reel I use to balance a short rod. I splice backing to usually half of a double-tapered line, or up to 60 feet of a weight-forward line. Sometimes I'll shoot backing line on longer casts.

How short a rod might you need to make a catch? At one time, hefty cover meant I could cast from only one place. I put the butt section of the rod on the grass, stripped coils of line at my feet, and kneeled to cast with only the tip of the fly rod. Shooting coiled lines, I arrowed a cast low to the water under an overhanging tree and 20 feet beyond to a feeding trout. Even in the mini-rod category, that's the shortest fly rod I've ever used to catch a fish.

Advanced 2-Weight Tactics
for Larger Trout

THE FIRST TIME I uncased my 2-weight, 7-foot 9-inch Orvis Ultra Fine some years ago, I called on the rod to perform well beyond its recommended use. Faced with large trout that wouldn't come up to feed on drys, I used the rod to toss hefty #8–12-weighted nymphs. I caught fish and the rod performed beautifully.

Since then I've used the rod extensively to land large trout with some special but simple techniques that allow this amazing rod to handle all manner of flies. It has revolutionized my angling on spring creeks and crystalline spring holes, where its sensitivity has proven to be a valuable asset in taking large, difficult trout.

Sure, 2-weight angling with a small fly is as delightful as it is efficient. I can attest to that from the many 20-inch-class and larger trout I've taken with the Ultra Fine in recent years on prescribed #14 and smaller flies. But the 2-weight's capability is by no means limited to small flies. I've used it successfully to fish outsized wets and drys to large trout when conventional wisdom called for heavier equipment.

Regardless of the fly size, trout (browns especially) are wary of a tippet, and I fish 6X routinely in limestone waters. Long a proponent of short fly rods, I find the Ultra Fine's 7-foot 9-inch length an extension of my arm that only eases tossing outsized flies. Adjusting the casting stroke to present such patterns exercises this rod's intrin-

I use my graphite 2-weight rod to ease in a big brown.

sic power, making it perform equally to rods manufactured for a heavier line.

The Ultra Fine's action smoothly transmits momentum of the line down the rod in a way that eliminates snapping off a heavier fly on the back cast. And when the fish takes the fly, the rod's same advantages work in reverse. A big trout is less apt to break a hairline tippet against the cushioning spring of its light but strong tip. In effect a light tippet becomes much stronger. The rod tip exhibits a delicate balance, providing the power to set a #8 stout wire hook and yet protect light tippets from sudden surges.

For much of my fishing, an Orvis braided leader butt is an integral connection in my 2-weight system. I like the "loose line" effect of the braid in achieving a lifelike natural drift with a sunken fly. It also has an accordion-like shock absorber effect that protects against tippet breakage. When the hook is correctly set, the braid's minimal stretch serves to sink the point rather than yank it free from the trout's jaw. I prefer using a sidearm hooking technique, transferring the momentum of the line with the direction of current and always into the trout's jaw instead of away. It's quicker to transfer the line's weight sideways than it is to lift it directly upward. This technique requires less than a tippet-snapping flick of the wrist and is also efficient in static water, especially with shallow or surface flies.

The proper cast propels a weighted fly much as a lure is cast with a monofilament line on a spin outfit. While a wide loop is often associated with heavy flies, my cast presents a tighter loop for accuracy. The trick is developing form and timing to build up fly speed smoothly. On a back cast, I extend my arm and drift the rod tip to halfway between the two o'clock and three o'clock positions on the casting clock until sensing a slight tug. I then extend my arm for a similar lengthy forward cast. During the casting cycle the rod wrist must maintain a straight-line path to keep the fly on course. A single or double haul, if needed, enhances distance and accuracy.

Delivering the cast, I stop the rod at 10 o'clock, or as low as halfway between the 9 o'clock and 10 o'clock positions; the lower the rod tip, the greater the degree of accuracy. Even as the fly drops, keeping the rod tip pointed directly at the target and just above horizontal, I lower my wrist a few inches. The last maneuver hones accuracy.

Though seemingly light, the 2-weight gives instant rod-tip control for presenting the fly. A few special techniques are especially useful. First, as the fly drops, I quickly slip line into the hook of my rod hand's forefinger, pinching line lightly between thumb and forefinger under the handle. From behind this viselike, sliding grip I retrieve line with my line hand. Second, a deadly method for trout lying bankside is to make an across-stream cast, directing the rod horizontally, tip barely raised above the water. Strip line so the fly moves broadside across the snout of the trout. Finally, in calmer water, simply let the fly sink and use only the rod wrist to twitch the rod tip; this jogs the fly enticingly in place on its way down.

A light tippet gets a fly down more quickly. Typical pockets are partly hemmed by cover or surrounded by problematic currents, and when the trout feed deeply the morsel must sink without delay. A trout lurking on bottom in a spacious pool has the largest window of vision in the stream, and showing a morsel in as lifelike a manner

This trophy brown was caught on a Wisconsin spring creek with a floating fly tied to a 6X tippet cast by a 2-weight rod.

as possible has an advantage and also gives the ultimate sense of sport.

One myth concerning light rods asserts that larger trout on the line have an insurmountable edge. Well, perhaps, but without this heightened sense of sport, angling wouldn't be nearly as exciting. Knowing tactics to counter the stream-wise trout enables you to play the sporting game. Angling the rod to direct a trout from cover, playing the fish off the reel, strategically timing slack-line methods, and having patience are critical. During an encounter with a 30-inch brown caught on a 2-weight, I fought the fish in near darkness and played it by a sense of feel. The lunker's customary last effort for freedom was heading downstream out of its home pool. Giving the fish slack line aborted the powerful run by eliminating pressure. The trout turned back and was eventually beached.

A 2-weight will often wear down a larger trout in a shorter time than heavier tackle will. The light rod counteracts a trout's strength in a unique way. The fish does not have a solid, unyielding force to pull away from. I've played large trout hooked lightly on a little fly by letting them swim, directing the fish only with the slightest rod-tip pressure and eventually coaxing them in. In waters without heavy current the 2-weight can be likened to a light aircraft in a calm sky; as a veteran pilot once told me, "This little plane practically flies itself."

The 2-weight is not a substitute for all the fish-fighting tactics you'll ever learn, but it gives an opportunity to apply advanced fishing skills. Even before making a cast, mentally map the water. I anticipate a trout's strong opening foray on the line and plot a way to counter it. With a knowledge of habitat and a trout's often predictable series of maneuvers, you can be ready early to counter the fish's movements and lessen stress on the tippet.

A shorter leader and a heavier tippet will ease casting a weighted fly. I'll use a 5X tippet on occasion, perhaps when it is necessary to haul a big trout through a wide border of vegetation or when a lunker lurks amid a field of sunken boulders. Browns that seem bent on slicing a light tippet or large fish that instantly dive for cover, especially in a narrow or heavily vegetated stream, are among light-tippet hazards. Using a 4X tippet on a 7-foot leader and a 4-inch Woolly Bugger tied on a long-shank, thin wire hook, I took a 23-inch brown on the fly's first cast. That combination, as subsequent angling showed, is no longer just experimental for me.

My ventures with the 2-weight Ultra Fine know few limits. I've even used a 2-weight extensively at night with drys from #8 down to #20, conditions where heavier rods and fly lines have been considered essential. When angling becomes demanding, going light in the dark has given the same angling edge as it does during the day. Frequent angling partners have accepted my idiosyncrasy for sport by adopting the 2-weight. You can decide on the waters, fish, and angling methods suitable for your own 2-weight challenge.

Favorite Fish

Same Trout Again!

KEEP RETURNING to a reach of stream for an ever-growing insight into the ways of trout. Over any given time period, many of the same trout are providing much of the action, and some individual fish feed on the surface more often than others. A trout encountered, hooked, or caught presents a renewed challenge the next time. Just bear in mind that a trout carefully released is less likely to change its established feeding habits than a trout gouged with a large hook or mishandled short of causing mortality.

Early in my fly-fishing, I doubted, simply because of inexperience, that a trout would take a fly soon again. A sage angling buddy mentioned a secluded pool where he had released a 3½-pound brown, advising me where to plant my wadered feet and the presentation to use. "It's the only brown of that size there," he added.

I chose an hour when large trout would feed on that lane in the wide shallows he had described and, of course, was amazed when I caught the thick, hook-jawed brown. In years since, I've been able to direct friends in a like manner, and they've often been just as surprised as I was. One fellow who was new to fly-fishing and the stream was astounded when the several *X*s on my sketch were transformed into trout of the respective sizes I had noted, rising to his dry fly. "How could you know?" he asked.

"Simple," I thought. I'd given him the time, the approach, and the presentation for that location on the basis of a number of envi-

A rainbow is gently released back to its home.

ronmental variables and on taking fly patterns. "I caught them all a few days ago," I answered. "You're a good fisherman to have done so well." In this instance, I had made a new friend, and he has become a dedicated fly-fisher.

Years ago, Joe Brooks, the late great angler and fishing writer, showed me how to properly revive a trout I'd caught. The impression this made on me has had a multiplying effect over the years; taking a few minutes to share such education should be every angler's good deed. Demonstrating that with a proper release a trout is no worse for the struggle may be more important to the future of angling than any advice on how to catch trout.

I remember one day when a 3-pound rainbow trailed a stubby, gossamer strand of membrane from its jaw after my partner's dry fly was removed. I revived the trout and happened to chance by the same spot a few days later. Sure enough, that 'bow, or its twin, finned in the identical place, now hanging a bit more deeply. It inhaled the nymph I drifted to its snout and put on a spectacular series of seven leaps, matching the aerial antics I had watched on my friend's line. Later, at my feet, the 'bow showed the telltale tissue edging the jaw. I again revived it, knowing the same satisfaction as when another angler has taken a trout I've released.

Trout are your teachers, too, as one dimpling rainbow demonstrated. With a hatch of size 16s and 18s again on the surface, this time I matched the smaller ones. The trout sipped my dry, and the springy little rod proved a sporty match for the leaping rainbow. While easing it in, I saw last time's tippet streaming from the #16 dry notched aside the back; foul-hooking is not uncommon when a trout rolls up but refuses or misses a fly. The lessons: (1) selectivity, (2) a trout's homing instinct. After nearly emptying the reel's backing, that 20-incher had returned through the vast river pool to its exact feeding station under the drift of insects. Marked for me by a snag on the bank, this chosen niche along broad flat water wasn't otherwise discernible from a distance.

The repeat angler can glean more about the feeding patterns of an individual trout. A larger trout may establish a lair, and while it'll feed on a given station often at about the same time of day, it also may cruise and use various locations within its selected range. During a good hatch, I've taken a large brown three times in little more than a week on different feeding lies all within 50 yards of its lair. One beefy, elusive brown that would lurk to feed along several edges in its pool from time to time had grown when I caught it a second time, nearly two years later.

As a trout becomes larger, it may drop to lower, roomier waters, though water temperature, feeding forays, and spawning rites are among factors that may influence an individual's whereabouts. George Anderson lost a 'bow the first time he saw it in a small Montana stream and observed it ranging upstream and downstream as far as a quarter mile before landing the nearly 9-pound trophy a year and a half later.

A trout should be landed in a way that avoids injury. Although a net eases the corralling of a heavyweight, the last time a partner handed me his floating net I tossed it aside, for the trout's torso obviously wouldn't fit. I prefer playing a fish to hand. Somehow I got into the habit of clamping thumb and forefinger (as with a bass) on a brown's lower jaw and would judge my brown-trout days by a scratched and often bloody thumb. Now I simply "tail" some cumbersome trout with an overhand grasp ahead of the caudal fin; this secures and steadies the tired fish while keeping it in the water. Or I'll beach a willing trout with a lead of the rod onto a smooth (not rocky) stream edge.

A few of the larger trout in a catch-and-release stream I ply regularly, however spirited until played in, have obediently snugged on a shallows, awaiting release. Trout that have learned the game frequently show another angler's fly in the mouth, tippet snipped. It's usually a deeply embedded #16 or smaller hook.

During the last few years, I've wielded a 2-weight outfit and usually a 6X tippet for innumerable 20-inch-class browns, some ranging up to 30 inches, in this public "fish-for-fun" stream. I've caught many of them two or more times and know that a light rod and hairline tippet don't have to be a killer of large trout. This is tackle that gives an angling edge in a large, sedate limestoner. And the thrill of the hookup—standing behind a wand of a rod while an eye-opening trout tethered on a gossamer strand takes a dry fly—is one of the ultimate experiences in fly-fishing. But since a large trout usually is near exhaustion when it succumbs, special attention is needed to ensure its recovery.

Using the two-hand cradle (one hand wrapped ahead of the tail, the other hand palming the underside just behind the gills ahead of the belly), you can steady the trout in an upright position, facing it into a calmer side flow. Let me emphasize that unless the trout regains equilibrium, revival methods may not be effective. Then, "washing" the trout a few inches ahead and back, gently, up to a half minute, will usually get the gills working naturally. Excessive artificial pumping of the gills can drown a fish by supersaturating it with dissolved oxygen. However, a fish allowed to rest for a minute or two may be in need of a second pumping procedure before the gills begin to flex naturally.

Should a trout want to swim away weakly, just a little restraint with the tailing grasp will keep it in the easier shallows. Resting a trout in comfortable shallows until it regains strength is helpful to its survival. For over 10 minutes I revived one notably hard-fighting lunker and, when it was breathing healthily, went about my fishing. I returned to check on it a half hour after unhooking it, and the fish departed speedily with a tap. The following year it still used the same feeding niche.

One chart has been devised to suggest a trout's recovery time in relation to its size, duration of struggle, and line weight, but there are too many variables to arbitrarily judge a trout's readiness to re-enter the mainstream. One should administer to individual trout. Ideally, a trout will give that little flip of its tail when ready to escape a cradling hold, as a 25-incher did in an award-winning video for Wisconsin Public Television. As always, I kept that one in the water with a cradling hold; with the tailing grasp there's never a need to squeeze a trout or to grip it over the back, a viselike lock that can remove the protective mucous membrane and injure internal organs. When you pose a trout for photography, cradle it lightly, balancing it in or over the water. I've hefted a few with the tail grasp for a nose-down photo, salmonlike.

Before taking a close-up or having another person take a posed photo, revive the trout a little until the still camera is ready. I prefer detailed photography of a trout's markings for identification. The clustered spot patterns on a trout's operculum and head are like fin-gerprints—unique. Other obvious features naturally mark certain individuals. Purposely "tagging" a trout or marring its anatomy as carefully as notching a fin may not be harmful, but neither appeals to me. If you are making a personal study of your trout or want to claim bragging rights, a little pinhole in a fin will do for a time.

The challenge of taking a trout again is an element of the sport we all experience, if only because someone may have hooked it. Often, a change in flies will take a trout that has mouthed a pattern. During a feeding spree, a trout may be hooked several times—not only when hatches are prolific. While I was fishing to other trout in between, one heavily feeding trout took the same fly three times until I hooked it the fourth time. In another instance, I didn't stay around to find what one native brown might take after it swam from my hands and immediately resumed rising to hatches. Recently a fellow I had taught to cast made a perfect drift with a dry to a hovering 21-incher and caught it. Some 40 minutes later I passed that way, and the trout was hanging near the surface; I caught it on a different dry.

This may seem contradictory, but a friend and I once agreed that a week is a good interval to try again for a lunker brown hooked in a favorite local stream. But in trouting, personal guidelines may depend in part on one's usual methods and flies. The big brown becomes wary of familiar fly patterns, and the wiliest of them will adapt feeding times to seldom-fished hours and when conditions move them to feed. The "science" of pursuing such long-located trout has had me on the water on a rainy, thunderous night when I knew the hatch would be only sparse—and then I've found the brown feeding.

The lunker may also feed briefly. One night, the same friend and I met after angling for located, secretive browns that had eluded us on earlier trips. We acknowledged, over his broken fly rod, that the big fish had fed for just 10 minutes. Mine had siphoned under a large dry as if it were a midge and sliced the tippet. Angling for lunker trout that are seldom seen in a local creek can be a patient version of the sport.

When hatches require small hooks and light tippets, even a cautious trout will feed again. Not uncommonly, larger trout persistently remain on station, continuing to feed as though oblivious of a wee hook that has slipped from the jaw more than once—or sometimes a snapped hairline tippet. In one example, a friend had broken off a midge dry in the jaw of a larger trout, and he suggested that I try for it. Minutes later, it fed sporadically again, having reverted to emergers. It wouldn't look at a #18 floating pupa on a 6X tippet, but then it took a #20 on 7X. I also unhooked the midge dry I had tied for him.

Trout I've caught earlier cause me to question the need to make subtle changes in even a hatch-matching fly or the need to use a contrasting fly. A week later some individuals have shown a liking for the same fly, while others that take the productive pattern with a slight change in color or silhouette make me think the new impression was convincing. I initially took one 21-inch native brown on a cream fly; I then mixed additional new shadings of dubbing into the fur abdomen each of the next two times I caught it rising in the same hatches. For a rising 24-incher, I used a hackled caddis, and two days later a no-hackle of the same pattern.

When a trout spurns a hatch-matching pattern, an attractor pattern can catch its eye. Often, a realistic fly used as a *contrast* to the hatch is deadlier. A nice rainbow was hogging the base of a riffle to rise in a variety of hatches along a heavily fished meadow stream. When I tried to take it a third time, it fed on minutiae, but I finally caught it on a #16 no-hackle dun of a darker color than any mayflies I've seen in that stream. That wasn't the only instance when a dry that size has taken trout feeding on the tiniest insects.

On a distant, famous stream I travel to, the same feeding lane gave me what appeared to be the same rising brown on a dry at about the same time a year later; detailing the second encounter would involve a carbon copy of the first, including a description of this trout's routine of unusual—learned—fighting techniques on the line. And on streams I fish more often, a particular brown's individual fighting way has hinted of the same trout again. I've caught such a trout in different locations as the fish moves about its pool or takes up a new lair or feeding site. Trout not seen for a considerable time symbolize the gist of this chapter, for if anglers have done their part it's possible to return later with quality sport to be had—and, I suggest, with a renewed appreciation and understanding of the ways of an individual trout. Catch-and-release expands such opportunities.

As a postscript, coming back with a lighter rod is one of my favorite sporting ploys. I've lost a large trout and then taken it on lighter tackle. Generally, I do best on the same trout again with lighter tackle; the light fly line and leader are a natural adaptation for warier trout. Further, you needn't be entirely practical in matching the tackle to the water and the trout—if you enjoy the challenge.

Small Wets for Big Bass

F OR MORE THAN A WEEK I watched a parade of lure-flinging fishermen saturate a nearby, small peninsula jutting from the shore into a popular fishing lake. During this brief time, I thought the bass in those shallows had seen enough metal, wooden, and molded plastic spinning lures to make them wary.

The small peninsula stood out from the even 100-yard lakefront. The boggy prong, bearded with marsh grass, bordered depths of 3 feet. I had an inkling this bassy-looking node was more than a feeding spot for fish cruising the shoreline. The bank was deeply undercut, a feature hidden by the grassy tangles draping its overhanging border.

On a pleasant evening I anchored my boat 50 feet off the promontory and began casting well off the shoreline, with an eye toward the bank. Bass reside in watery undercut caves and haunt dark shallow places. I hoped for one that would feed on the surface along the edge. Thus, I saved the margins.

My fly was nothing fancy: a #8 Woolly Worm tied with a fluorescent red yarn tail, an attraction that in my experience often makes a positive difference in the catch. My leader was 9 feet, tapered to a 4X point. I used an 8½-foot fly rod with a soft tip and backbone in the butt. The right tackle for presenting a smallish fly for bass, and for hooking and parrying the pugnacious fish over bottom snags, may vary. This combination is a basic outfit.

The sun had nearly set on the western horizon, and shade spread

from the grassy point, darkening the calm shallows. As I fished leisurely, enjoying the late day, my vigil was rewarded. A yard from a
bush on one side of the point, a splashy rise spangled the water. It
was definitely a bass taking an insect, which occurs more often on
this heavily fished lake at night.

Seeing a bass rise stirred my instinct as a fly-fisher. Had the fish
nosed from the deeply undercut land and ventured under darkening
water for an impulsive take of a single insect? Was the bass tarrying
or cruising? The way to answer those questions, I learned, was to
present the fly as quickly as possible while the fish would likely be
there. My cast didn't show the fly in the ring of the rise, but seconds
after the water had flattened, the soft fly alighted on the hub where
those concentric rings had spread.

Dry, no. Wet, no. Simply soggy, yes, in the surface film. The
Woolly was taken deftly, with a small splash, as I had seen previously.
I set the hook solidly but with a light hand so as not to snap the
tippet. All at once, the largemouth cavorted like an energetic small-
mouth. It jumped suddenly, stiffly, falling back in, then scampered
in a tail-dancing foray for 15 feet, broadside across the point. When
it settled into the tugging runs and slower head-shaking mannerisms
of a largemouth, my springy rod bowed deeply. I applied the
strength of its backbone while coaxing the fish to urge it from mir-
ing into bottom vegetation.

On the comparatively light tippet, it jumped again. The sport
was exciting because of the circumstances. When I eased it to the
gunwale, those factors that I had come to believe were notable,
namely, the fishing pressure with lures became apparent. As I lowered one hand to grasp the fish's lower jaw, I saw it was split down
the middle, from fighting off tenacious treble hooks. I inserted my
thumb more deeply into its jaw, bent it downward, and rested the
weight on my forefinger, immobilizing the bass. I lifted a chunky
17-incher.

Yet, that bass, which may have been dieting on smaller morsels
because of its mangled jaw, was not a unique catch. Bass will feed
on insects simply for a supplement and because of the fish's inquisi-
tive nature in foraging. A bass has a somewhat insatiable curiosity,

so even if one has become leery of artificials, it'll still take a gently presented fly.

When I first began bassing, I assumed good-sized fish were gluttonous and took only large offerings. One episode cued me that the small wet fly has its place. We were casting to a shoreline, and my buddy had let his wet fly sink in the shallows. Our boat then drifted very slowly along with the slight current in the river neck of a reservoir. As the sunken fly began to swim parallel to the shoreline dropoff, a sizable bass appeared and siphoned it in. The visible, easy take of a #12 fly at the time seemed uncharacteristic of this fish with a gaping maw, but it nonetheless led me to techniques with the small wets.

Permit your wet fly to sink in a bassy pocket, such as the openings and notches in reed lines, under a bush, or along a dock. Bass will take the fly on its slow descent. A fish eyeing a tantalizing morsel will generally take it gently.

When the wet has sunken to the desired depth, I use a slow, steady retrieve. A hand-twist retrieve makes the fly appear alive. With palm of the line hand upward, grasp the line between your thumb and forefinger. Then roll the wrist toward the fly rod until it is palm down, fingers reaching forward over the line. Pin the line under the little finger, and twist the wrist away from the rod so the line loops around your little finger and slides in, cradled on the middle two fingers as the palm turns up. Fold in the hand-wide length of line by forming a fist. Anchoring the length into the thumb-forefinger vise, slip the little finger out of the bow. With this wrist-roll you can vary the pace of the fly. Several hand twists will gather a number of figure eights of line in hand. Drop the handful of line and continue the retrieve.

In this fishing, both while the wet is sinking and during a retrieve, the take of even a good-sized bass may be light. One guideline, then, is to fish a straight line to the fly.

Borrowing an aid from nymphing for stream fish, wrap a piece of bright-colored wire-core chenille on the leader tippet a foot or more ahead of the fly. White and fluorescent orange are two colors that show up well. If you find such an indicator helpful in detecting a light take, you may wish to tie in a piece of chenille with thread and cement it with an adhesive. When probing shallows in waters that give enough visibility, such a "light" on the line may merely stop in the water, signaling that a fish has the fly.

When using smaller flies on a light line, I do not strike hard. I hold the rod tip low to the water, pointed just aside the straight line. The low rod also is in position for hooking gentle-feeding bass. When the connection becomes "heavy," I simply roll my rod wrist sideways, extending the rod horizontally at a right angle to the fly line. This is a somewhat automatic hooking technique when fishing a slow-paced fly. It works with any tackle.

A #8 fly pattern I tie has a way of attracting fish. The underbody is a fluorescent material, such as wool. The overlay is a thin strip of plastic cut from the translucent carrier for a six-pack of beverage cans. A paper-thin tip of this plastic is bound down at the bend of the hook. The remainder of the strip is spiraled forward around the shank to the front of the hook. The see-through qualities of the plastic give a distinctly segmented appearance. In various lighting, either the softly shiny plastic or the underbody color shows dominantly. A slow presentation of this home-tied, chameleon-like fly has caught the eye of many bass.

Bass perceive color remarkably better than other freshwater game fish. This has been proven to me when a sizable fish paces a little #14 wet. In my experience, the individual bass is attracted most often to fluorescent yellow and red. Flies having one of these colors for the abdomen are my favorite choices when flies matching natural foods may not be taking fish. Bass are highly perceptive and attracted to red. A red ant and the standard red-banded Royal Coachman are effective.

When bass cruise along cover harboring small fish, a bucktail or a streamer can be a "hot" pattern. I usually present one on a slow retrieve to mimic a feeble, swimming minnow rather than an escaping fish. I use 3-inch-to 1-foot-long strips with pauses. These patterns can be presented at all depths with the aid of modern fly lines. You can, for example, use a weight-forward bug-tapered floating fly line for presenting unweighted wet patterns several feet under the

My chameleon wet fly, #8, in the jaw of a hefty bass

surface. You might then want to try a Wet Tip line for depths of 6–10 feet or even a full sinking line to reach the bottom in a hurry.

A friend of mine likes to fish in the late afternoon shade of a river channel beneath a city bridge. "There are a lot of fingerling northern pike there," Steve told me, "and the bass take them." He uses a black-over-green streamer to imitate the little darting pike.

I once tied a larger-than-usual bucktail to imitate a sucker and other minnows that have a dark back and a little color on the flank. I added gold bead eyes on this pattern. On a bright August morning, its christening swim along the edge of a drop-off where bass cruise in crystal-clear water attracted a sizable beauty.

Many a time a bait-fish fly has taken bass when they would not go for other offerings. I reaffirmed that when I tied a lightly weighted, chenille-bodied black Matuka streamer with the two split, long hackle feathers as tails. Retrieved at a snail's pace over weed beds, that "new" pattern proved to be lethal. It was a fly these fish had not seen before, adding to the lore that a bass feeds with a considerable degree of curiosity.

A similar fly, my All-Marabou Leech, is one of the deadliest bass enticements I've ever used. While #6–10 Leeches can be regarded as small wets for bass, smaller Leeches on #12 and even #14 hooks attract the wariest bass well. Ease them along in shallows or present them on bottom. They're naturals for sight fishing to bass lurking in shallows, and I'll go as light as a 6X tippet and fish a 2-weight rod. On ultralight tackle, bass of a pound are impressive, and truly larger bass become tackle-testing trophies.

When I was a teenager, I waded a 90-acre, bowl-shaped lake with crystal-clear water. Back then, bass frequently fed in the reedy borders and a few weedy bays. They were not as wary then as they are today, because increasing numbers of anglers have taken to the once lightly fished small lake. I still fish that lake. When bass are in these shallows during daylight hours, like during the cooler waters of spring and fall, often under overcast skies, they present the greatest challenge ever against the light sand bottoms and sparse cover. Small wets have become a panacea. Flies on #6–14 hooks are surprisingly productive not only on such local waters but also wherever and whenever bass in shallows aren't going for larger offerings.

You may label these bass offbeat, but they have become a bit smarter in the steadily fished waters. By adapting your times and flies, there's angling for bass in shallows, though the fish may have been shown any number of artificials. Whenever you seek this prized game fish with the fly rod, it will feed with a curious eye.

Match the Hatch for Bluegills

ABUNDANT IN A VARIETY of habitats, including lakes, ponds, river backwaters, and streams, the bluegill is one of the most commonly sought game fish in America. Its well-known eagerness to take an imitation and give a feisty battle on light tackle especially endears this brightly colored little fish to fly rodders.

However, that eagerness to smack an artificial is not the bluegill's only attraction to fly-fishers. For example, when feeding on insect hatches, this popular panfish will frequently display selective feeding habits that often are attributed to trout. This choosy preference, though, is not necessarily for any one insect, but rather for a floating fly, and not only during pleasant summer days.

I used to believe that the surface bug was used only when numerous varieties of insects are on the water and the fish are accustomed to rising for them. Not so, I learned. In chilly water of spring and autumn, a bluegill will come up to take the one insect on the water. I had seen sizable 'gills do this often enough that I began using a patient method with the dry fly several years ago. I adopted this leisurely angling technique during a stint on a lake near my home.

I cast a dry fly to the edge of an old sunken channel marker in the 3-foot-deep shallows. A minute passed before I saw a hefty bluegill tilt slowly upward, look over the dry fly nearly snout-to-hackles, then sip it in. I tightened the line, and the hooked bluegill took off, planing its flat side against the bowed fly rod in a lunging run.

A dry fly that sits on the water for a few minutes can be enticing to cautious bluegills and is most practical when cast near cover and to sighted fish. Even on a chilly day when the sunken fly should normally be productive, bluegills will show a penchant for the easily captured dry.

Bluegills rise to one insect or another throughout the season. In southern Wisconsin, where I do the majority of my bluegill fishing, hatches bring up the fish as early as in the days after ice melts in spring, through summer, and well into autumn. As with all the hatches, the abundance of a particular insect may vary from year to year, but the comparatively fewer numbers will still attract bluegills.

Early one evening bluegills dimpled the mirrored waters of a bay. They were selective to the emerging midge pupae in the surface film. The presentation was as important as the fly that simulated the natural insect. Swimming a #16 pupa evenly for 6 inches to a foot, then pausing, resulted in a gentle take. Those bluegills were partial not only to the form of the insect most abundant at the time but also to pupae that were struggling to hatch. In this instance, the naturals were so abundant that a retrieved fly caught the attention of the fish.

Midging bluegills offer challenging angling and may require various presentations. During the onset of hatches, the fish feed more deeply, at the edges of vegetation and near the bottom. One technique is to let the weighted pupa sink to the source of the hatches, then slowly raise the fly rod. With the floating line sliding along, the pupa rises through the water as the ascending natural insect does.

The majority of bluegills will feed at the exact level where the insects are concentrated. On one cool day, I watched an occasional 'gill dimple the surface during a sparse hatch. Midge pupae were dallying in the water near the surface, though not many were emerging on the lake. I cast to one of the fish, and the lightly weighted fly sank, then hung inches below the surface, buoyed by the leader plainly visible on flat water. (You can grease the leader with Mucilin to present a hanging pupa at the feeding depth of the fish.) The fly hung suspended for 30 seconds or so before the end of the leader barely twitched on the water. Tightening the line, I put a scrappy 8-inch bluegill into its act.

"Hidden hatches" of emergent insects also attract bluegills. Some of the larger bluegills I have caught were feeding on ascending nymphs of mayflies. During a sparse hatch of drakes in late spring on the lake I fish, the pattern of angling is highly consistent. As dusk deepens, the nymphs begin to swim from the bottom, and sizable bluegills begin to feed avidly. I fish a #8 brownish-black fly that simulates the nymph. I allow the fly to sink 5 feet or deeper, then retrieve it slowly, finally raising it toward the surface. Throughout the two weeks of this hatch, most of the larger bluegills succumb to nymphing.

In the twilight and after dark when mayflies are on the surface, I present a high-winged dry fly to rising fish. When the mayflies return to the water to lay their eggs, the bluegills are partial to a spent-winged dry, which floats flush on the surface. Following the opening days of the hatch, flies are on the water in increasing numbers. Last season I was fortunate to catch an 11-inch bluegill by casting a spentwinged dry fly into an audible rise.

In heavier hatches, many night-feeding bluegills slurp thumb-sized mayflies. Most of the hatches of larger mayflies that cause extensive surface feeding at night occur in various regions from late spring into summer.

For a change of pace, stream fishing can be delightful. In a mild flow, bluegills feed with a degree of selectivity that can be remarkable. My favorite part of one stream stretches for a couple of miles below a spring-fed lake and meanders through a meadow. Seepage springs filter in from the wetlands, as well as from the hard bottoms of sand and gravel. This reach never muddies, and bluegills rise for hatches from spring to autumn.

One chilly spring afternoon, 1-inch, blue-winged mayflies hatched from sunken mudbanks along a sluggish, widely sweeping bend. In the brisk weather, they drifted a long way, flopping their large wings in their attempt to raise themselves upright. Bluegills took them in splashy rises.

During the season as the hatches change, so does the preference of the bluegills. If they're ringing the water taking #16 dark mayflies, a facsimile drifted naturally does best. If they're splashing for scampering caddis flies at dusk, fishing across and down with a caddis dry fly and inching it across current on a slack line takes fish.

One fishing venture gave me a special appreciation for bluegills and the hatches. During an evening several years ago when I did not have my small hatch-matching flies along, I encountered an eye-opening complexity of insects. As I waded the lower end of a smoothly flowing pool, the flies became as abundant as confetti. *Baetis* mayflies hatched from the stream, with several other varieties of mayflies in lesser numbers. Midges sprinkled the air, and many dropped onto the surface.

A bluegill 10 inches long appeared in midstream at the tail of the pool. Hovering at the surface, it sipped to feed in the surface film. Then, it slowly finned toward the top of the pool, feeding every foot of the way. As it turned and swam down to its original position, it began another upstream foray. How I wished for a #24 spentwing no-hackle midge spinner! That tiny fly would have imitated the most abundant fare on the water, and the bluegill was taking only those flush-drifting tidbits. Presenting what flies I did have proved to be as frustrating as the bothersome mosquitoes, which soon joined this otherwise classic profusion of hatches.

Locating habitats of insects provides optimum fishing, whether the food is aquatic hatches or terrestrials. Bluegills migrate to feed in areas where they expect insects to be numerous on the water. One of the terrestrials that are relished is the ant, a perennial that bluegills feed on anytime. A friend first showed me this one chilly day as we fished a brushy shoreline. "One more bluegill, a big one," he said, knotting a red ant onto the tippet. The bright fly beneath the foliage was taken with a solid strike, and later he cradled the 'gill that overlapped his palm.

Bluegills lurk beneath overhanging cover for the wide variety of terrestrials that drop to the surface. It's worth taking the time to determine which ones are most plentiful and favored by bluegills. Inchworms and innumerable beetles are a few that may be abundant from time to time.

Various insects will disperse with the wind. Thus, terrestrials, as well as aquatic insects, may be scattered over an expanse of water. The funnel effect of winds and mild lake currents tends to congregate insects on protected areas of water. Bluegills will convene and rise where insects become temporarily abundant. They will feed on top even in mildly rippled water, so "drifting" a dry over a rising fish is productive.

One breezy day in late summer while parading a #18 Midge along ripples to rising bluegills in the lee of a bay, I spotted a lone 1-inch grasshopper well out on the lake. It had drifted and kicked from the far shore of the small lake. Moments later, a bluegill took it in a splash. I changed to a hopper and caught the fish. The others rising to numerous but scattered midges would take only a small dry.

Hatches of pudgy beetles can bring excellent offshore rises of bluegills. Typically, the beetles are strewn on the water in deceivingly large numbers, somewhat concealed by their humplike, low, floating silhouettes. When mixed sizes are present, usually smaller beetles are more abundant. Often bluegills sip #18 beetles exclusively, even though some half-inchers are afloat.

One of the notable terrestrial hatches is the annual fall of flying ants. Starting in mid-September, these winged ants offer several weeks of angling along a lake edge I wade. The rounded point is bordered with tall overhanging trees harboring the ants. They'll flutter downward, dropping lightly onto the shoreline shallows and the deeper waters, the distance of a long cast onto the lake.

Overcast, calm days produce squadronlike flights, and the ants dot the surface in considerable numbers. I've tied a #16 winged ant to match them, settling it low onto the water. The bluegills are selective to the near flush-floating insects at rest and take one with a gentle rise, leaving a small ring on the water. I wade in place, watching for a rise and keeping plenty of loose fly line coiled on the water. A 'gill may feed 20 or 60 feet away. Casting the fly accurately on target within seconds after a fish has fed is the steadiest technique. Leaving the fly motionless for a time takes the most fish.

The 8-inch and larger bluegills tend to feed alone. They cruise slowly along near the surface to spy an insect. While you can always

A bluegill tilts up for a late-season flying ant. (Artwork by Richard Fendrick, based on an original sketch by T. Wendelburg; reproduced with permission)

skim the fly slowly along to a new spot, usually a fresh cast and fishing the fly at rest is more productive. These bluegills can be incredibly shy of any line movement, even with a light tippet.

The selective bluegill is line-wary, and a light leader tippet is best. Use a 4X or 5X leader tippet to turn over a #8 fly when the fish are taking larger insects. However, I do the majority of my bluegilling with #12–20 flies on a 5X or 6X tippet. When bluegills are finicky, a 7X tippet has given not only a feather-light presentation but also the obscurity that can make a difference to the sharp-eyed 'gill tilting upward to a little fly.

For fishing pocketed waters amid snaggy cover, a leader of 7 feet is fine. In calm clear water a 12-foot leader often is not too long for wary bluegills. A tapered, floating fly line of 1–4 weight will delicately present the fly. A small-diameter, light line is an aid in hooking fish, for it offers less resistance when sliding in across the surface or when raised from the water.

Choose a fly rod that balances with the line. An 8-footer is an all-purpose stick. A rod with a light tip presents a small fly quietly and has the sensitivity to hook the fish when it gently siphons in the fly. If you like a short fly rod, as I do, the bluegill will give you an increased sense of sport as it bends the little rod. Yet a pugnacious bluegill planing its high-side broadside against the leverage may bow my strong 8½-foot fly rod as deeply as it would the 5-foot wand.

The bluegill has many qualities as a sport fish, not the least of which is the selectivity it frequently shows when feeding on insects. Try matching the hatch for bluegills.

Skamania

Late Summer's Glory

IN SUMMER MONTHS and continuing into early autumn, the sleek Skamania steelhead ventures up rivers on the Pacific Coast and into certain Great Lakes tributaries where they've been introduced. This sporty steelhead feeds willingly but deceptively, and the knowing angler adapts to its ways. Developed at Washington's Skamania hatchery, no other strain of anadromous salmonid returns to its spawning river so early, providing action in shirtsleeve weather.

Water conditions dictate the timing of the runs. Summer rains that freshen sometimes low, paltry rivers encourage Skamania to leap low dams, surge across shallow gravel bars, and continue upstream to occupy favorable habitat. In my home state of Wisconsin, main-stem rivers that enter the west shore of Lake Michigan, as well as many rivers throughout the Skamania's range, provide concentrated steelhead populations upstream to a dam. Dry spells, typical of late summer, cause water levels in most rivers to drop precipitously, in turn causing steelhead to disperse, many heading back downstream. However, those rivers offering suitable summer conditions and cover are like magnets, holding secretive Skamania and bright new fish that sneak into the rivers on their own schedules.

Follow the Oxygen

A steep gradient in a stream produces a riffling, choppy run, called a staircase by some. As the water tumbles over stone and rock, it

I caught this beautiful Skamania steelhead on a Lake Michigan tributary using 6-weight tackle and a #6 chartreuse Woolly Bugger.

mixes needed oxygen into the tepid stream. Some steelhead will hold in pocket water behind large boulders in the center of the fast water, while others will hold in the dark-bottomed hole below. A deeper, cooler hole with steady current may hold steelhead throughout summer, provided the critical oxygen content is there. Similar, but barely chest-deep, base pools shaded by dense foliage also are productive. Dark bottoms attract steelhead in shallow or deep water, as areas of interspersed submerged rocks and rooty, undercut edges do.

An upwelling spring, cool to the wading angler, is like an oasis in the summer river. So, too, is the mouth of a cooler entering tributary. Steelhead may nose into these oxygen tanks or fin nearby.

Some rivers contain many areas of typical summer habitat for steelhead but frequently stay discolored long after it rains. Their stained nature, ironically, is one reason they offer crops of Skamania, and they provide camouflage for the angler as well. Make no mistake, visibility through stained water is adequate for the steelhead to be just as sensitive to fly color, style, and presentation as it is in clear water. A river tends to carry particles of silt or root sap in suspension high in the water column, while the waters along hard bottom, slower or shallow edges, and riffles can run clearer.

Cool Mornings

While steelhead prefer water temperatures in the mid- to upper 50s, many summer rivers flow with warmer water. Temperatures in the 60s may be ideal, though the Skamania is tolerant of temperatures into the 70s where enough dissolved oxygen is present. The summer steelhead adapts to warmer daily temperature ranges by seeking the darker, cooler spots. When the water temperature drops but a few degrees, look for fish easing into shallower lies. In either stained or crystal-clear streams, early morning hours produce the coolest waters of the day.

One recent late-summer morning, I began in a forested pool on a favorite Wisconsin river. A Woolly Bugger presented upstream and drifted deeply under a high rod tip was ignored. The weighted Woolly Bugger is a fly of many disguises, so I flipped mine to the head of the pool and, with a lowered rod tip and a little slack in the line, sank it to the bottom. A jigging action with the rod tip hopped it in short, steep jumps through the water back toward me. As the billowy fly settled the second time, the subtle tic marking a steelhead's take revealed that a change of presentation is often all it takes to fool a steelhead.

A few minutes later, the Skamania at my feet lay beached across a gravel bar. The muscular fish spanned a man's arm length, its metallic sides a bit tarnished. A long-time river dweller, it showed a gnarled membrane from a recent hooking in the cleft of the jaw opposite my fly.

An elderly angler walking the river had watched the quick action, looked at the fish, and offered, "Hardly anybody's upstream. I just turned a bright fish in the big pool a ways up. Sure got the old ticker going. I'm headed back to the barn, so it's all yours."

I had to go some distance to find the wide, deep pool formed by a bend in the river. Switching to a smaller chartreuse Woolly Bugger, I carefully waded the lower end of the large steelhead sanctuary. My sidearm, upstream, curve cast dropped the end of the floating line in a nearly right-angled, inverted L, slanting the weighted fly sharply but with minimal disturbance toward the steep bank. A gentle 20-inch strip of line swam the fly broadside into mild current in a mannerly fashion without straightening the angled line. The Skamania's pickup of the fly visibly twitched the floating loose-line hinge, and I set the sharpened hook firmly into the jaw with a side-arm motion.

Steelhead new to the river are unsurpassed fighters, and now incredible acrobatic leaps occurred against a backdrop of lush green foliage. Then, in seconds, the entire line shot far upstream. Eventually I played the fish back down, subdued by side pressure of the rod. Stepping to the shallow side and turning downstream, I led with the canted rod so the fish's tiring thrashes gave it momentum to slide it onto the flush bank.

I eyed my prize. Olive on top, the 5-year-old's sides shone like quicksilver. Balancing it across my arms, I lowered the 33-inch 12-pounder, facing it into moderate current. I needed to give it extra time in the warmer water. Those minutes of washing the summer fish back and forth gave me pause to consider the morning's peaceful steelheading.

Bonuses

An added attraction to summer steelheading is the presence of other salmonids. Along the way, I had taken a brown that would be regarded as a lunker on any inland stream. The butterscotch-flanked brown may have entered the river last autumn to spawn, overwintered in the stream, and become a resident fish. Hovering high in sunny waters, it had snapped the Woolly Bugger when twitched near its eye.

A lesson can be drawn from these experiences. Each fish responded to a fly exuding breathing materials given enticing action by rod or line manipulation but only during a tension-free pause.

Yet it would be a mistake to discount the natural drift, which is the acknowledged presentation for steelhead.

The natural drift can be used with traditional nymphs and wets. Or for a different look, try a marabou or another streamer drifted naturally. Adept wet-fly anglers can detect the steelhead's light take. Many, however, use a floating strike indicator set a selected distance up the tippet or along the leader. Adjust the depth to give the fly a lengthy drift along bottom or higher through the water (a deadly summer presentation). Keeping a loose line to the float removes tension and allows the fly to be presented naturally.

Imitations and Impressions

Summer steelhead that have settled in will feed on aquatic insects and crustaceans, and sampling the larder in a river will help you choose productive patterns. For a general rule of thumb, stick with buggy-looking impressions. The subtle use of a soft material makes a fly appear lifelike. A fur such as hare's ear produces effective imitations of nymphs and scuds. Tails and legs that sway can be impressionistic (marabou or soft hackle) or realistic (turkey or other fibers). Nymph patterns with a loose clump of ostrich herl or muskrat fur and the heads of larval patterns formed with turns of peacock or ostrich herl pulse even on a natural drift.

Spare use of flash material will often attract steelhead and in tinged water, especially when coupled with a blend of Antron and fur dubbing. Tinsel ribbing is one option. Just a few strands of a flash strip, such as thin Flash-a-bou, twinkles and undulates when tied longer on streamers, but such materials should be tied short on nymphs, wets, and drys.

Patterns that combine a "meaty" abdomen with softer sparse tailing and winging or hackle generally are the most alluring to steelhead. My friend Gary Nimmer efficiently plies the rivers near his home in northeastern Wisconsin with a pattern he developed that is suggestive of stone flies. He ties it on lightly weighted #6 and #8 up-eye Partridge salmon hooks. Dubbed the KO for "knock-out punch," it incorporates the mentioned requisites: short, sparse, black marabou tail, black glittery chenille abdomen, just a dozen strands of blue Krystal Flash for a short wing pad, and a sparse, soft, black hackle.

Successful summer patterns, both traditional ties and innovative creations that exhibit "breathing" qualities, may be encyclopedic in number. But I most enjoy steelheading with a versatile Woolly Bugger, some having a softer-dubbed marabou body, or the hackleless impression of an All-Marabou Leech tied simply of tail and dubbed body. Both are deadly in all sizes and are among the most versatile of patterns in suggesting natural aquatic foods and in the innumerable methods of presentation they afford the angler. They can represent bait fish, crayfish, leeches, and even nymphs and larvae.

Preferences of the enigmatic steelhead may often be matched by changing to a different size or color. Once, for a fish hovering high in a placid, crystal glide, I switched from a #8 white Leech to a miniature #14 claret Leech. A steelhead's known weakness for red produced again. The fish inhaled the little fly paraded broadside with short, puffy swims across its snout.

Presentations

A broadside presentation is productive, however accomplished. One that's easy to do is effective in water that would seem a difficult prospect—a broad, subtle current. Cast straight across, let the fly sink to the bottom and strip it back upward. One time, a steelie, coursing about, disappeared in deep water across stream. The cruising Skamania then came out of nowhere, swimming fast and long, to take the marabou tie during its brief pause near the surface. Long, snappy strips of line worked that time.

Casting at an angle across river and swinging the fly across and below can be the most effective. The proper presentation will feel virtually weightless when you lead with the rod tip. Ideally, set up the presentation so the strike should occur at a 45-degree angle across and below. After the fly drops on the cast, a drift-free swing may be started by mending line downstream. Repeated downstream mends during the swing will reposition the fly broadside. Expect the take during the fly's natural broadside swim while leading with the rod angled downstream in tempo with the swinging line.

Don't neglect the surface fly. A friend entertained me once with stories of summer steelhead taken on hairwing drys in west coast rivers. Ever since, I've angled to midwestern Skamania rising selectively to feed on hatches, notably caddis.

Prospect the water by skimming a dry broadside on an across and slightly downstream shallow-water swing. Shake the fly by waggling the rod tip horizontally in rapid side-to-side vibrations while making quick, short strips of the line. The wriggling fly appears loose and natural on this imparted retrieve and will trigger takes. Imitate the actions and appearances of natural surface prey—insects to voles.

Spun-hair body attractors like the Bomber, or a tapered mouse I tie, churn the water and bring takes. A sloped-back, single hairwing Goofus Bug–type, which I created with long hair tails widely split and knotted, gives a less disturbing V wake.

Summer, too, is a time to use lighter tackle. I consider the 9-foot, 6-weight rod I usually fish as my figuratively "heavy" outfit. While 2- or even 3-weight outfits can be used, for more direct control when going light I use an 8-footer with a 4- or 5-weight line.

I use weight-forward floating line in a tone no brighter than ivory. A leader of 7½–8½ feet eases the casting of bigger flies. In tinged water I've done well with a leader as short as 5½–6½ feet and stout tippets of 0X and 1X. A 2X or 3X tippet is standard, but lighter ones for summer steelheading with sparse and smaller flies may be as fine as 5X. Longer leaders have their place, prominently on low or crystalline waters holding spooky fish.

While tackle should be matched to the water, and presentations with the range of flies used, guidelines are arbitrary. Taking the Skamania a new way and with lighter tackle is a quest worthy of this sporty fish. There are few angling adventures quite like earning a large, brilliant, wildly leaping, tackle-testing summer Skamania.

Surface Tactics

Bountiful Spring Creeks

AMONG TROUT STREAMS, the steadiness of a quality spring creek is unmatched. Trout feed extensively on insects and other foods that can be imitated with artificial flies. On almost any day of the open season, even if it's a year-round season, there's fishing for the fly caster who casts a light tippet and small flies.

Typical of the secretive nature of these small waters, the first little spring-fed creek I fly-fished remained obscured even in the open meadow until I was within yards of the bank. Kneeling to remain concealed, I looked up the smooth water that meandered in snaky switchbacks through the Montana meadow grass and shone with the chalk-blue tinge common to limestone creeks. A trout dimpled the surface as it fed on tiny insects 35 feet upstream, completing the picture.

I was traveling through the area and had a day to fish. But the rivers and even the small freestone streams were bank-full or flooded, most muddied with June snowmelt from the high-country mountain watersheds and further swollen from recent rains.

Watching the trout dimpling this clear, tranquil water, I silently thanked the fellow who had directed me here. The tiny creek, only a few miles in length, welled up from an aquifer on the valley floor that poured thousands of gallons of clean water per minute through a narrow channel, giving the creek a stability unknown in other types of water.

For my first trout I selected a #20 Jassid, a specklike fly that would drift flatly on the surface. After knotting it on 5X tippet of the 9-foot leader, I stripped lengths of line from the reel, letting them coil loosely on the ground. My cast angled upstream, the fly alighting a yard above the trout. The Jassid drifted directly over the narrow feeding lane, and the trout sipped it. I tightened the line, nudging in the hook. Suddenly, the leader sliced through the water and the reel spun when the trout zipped ahead. Then, beyond my bowed fly rod, the fish leaped, somersaulting like a flapjack and falling back on the skillet-flat water. The fish was a sleek rainbow, which I soon brought in and released, cradling it facing into the current till it wriggled and swam upstream.

That day opened a new world of trouting to me, the world of small spring-fed creeks. These creeks are found across the country. They are born where underground rivers well up, sending cool, mineral-rich waters at 48–56 degrees upward through fissures in the earth's surface. Most emerge at low elevations and trace a gently flowing path along valleys often shouldered by rugged hills. Sparkling creeks grace even arid sagebrush desert. Some, notably in the West, are found on high-country meadow plateaus. A creek often surfaces near the base of bluffs or outcroppings, while others well up in an arroyo in the midst of a meadow.

Most spring creeks are only a few miles in length. Those that are longer are often richest in trout along their narrow upper miles. Many spring creeks flow on public lands, not only in the West, where areas of vast acreage are federally owned, but in states around the rest of the country as well. Realizing the value of spring creeks, state fish and game departments, other agencies, sportsman organizations, and even municipalities have ensured public fishing rights on numerous small streams. But even when the spring creeks meander through private land, a polite request for permission to fish is often honored.

The productivity of a spring creek is ultimately derived from its water quality. Trout will lurk in chill waters at the source of these creeks. One I have fished in recent years spills from a crack in a ledge above ground and tumbles into an instant, full-blown stream. In many instances, a bowllike small "pond" (or several of them) laden with emerald vegetation marks the beginnings of a spring creek.

One such spring wells up to form a bowl the size of a large room at the base of a limestone outcropping. It lies hidden in the partial shade of a woods on one bank. Wild brown trout feed in the crystal waters. Smaller trout, including a 3-pounder I once observed, leave the open and lurk in side pockets among the underwater jungle of crisp vegetation when the resident lunker begins circling the pool in a clockwise route. This hulk of a brown tips up now and then to an infinitesimal caddis, a midge, or a little terrestrial. Once the brute delicately sipped my #20 black ant. This spring pours icy water into the stream at 2,700 gallons per minute a little way below the headwaters.

Creeks regarded as the most bountiful in aquatic life well up from limestone substrata. Other minerals, such as magnesium, also tend to increase the productivity of various spring creeks. The dissolved minerals in such natural springs fertilize the stream, and vegetation grows abundantly in the alkaline waters. Leafy clumps of watercress are a sure sign of a cool spring creek. Other plants common in alkaline waters include *Elodea, Potamogeton, Chara,* and *Callitriche.* The vegetation provides cover and is the base of an enriched food chain.

The prolific spring creek sustains a concentration and variety of natural trout foods second to none. Staples include small crustaceans, such as shrimp, cress bugs, sow bugs, and snails; a great variety of aquatic insects; and, in certain creeks, various minnows. I've seen sculpin beneath matted duckweed over an area of rocky bottom. In some creeks crayfish beef up the larger trout.

With a constant flow of cool waters year-round and a bountiful larder of natural foods, enriched spring creeks support more trout per given area than freestone streams do. Trout in some spring creeks grow as rapidly as 4–6 inches in each of their first few years. Various kinds of trout have their own growth potential, yet as a rule

This brown was released to its 57-degree spring creek environs after a spirited fight.

one of the attractions of a quality creek is that many sizes of trout await the angler. Because of the variety of foods in these creeks, anglers have a wide choice of flies and methods. If you like dry-fly fishing, the spring creeks have a charm all their own.

Since the water in these creeks seldom varies as much as 10 degrees on any day, aquatic insects emerge with a rise of only a few degrees. I like to be on the water during a pleasant morning, for good-sized trout quite often rise in the first hatches of the day. Spring-creek trout may lurk almost anywhere in narrow lanes between instream vegetation. Hatches emerge from the spinach, too, and a trout often merely rises from its lair to feed or takes up a feeding station at an edge under the floating insects. In these chilly creeks trout tend to feed avidly while water temperatures are on the upswing during the day. It's been my experience that while waters are rising from the low to upper 50s, hatches of many aquatic insects are steadiest. This swing is common to the majority of spring creeks during late spring.

A change in weather can trigger hatches on these creeks. One bright June day after the morning rise had waned, an overcast swept the sky during the noon hour. Suddenly, hatches began and trout started rising once again. I carry a wallet photo of a brown that took a dry fly during that time.

Standard dry flies that take trout of spring creeks include midges, tent-winged caddises, Adams, Blue Duns, and Olive Quills. Some seasonal hatches are represented with larger flies, but the majority of spring creek insects are matched by #14 and mostly #16 and smaller flies. Lightly hackled patterns, as well as no-hackle imitations, are highly effective on trout in placid creeks.

On enriched spring creeks the smallest of aquatic insects, the midges, attain their greatest abundance and are steady hatches. You'll also find delicate varieties of small caddises and mayflies that do not exist or may be present only in sparse numbers in freestone streams. Insects may be on the water at any season of the year. Multiple hatches, as well as sometimes quick changes in hatches, keep the observant angler alert for what fly the trout are taking.

One spring day in the Midwest, while I fished to trout rising for small caddises, Hendrickson mayflies suddenly began to emerge, and larger trout started feeding, taking only emergers near the surface. A sunken imitation caught trout, although that time the mayflies hatched for only a brief half hour. It was the time of the season for Hendricksons to emerge; however, unexpected hatches have resulted in angling to remember.

An unexpected hatch of small flies occurred on a creek where they usually appear in spring and again in the cooling weather of approaching autumn. On one particular summery day, as the dry air warmed to 75 degrees, sparse numbers of mayflies emerged from vegetation in swift, well-oxygenated shallows along a section of meadow creek. *Baetis* duns as large as #16, others as small as #24, free-floated while drying their wings on placid waters where browns took them.

My partner that day, Roy Swanson, a highly skilled nymph fisherman, changed to a no-hackle dry fly and caught beautifully colored, large plump trout. Toward the end of the hatches, a 2-pounder siphoned under my floating emerger pattern without even ringing the surface, and I played the trout to hand on a 6X tippet.

The insects and visibly feeding trout keep spring creek angling a continually interesting challenge. On mild days in late winter buddies and I have fished for trout rising to mayflies. The gist of post-angling talk usually goes something like this:

> Partner: I had never seen winter-hatching mayflies before the creeks were open in the cold months. We should keep these hatches secret!
>
> Me: I've fished hatches of small mayflies in other regions, and they were unknown sometimes. We've fished the same hatches for some years in a row now on spring creeks, and they are as consistent as the weather.

During one late-winter thaw, many streams were high or muddied with cold snowmelt waters, so I headed for a miniature limestone tributary. The sliver of clear water about as wide as the shoulder of a highway flows steadily, ankle to occasionally thigh deep.

My boots crunched along the snowy bank near the creek's mouth at the mainstream, and I waited a short time. Forty feet upstream a trout swam from beneath one of the logs lining the banks. Its fins rippled, I thought, as it spied a floating midge and tilted up to take the fly. A while later it sipped my #28 midge on a 7X tippet, and the feisty brown tugging against the light rod broke my cabin fever.

As midges emerged more trout fed on top. I took a couple of hours to fish up the entire 800-foot length of this tiny feeder creek in the quietude of a valley white with snow. At its source, water in the upper 40s tumbled from a fissure in an outcropping. Spring creek trout, like the inveterate fly-fisher, know no season.

The smooth waters common on spring creeks have a tenacious surface film, which means emergent aquatic insects frequently drift a considerable way in their shucks, floating low until the winged insects are able to hatch. Emergers are often the form of an insect available to trout during the early stages of a hatch, and trout often feed selectively on them for the duration of the emergence.

I release a Loch Leven strain of brown, caught on a Wisconsin spring creek.

I used to float dry flies, unheeded, over brook trout that were sipping floating emergers on a placid spring creek. It wasn't till I switched to a floating emerger that trout readily took my imitation. Fish this as you would a dry fly.

One simple, but deadly, impressionistic pattern is nothing but dubbed fur spun the length of the hook. A grayish fly of muskrat fur is universally effective. Rabbit fur is useful for matching specific insects because it is available in several colors. These are quick flies to tie. After anchoring the thread to the rear of the shank, spin small bits of fur on the hanging thread under a little tension. Then, spin the thread to tighten the fur. Simply spiral the dubbed thread the length of the hook shank and tie a small head.

In proper sizes, the flies are effective as floating mayfly nymphs and midge pupae. Doug Swisher suggested a chubby, "buggy" version as a floating caddis pupa. Such flies have often meant the difference between having a great day and being left high and dry with the dry fly. Emergent imitations have taken perhaps 50 percent of the trout I've caught in aquatic hatches during late spring.

As with the nearly flush-floating emergent aquatic insects, many terrestrial insects that trout take on the surface of meadow creeks show low silhouettes. Hatches of various terrestrials, including beetles and even the first little grasshoppers, may appear in late spring, especially at lower elevations.

Ants are common along meadow edges, and trout relish them. One day an early-morning deluge had somewhat roiled a spring creek, and the expected aquatic hatches did not appear. But in late morning, when the waters had cleared to a tinge, trout began rising to assorted little terrestrials that had washed in. Most trout fed along grasses draped over the stream banks. But one brown held boldly in stronger flow to feed below the mouth of a narrow spring entering the creek. Here, additional terrestrials washed in from the 4-foot-wide brook, which also supplied clear, fresh water. That trout took a #16 ant.

Entering waters such as the one just mentioned are always worth exploring. Trout in even a 15-foot-wide main creek will fin up to these feeder springs to dine, and the little tributaries frequently have populations of native trout. I've happened upon a number of crystal, watercress creeklets colder than the main-stem stream and only several hundred feet long to their source. Herb Oechler, a frequent fishing buddy over the years, told of hooking a trout in one such narrow creek. The fish leaped onto the bank, wriggled back into the water, and soon jumped onto the other bank.

These creeklets can give you surprising action. As along any small water, keeping well back on the bank, extending the rod tip over the stream, and lowering the fly will take trout. I fished up to the source of one such spot, a circular springs where the mineral waters welled up, filtering visibly through little puffs of sand. A palletlike weed bed spanned its outlet. From the bank, my cast draped line across the surface vegetation, setting a fly on the water beyond. A trout took the offering.

After sliding the fish in, I measured it along the markings on my fly rod and took an admiring look at a rare catch. That chocolate-backed, golden-flanked beauty was thick and robust, and heavier than any stream trout of the same length I had ever landed. For moments, the place seemed a piece of wilderness. But like many quality spring creeks, these waters were only a short hike from a paved road. I released the trout.

Spring creeks are uniquely productive, and even those not far off the beaten path can also be uniquely enjoyable for their quiet and peace. Since that first day on a creek winding like an oasis of trout in a Montana meadow, I've returned to many other spring creeks. They give angling of a quality that hasn't changed much with the passage of time.

Low-Water Camouflage

SOLUTIONS TO THE MYSTERIES of catching difficult trout in low, clear streams of the lengthening season lie in lore gleaned over years of angling. Certain aspects of this lore may be new to many anglers and long forgotten by others. Clothing, tackle, approach, fly choice, technique, and timing of presentation all can be grouped into a single category critical to success: *camouflage*. The need to be unobtrusive can inspire innovative modifications in tackle, flies, and presentations. I've seen these trout of thin water spook from a low-winging bird, so let's begin with a checklist of camouflage beyond a broad-brimmed, earth-tone, shielding felt hat and the polarized sunglasses that are indispensable to cut surface glare and give you a trout-revealing window beneath the surface. In my experience, the best camouflaging color in apparel is a dull, light grayish pale blue, available in shirts but, as far as I know, only in custom-made vests. A sky hue is masking even in reflections on water.

Light lines and rods are the choice for delicate presentations with a light leader, and not only with the small flies that match numerous insects of the season. My own angling system includes flies that are a hook size or more larger than recommended for the tippet, which I tie for easy casting.

"Sparse" is one concession to camouflage and castability, but a sleek pattern also cuts through the air with minimal drag on a cast. Sure, a stout tippet is less noticeable when fished on a larger fly pattern, and 3X and #10s have given me great days when fine and small would have seemed the way. Yet I'll often use 4X or 5X with air-resistant patterns tied sparsely. More often during demanding conditions and routinely on limestone waters, however, I'll use 6X with sleek-formed silhouettes tied sparsely; the largest of these is a 1½-inch spent-, delta-winged no-hackle hopper I designed for tippet-shy trout that have seen just about all the hopper patterns.

Today's weight-forward tapered fly lines make it easier to push out oversized patterns without sacrificing delicacy, and a good fly caster can adjust line speed and loop configurations to deliver a dry in a lifelike manner, just as a natural terrestrial would tumble. A dry fly that's a bit air-resistant for the tippet will also float more naturally, since it's less hampered by the tippet on the water—another aspect of camouflaging, in this case accomplished by enhancing its appearance as a natural. The concept also applies to the sunken fly that drifts in a freer or more natural way, unencumbered by the tippet. These modern weight-forward lines exhibit fine front tapers, not only for delicate presentations, but also for tilting the cast forward to drop a terrestrial imitation solidly with realistic impact onto a trout's snout before the tippet falls imperceptibly. This presentation with a terrestrial, large or small, will alert and convince a trout that earlier ignored a drifted fly.

Line Weight and Color

On limestoners, I regularly wield a 2-weight rod, often with a 3-weight, weight-forward line to ease the casting of larger flies. Similarly, depending on choice in tackle for various waters, a 3- or 4-weight rod, in combination with a preferred weight-forward line, will provide versatility without sacrificing delicacy. A 2–5-weight system gives delightful angling on big rivers during low water. Modern graphite rods simply enhance the line weights that can be used to advantage without sacrificing versatility in fly sizes and presentations.

Gray and olive lines are the least noticeable hues on the market. In a brighter line, I prefer buckskin to ivory tones. When using the

Light tackle was the only way to fool this brown, caught in very low water.

proper leader, the line color shouldn't be a factor in making a presentation to a given trout, but a muted fly line is less apt to spook *other* trout.

Low-Profile Casting

The whip of a visibly slicing fly rod is a factor in low-water angling. A thorough knowledge of the trout's window and adjusting the casting plane from vertical on longer casts, to quarter-arm, to sidearm, as needed, will keep the flailing rod always within the 10-degree blind zone that angles upward from a trout's acute cone of surface vision. Kneeling in the stream figuratively shortens a rod.

On a placid pool I frequent, 15–35-foot casts will reach trout that feed continuously on midges. I've compared the difference in 2 feet of rod length when making vertical casts. When I use a 5-foot rod, even after repeated casts, trout never shrink from view. There's no doubt they can spot a 7-foot-plus rod at such ranges if it arcs high above the water. Even the hatch-conscious trout in the catch-

and-release stream where I made these comparisons become leery of a section of flailing fly rod (and line). In recent years I've used a 7-foot 9-inch rod here most often, mostly casting sidearm with the rod canted.

Leader Length

When you're fishing placid water, a longer leader is advisable *in relation to the length of fly rod*. A general rule of thumb I use is that a leader twice the length of the fly rod not only tends to keep the rod and line hidden from a trout's view but also enhances a balanced cast. I've fished leaders up to 18 feet with a long rod in low water, but unless such lengths are needed I like the shortest practical leader for the waters and rod I'm using. For example, on one of the wider limestone streams I normally fish a 10-footer, which is satisfactory most of the time and always seems to give better results than even a 9-footer.

If you're a specialist, stream size is not as important as water type in choosing leader length. Long leaders camouflage midging along a narrow, flat, gin-clear creek, but on a creek 20 feet wide with continuous bends, corners, nooks, and crannied pockets, I've wielded a hidden 5-foot rod and a mere 6-foot leader for fancy casts, including curves, and ripped up the native browns with #16 no-hackle drys just when fishing would seem to be most demanding.

A short rod naturally enhances accuracy, arcs through a short casting plane, and permits me to exercise line control in a confined space that's also apt to be shrouded with summer's foliage. Such angling adaptation can be intriguing for 6X fishing. The short rod, however, is not limited to short casts, and as you wade midstream it always gives a low cast near the water, ideal to toss a fly under overhangs. The entire presentation occurs beneath a trout's angle of vision. A short rod can be enjoyable to probe shrunken rivers, too. But the concept of using tackle that naturally remains hidden is just as important when brandishing a longer rod and making longer casts on larger waters.

The primary function of leader length is to keep the fly line beyond a trout's window of vision. But tippet length and diameter are generally more critical in a natural presentation, because the tippet competes with the trout's attention to the fly. Although variously formed casts serve to conceal the tippet in part, about the only time the tippet is all but invisible is when the fly drifts directly forward of it to a trout hovering to feed nearly on the surface. On many occasions, picky low-water trout in a sliver of a creek have taken my #22 fly cast straight upstream only when the seemingly flat but subtly mixing current naturally formed a curve. By leaning low to the water, I could then detect the candy-caned 7X tippet that drifted the fly first. When there's space to execute a fully tight-looped curve cast, it's an ideal way to create this presentation.

Angle of Presentation

Simply a change in angle to present the downstream dry fly can give you big elusive fish. I've waded up and fished across, casting tightly to the stream edge, but I've taken the largest trout only when I re-traced my route, making downstream casts. Drag never entered into the presentations from either angle, but angling downstream with the dry and presenting the insect silhouette tail-first, which was enticing to the trout, with the leader extending upstream and less visible, indeed seemed to make all the difference. And what about the downstream dry fly also drifting unhampered at an almost unnoticeably slower pace, too, brushing along the edge cover? Such accuracy is easier to achieve with a straight cast tight to foliage, but sometimes I'll add a short hook, flicking the rod tip horizontally and upstream an instant before the fly drops. This miniature curve cast bows just a foot or so of the tippet upstream of the fly.

With the downstream dry, big Montana browns have seemed suddenly gluttonous over the same #8 that was disdained while I had fished upstream. Last season on a wide Wisconsin meadow stream, a 26-inch brown, snugging under a flotsam outcropping over 4 feet of water, lifted completely, horizontally, over the edge water in a head-and-tail form I've never seen before to take a pale olive #16 leafhopper solidly.

I had tied the fly to match pale naturals of the deepening season, little and obscurely colored terrestrials that could easily be missed but for patient sampling amid the glut of larger, more colorful varieties of meadow hoppers. By this time of the season, the trout had had their fill of larger hoppers for a while, and many had sore jaws from cricket patterns and beetles. Small hoppers on #14 and #16 hooks, and #18 crickets if they're present among the broods that have grown larger by late summer, give me larger trout each year.

Leader Construction

My standard leader for limestone angling is a 4-foot braid designated for the proper line weight. If it's packaged in a longer length, I shorten it from the butt. I carefully blood-knot 17 inches of supple 3X tippet to the braid and Super Glue the connection; a 10-inch section of 4X is then added. The remainder of tippet sections can be added to suit. My usual 10-foot leader consists of equal lengths of 5X and 6X. The loose, accordian-like quality of the braid enhances a natural presentation with both dry and wet flies, and its stretch is a shock absorber to minimize stress on light tippets and small, fine-wire hooks when parrying large trout.

The ultimate midging leader I've come up with has a full 6-foot braid, two transition sections of monofilament, and a triple tippet (20–30-inch lengths) of 5X, 6X, and 7X. Each of the tippets should be the same length to create a long leader that is perfectly balanced, casts like a silken thread, and increases your hooking percentage with flies as small as #22s to #28s on longer casts. To emphasize an earlier point, I usually tie this leader twice the length of the rod.

Fly-Rite's Hi-Viz flat-butt leader is excellent for low-water camouflage. Its thin, flattened, oval diameter turns over beautifully and enhances the forming of in-air mends, including curve casts. This design lessens air resistance during the cast and reduces potential drag on the water. Its extruded, knotless taper slides on surface vegetation and sheds particles in the water. When I want an ideal shorter leader, I trim the thick butt to create a "quick-taper" leader.

I'll use a length as short as 4 feet, with up to an equal or greater length of progressively finer tippets.

When trout are most difficult on flat water and in low, clear streams, I want tippets that have a dulled, nonglare translucent appearance. I've made on-the-spot changes over the years from clear, sometimes shiny tippets to less visible tippets, and the nod unequivocally goes to the latter. Tippet material dyed a translucent, watery hue matching the stream coloration, with grayish blue the best single choice, is the ultimate in an obscure connection to the fly.

The simplest tippet change can fool a trout that has spurned your efforts; add a length of the next finer "X" designation. Now the same fly drifts between the trout's eyeballs on a less visible, looser connection.

Dressing the Tippet and Fly

During intensely lit hours when a floating 6–8X tippet casts a rope-wide shadow on light, shallow bottom, try rubbing it with a thin film of streamside mud or leader sink and then presenting it just immersed at least to diffuse the shadow. If needed, a pinch of flotant an inch or so up the tippet will buoy the dry fly.

When trout develop a critical eye, only a quality dry-fly flotant should be used. Fly-Rite's Dilly Wax, for one, gives an added but not unnatural luster to the most delicate of drys without gumming a fiber. For uncooperative trout in lowest water, use a dry without flotant. And whenever insects flutter, especially on quieter water, an undressed dry tied with longer, softer hackle can create a deadly, ethereal, high-floating silhouette. Fetching fly types include a variant or spider the circumference of a golf ball, a #18 long-hackled Griffith's Gnat, or something as small as a #24 midge.

Staying out of Sight

The trout are keenly aware not only of predators but also of flashes of glint and movement over the 10-degree blind zone. Walking a high bank or walking tall along a low bank over a shallow stream will spook even distant trout. Always keep low and approach a stream from a right angle. There are opportunities to fish from well back on a low bank, delivering only the tippet and fly onto the water at an angle that presents the fly to a sighted trout.

Trout lurk in odd, often shallow locations during low water, frequently holding near the shallow bank to wait for food. One time I had raised a leg to slide into the stream when I belatedly spied the rotund shape of a brown not 20 feet upstream, finning behind trailing grasses in a foot of water. I teetered back, knelt, and with a sidearm flick cast—a short and unalarming stroke—dropped the fly upstream on a threadline tippet. That one I unhooked at my still-dry feet, and it was larger than any trout encountered while subsequently stalking heronlike in the water.

I'll assume a vantage and remain still before expected aquatic hatches, often in the early morning, when stream-born emergences occur in the summer. Not only do the well-known *Tricorythodes*, or Tricos, and prevalent midges emerge from streams in the cool water of early day, but a progression of hatches can occur. It usually starts with midges, but sometimes with fluttering caddises (which a large trout eagerly awaits and splashes for) followed by small mayflies and stone flies.

Ideal Early-Morning Waters

I've fished well-oxygenated, stony streams with varied bottoms and habitat that produce a progression of morning aquatic hatches— mixed habitat that gives some of the year's best angling. The angler who's in place prior to hatches becomes no more a threat to trout than any other inanimate object. And besides observing the water, an angler who eyes streamside cover may spot previously hatched aquatic insects such as caddises beginning to scramble along stalks and debris, as well as early terrestrial activity. Insect life begins to stir with the diurnal shift of increasing light and with the warming of the waters by as little as a degree or two, giving opportunities more varied than you might imagine.

One such ideal location is the freshened water from a cooler tributary trailing into the stream; another is a lane of cool springs filtering from the streambed. During a full day I took water temperatures at intervals across a shallow, gliding river, and my thermometer showed the water over sand-gravel bottoms along the far bank to be several degrees cooler. This led me to cross the river early the next morning. Sure enough, hatches emerged and larger trout fed deftly along the gliding lane of cool water filtering through the streambed. Naturals drifted along on the surface film, and a little No-Hackle suggested their posture and easily captured forms.

Exploiting Morning Hatches

Morning hatches generally burgeon first in shallow areas, and trout will feed below mildly eddying breaks. An angler needs to learn habitats where specific insects emerge and to recognize feeding lanes. Not all the aquatic creatures that become active are a part of hatches; one example is the coleopteron known as the back swimmer. This small, flattened, oval aquatic beetle oars its way through quiet edge water, each one like a one-man varsity crew. Observation and sampling both take time, even involve giving up some fishing time, but one such venture resulted in my tying a lightly weighted #18 facsimile with turkey-fiber "oars" extending flexibly out from each side and subsequently questing for the sizable browns feeding on the naturals.

One morning I greased the leader within a couple feet of the fly, and when the trout began feeding, I drifted it sunken in this microhabitat edging the stream. The pinpoint end of the floating portion of leader paused, I tightened the line, and the line zinged away. Catching an earmarked trout is a satisfaction of study common to low-water angling.

The most common vantage for morning hatches is a pool fed by swifter shallows where insects emerge and drift or flutter along to dry their wings. The early angler fishing from the shallow side is in place to fan casts over a wide angle at the top of the pool, and can step one way or another without spooking fish. Sizable trout shoul-

A leaping brown trout rewards the light-tackle angler.

der to the head of the pool, and it's not unusual to see a beauty launch from a deeper, darker slot in the riffle to capture the first fluttering, hopping caddis of the day.

I fished one such spot on two occasions seven years apart. On the first visit, my quickly cast dry took a large brown that had just nailed an early-morning caddis, and in the same riffle cut seven years later a similar trout did likewise, though the hatch was a small fluttering mayfly. I used the same fly both times, a Red Variant. Its quill wings created the impression of a fluttering insect over the surface, and that wasn't its only attraction to this river's trout. The spidery, sparsely hackled pattern closely suggested a crane fly, relished as an elusive insect. Camouflage in a dry, or showing the trout a lifelike bit of the insect it's feeding on, is one important aspect of suggesting a hatch. And with the onset of hatches from quick water on a pleasant morning, I've known all varieties of aquatic duns, including midges, to flutter immediately in an attempt to gain balance.

The Trout's Window

With its high, side-mounted eyes, a trout can clearly see the surface and over the water within its acute window and can detect motion above the 10-degree angle of refraction extending like an imaginary cone around its 330-degree range of vision. A trout is capable of exercising both eyes (binocular vision) and one eye (monocular vision).

Since you're most concerned with the distance between you and the trout, the "half window," expressed in terms of monocular vision, is a handy guide to determine a good casting vantage. The experienced angler can accurately estimate a trout's range of vision and fish from its blind area below the 10-degree angle of refraction simply by judging the trout's depth. The "ruler" at first sight is that the half window extends from one eye across the surface approximately the same distance as the trout's depth; this is a 45-degree relationship. But in fact, a trout's actual oval window extends as low as 48½ degrees, so its actual acute window is a bit wider. (A trout hovering 3 inches under the surface has a half window a half inch greater than its depth; this expands correspondingly at increasing depths, until a trout holding at a 5-foot depth has a half window of 5 feet 8 inches.)

The trout's only fixed blind area extends directly behind. I've seen this described as 30 degrees or wider, but experience shows that the wedge of this zone shrinks severely in low water. This should tell the angler who casts upstream to keep low and avoid a high rod at short range, and at any range always avoid a high cast that encroaches over the cone of vision.

For a trout upstream in shallow water or hovering near the surface, you can edge just a step or two aside and angle your cast so the rod stroke and line will stay within the 10-degree blind zone close to the water. It's low-level, precision casting from any range with the line safely off to the side. Thus, a canted cast and straight-arrowed tight loop tilted toward the target can be deadly. Only the gossamer tippet slides through the narrow wedge of the peripheral blind zone extending from the trout's surface window. On the basic presentation, the fly alights shortly upstream and drifts into the window. The same delivery is used to drop a bug with light impact—onto the snout if desired. You can do well from any hidden angle with a straight cast and pinpoint placement of a fly for a short drift to a trout in water where fancy casts might otherwise be prescribed.

When a trout is feeding on a narrow overhead lane but refuses accurate presentations, you can often elicit a rise by showing the fly along the obscured *side edge* of the acute window. Trout feeding in shallow water on overhead hatches as small as Tricos have then taken my #24 imitations. When fishing from an angle, I've often presented the fly on the *far side*, so when the trout turns to take, the fish is heading away and definitely won't see me.

But low water produces many anomalies. One day as I stood in gentle, calf-shallow, clear water and fished across, my peripheral vision revealed a large brown back-finning easily with the current and holding just 15 feet upstream. Kneeling, I used a low sidearm cast to swing in a fully bowed candy-cane curve that drifted the fly into the window, the leader loop and line having fallen well away. The brown nosed up without hesitation to take the little Adams.

A trout in any depth of water might hover near the surface in anticipation of naturals and will often dine steadily. With its concentration on the numerous insects afloat, the fish may seem oblivious of the angler, but actually it's limited by its acute window of vision, which is now confined to a small oval on the surface. With care, the angler who stays low to the water can fish from a chosen angle for a fly-first presentation at short ranges of 25–30 feet.

An individual trout that's hunkering deeply may ascend a considerable distance to take an insect on the surface. Browns in particular will develop this manner of feeding cagily, either coming up once to a lone insect or at predictable intervals to numbers of floating insects. In such instances, the fly line should be kept well aside the expanded cone of vision, with only a long leader and the fly in the window. A lengthy, light tippet is advised, and you should fish from well away, making longer casts.

In some instances I've seen trout select only mayflies that floated perfectly at rest, rejecting any that fluttered. I watched such a learned brown for a time. It held 4 feet deep, its full window encompassing 9 feet, on a crystal-clear flat-water glide. This fish actually rippled its fins when selecting a dun well upstream of its 4½-foot range of vision, enticed by legs piercing the surface and a wing shadow on the underpane. It scrutinized the behavior of individual insects as they drifted slowly into view and, when convinced, made its always identical, measured ascent, lifting into a nearly vertical pose. Sometimes it then drifted downstream a short distance with snout under the fly while virtually hovering on its tail, finally siphoning the winged dun. Then with no more effort than a stabilizing brief forward roll, it dropped back to bottom. Over minutes I noticed these selections on its chosen narrow feeding lane directly overhead. I knotted on a no-hackle, upright, single polywing match of the natural and, with a backhand 40-foot reach cast, set it down lightly 10 feet upstream of the trout, for delivery about the time the trout was due to rise again. As the fly drifted into the window, the trout's fins rippled. It blimped upward, arcing its head to stand on its tail, and took the fly in form.

Drifting and Twitching Terrestrials

Low-water trout will feed as cautiously on terrestrials as any trout selecting mayflies, and I rely on realistic patterns presented on a natural drift. Yet by the end of the season, my notes are filled with examples of recalcitrant trout that fall to a convincingly activated imitation of a leg-kicking insect on flat water. The deadly little twitch as a hopper or cricket enters a trout's window is well known. One time I happened to cough at the right time, suddenly nudging a cricket imperceptibly in a manner hard to accomplish with rod-tip action, just as it neared the snout of a big brown rising sporadically in deep, gliding water. It had ignored a few drifts, but with the odd twitch seen through its window it came up and quietly took the chunky #16 cricket. Smaller terrestrials, as mentioned earlier, become highly palatable as trout become more cautious about feeding.

Further innovation can be required to convince wary trout to take the fly when they ignore previously effective methods. With a cricket, I'll show a change of pace in the manner of kicks interspersed during a natural drift. In one instance my cast across and slightly downstream dropped the fly beyond and up-current of a trout hovering in slow flat water. I added a few punctuating kicks to ease the cricket broadside into the window and short-drifted the fly. But when it had drifted over and was still near the trout's eye, I twitched the cricket a bit suddenly; the trout turned for it hesitantly, I gave a second twitch, then the brown rushed headlong toward me, engulfing the terrestrial escaping toward shore.

The trout's appetite is notable, too, for a terrestrial helplessly awash on slow current, imitated with a flush-drifting pattern. A cricket tied with a few fibers of leglike deer hair camouflaging the hook point suggests the drowning natural, and a drowning cricket can produce action during slow angling periods. My largest rainbow last season took an awash cricket after it had drifted for a full minute over 30 feet of sluggish, deep edgewater.

During lulls when the meadow stream seemed fishless, I would take a vigil well back along a low bank overlooking a long quiet pool. Widely scattered one-time rises now and then ringed the satiny flat water, always at a distance. When a boil spread on the surface, I would run in a crouch, kneel, and fire my cast, dropping a flush-floating cricket onto the spot of the rise. The fly had to be presented within seconds. Only while the moody trout was momentarily aroused after taking a natural would it rise to the imitation. Even a drowning cricket has one belated kick to give, and this often triggered the take when the ruse floated nearly still on barely flowing water.

Remain as inconspicuous as your presentation of a light line, and you'll often find that a change of approach, method, or fly based on a knowledge of naturals will stir trout that have become wary in the shrunken, clear streams of the lengthening season. Each time on the water is a new and welcome chance for observation.

Fly-Fishing the Wind

THE MOST FRUSTRATING CONDITION facing most anglers is not sparse fly hatches or roily water but the wind. However, when winds ruffle the surface of a lake or stream, trout will often feed heavily under the added cover or on surface flies and other food forms that have been blown and concentrated against a stream bank or into a lee-shore area. With some basic tackle modifications and adjustments in technique, combined with a little common sense and ingenuity, there may be excellent fishing awaiting you on a windy day. In some cases, it's even possible to use the blustery conditions to your advantage.

A shorter-than-normal leader may be helpful. For example, a 7-foot leader will straighten on the end of a cast in wind that might whip a 12-foot leader around like a lariat. The shorter leader makes accurate presentations easier, and it handles large, air-resistant flies better. A heavier tippet is another modification that might help. If the wind is strong enough to require such changes in the leader, the need for a long leader with a light tippet is usually not paramount; the wind's breakup of the water's surface diminishes the need to fish "fine and far off."

However, when the wind is generally gusting or isn't actually affecting the water's surface but is still fouling your casts, the usual-length leader might be required for finicky trout. With a long leader, there are ways you can work *with* the wind instead of against it. On one occasion I was casting upstream into a gusting wind, and

I discovered that when the leader straightened, the wind-blown tippet usually fell in snaky curves, even "piling up" at times. The extra slack permitted the fly an excellent drag-free drift on the tricky stream currents—currents made even trickier by the occasional gust that swept the water's surface. This difficult situation resulted in fine fishing once I got the hang of controlling my cast and letting the wind pile up my tippet.

Stepping up to a heavier line weight is a basic on-stream change in tackle that can make fishing in the wind easier. A fly rod I often use is rated by the manufacturer for use with a 4-weight line. But this line often flutters around on a windy day, and I've discovered that the rod handles a 5-weight line satisfactorily. Most fly rods will function well with a line one weight heavier than the line you normally use. On days that threaten to be windy, I carry an extra spool with the 5-weight line on it. The difference, even between the relatively light 4- and 5-weight lines, is notable, and the 5 will cast more easily into the wind than the 4.

A final tackle recommendation for fishing on windy days is the use of a stiff-actioned rod. This should give the angler maximum line speed for casting in the wind. Opting for both a stiffer rod and a heavier line may give the caster his best chance to punch a cast into or across the wind.

In addition to tackle modifications there are certain basic tactics that can help the angler on a windy day. Short casts are always practical, when possible, but they are even more so in the wind. You may also be able to approach more closely to the fish than you usually would, using the wind-ruffled surface for cover.

When you find yourself in a position in which you must cast directly into or across the wind, it is desirable to lower the trajectory of the forward cast. This will help you to get "under" the wind. Normally, the wind velocity is lower closer to the water's surface. A sidearm or backhand cast may be required to do this effectively. Remember that the best casts are always tight-looped casts—on windy or calm days—and on the power stroke (the forward stroke) the rod tip should travel in a straight line as you move it forward. Sometimes, under normal conditions, you may intend to make a

I ease in a large rainbow on a wind-rippled Montana spring creek.

wide-looped cast, but in the wind you should pay particular attention to applying the power stroke properly and keeping your loops tight.

In many instances it may be practical to let the wind make the cast—the forward cast or the back cast—for you. Often you can work yourself into a position where you can lift a wind-starched line into the air and simply drop it to the water's surface with a quick downward snap of the wrist or let it unroll behind you for a back cast.

Wind direction and velocity may vary dramatically on different days, but if you take a commonsense approach to tackle modification and tactics you should be able to find a way to adapt to the conditions and buck the wind as best you can or use it to your advantage. Wind is simply another fishing condition that must be dealt with by the angler, just as bright sun, water level, or fly hatches must. In some cases its effect on other factors will actually improve the day's fishing.

When fishing on a windy day it is especially important to re-member to wear a hat and protective glasses—as you should when-ever fly casting—to protect against errant casts. When it's blustery, just pull your hat down a little more tightly and use a little common sense and ingenuity to beat the wind.

Fishing the Edges Dry

THE ANGLER who can read stream edgewater and know in all likelihood where a trout will be not only can readily spy a trout that others pass by but also can develop the knack of attracting an unseen trout to the dry fly on the first cast. Looking carefully to the stream edge and using techniques to present a fly accurately gave me larger trout early in my fly-fishing. To the serious angler, the diversity of edge cover and current configurations creates opportunities for a greater variety of techniques and innovations than angling other waters along the stream.

Consider that on many streams the greatest diversity and concentration of insects occur along the edges, where larger trout lurk to feed or lair away from the main flow in the seclusion of bankside cover. Studying natural insects along the edges, learning of effective flies or designing them at the vise, and selecting a taking pattern for the moment are an ongoing, always intriguing aspect of fishing dry along bankside waters.

In my experiences over more than three decades, the largest of trout lurking along bankside edges to feed often rise during quiet times, even though few insects may be on the water. During one such hour, moderate rains had dampened a sultry late afternoon, and with early evening a strip of light fog hazed the wide Wisconsin meadow stream. But barely a mist hung over a single pool that was wide, deep, and sunken a bit in the terrain forming a dogleg bend.

From the bank I scanned the darkening water, and eventually the lone ring of a rising trout spread on a gliding bankside flat an easy cast ahead.

The trout took on my dry's initial drift. As usual, I angled the rod to let its spring coax the trout away from bank cover. Soon it leaped twice in forward vertical lunges, and I gasped at its silhouette near midstream against the silvery, rambling, broad riffle base. A stream-canny brown resorts to every trick on the line and heads into known crannies in its domain; only my playing this one off the reel and slack-lining the fish at crucial times kept it tethered—and from leaving the pool. Unlike many a lumbering, bulldogging brown, this spirited trout's runs screeched line off the reel until I was playing it by a sense of feel in near darkness. Finally, with a lead of the rod, this one all but beached itself on a low bank.

The perfectly formed trout shone resplendent, blackish well below its back, typical of a trout that resides in an inky overhead lair. Its brassy, black-spotted sides glistened over pale butterscotch flanks and amber lower fins, leading edges banded starkly black and white.

Measured at 30 inches, that 1989 catch may be a record brown for a 2-weight outfit, 6X tippet, and small dry fly. I revived and released it unweighed, but not before Jeff Mayers, my partner, captured its silhouette on film over my outstretched arm against the last tinge of pale blue twilight. For all the detail that's important in our sport, basic angling on bankside edges can produce the exceptional trout.

The larger-than-average trout, especially the brown that stakes bankside drifts and pocket niches, displays individual habits, its feeding wiles not always coinciding with those of others. A patient, observant approach for a large trout rising along the stream edge is often deadly, as well as when trying for a sighted, lurking trout.

A bankside trout hovering near the surface, especially if it hangs with snout tilted upward, is eager for a surface insect. I've waited patiently for the hovering trout to feed and have been rewarded. But in the absence of a rise to a natural, I've taken the trout on a realistic match of an insect the trout would see at that hour. A hovering trout,

I admire 30-inch brown in twilight, taken on 2-weight rod with a 6X tippet and a small dry fly.

or a trout holding bottom, or one hidden in a pocket can be just as choosy over a realistic impression of a natural insect as the rising trout keyed into a parade of naturals.

Windy conditions and the commotion of nearby rising trout are two spurs to better action when lurking trout anticipate naturals. Though I had been pumping up trout to a dry along freestone streams previously, some 15 years ago I doubted the same could be accomplished with trout of a certain sedate spring creek in lieu of their daily plentiful hatches of small mayflies. Such conditioned native trout anticipate dependable hatch times, and so did I that sunny, blustery, late-autumn morning. But as winds up to 50 miles an hour blasted through the Montana valley, ruffling the smooth creek, stemming the emergence of pale morning duns, I edged to a lee area, a narrow slick protected by hedgerows of bankside foliage. I opted to match the absent hatch. Starting at the lower end, I worked low, hard-driving casts upstream under shifty breezes with my light fly rod, drifting a #18 Light Cahill along the edge. Placing each succeeding cast a yard or two upstream of the previous one as I went raised nice trout that had lined up expecting the hatch.

Hatch-conditioned trout aren't easily fooled by drys that lack the subtleties of realism; this stream is a test even for no-hackle duns. But now a hackled match suggested a quickly fluttering mayfly, the common sight of newly emerged *Ephemerella* drying their wings on a breezy surface.

As an aside, let me note here that hatches of daylight duns seldom are associated with bankside drifts. Yet locating quality mayfly hatches can lead the angler to the bank. As one example, on a 200-foot-wide river pool I fish, *Baetis* emerge along edges of the broad riffle but then drift the funnel-shaped current that skirts only along the deep bank. Additional mayflies hatch from the narrow edge along the straightaway. The large rainbows rise in line along that narrow bankside lane, though the entire vast pool is vacant of action.

Even when lesser trout rise to feed, often spashily, that larger trout lurking off to the side is aroused, receptive to a fly presented to its snout. If you can muster the patience, pause from fishing to the numbers of feeding trout and look to the streamside. Often a bankside fish feeds in a quiet manner belying its size, and having a large belly to fill, it continues rising as the hatch wanes, holding on station for a time afterward. I've spied a brown rising imperceptibly under overhanging boughs to insects as fidgety as caddis-look-alike spruce moths of the Northwest while the river was alive with splashes of lesser trout gorging on a feast of variously drifting, fluttering, and hopping cream moths.

Although a bankside drift or pocket may not reveal a trout, fishing selected edges has given me the larger trout. It's happened amid all types of hatches; often the taking fly represents a stray of an aquatic hatch far adrift to the bankside edge. Other bankside individuals have had their fill or aren't interested in the present hatch but, aroused by the activity, have risen to an imitation of another insect clinging on streamside cover.

A leaping trout under the branches is the reward for a good presentation.

Even the commotion of a trout splashing on the line can stir lurking fish to rise and feed. There's evidence too, in experiences of others and myself, that noise emitting vibrations through water can trigger a few insects to hatch. One dead-still late morning on a long, placid pool along a broad Wisconsin limestoner, a lone rainbow rose below a riffle corner along the bank. I eased into place near the top of this pool, which was too deep to wade in below, and, casting across, hooked the energetic trout. It flipped over the frying-pan-flat pool loudly, and its crisp splashes triggered another trout to rise once along the bank 10 feet farther downstream. From previous episodes, I had become accustomed to looking beyond a trout on the line. Quickly releasing the 'bow, I angled a longer cast, and the trout that sipped the drifting fly turned out to be a swashbuckling 16-inch brown. Then the same scenario happened again, another 10 feet downstream. This was a 17-inch brown. If I was having a hard time acknowledging this chain reaction, well, yet another repeat: Casting 50 feet downstream to a dimpling rise produced a heavyweight brown that twice nearly went into the reel's backing—successive longer casts in a downstream fan, each fish caught larger than the previous one. That quartet was a tribute to a durable but realistic little no-hackle I had designed to match present caddises.

Sample Aquatics and Terrestrials

Timely angling to expectant trout along edges by using a fly that matches a current natural not on the water is not limited by the source of the hatch or the fly size. The angler should know the current crop of natural insects—both the aquatic, waterborne forms and those land-based insects that fall onto the stream (the adult aquatic flies and spinners as well as the true terrestrials).

Trout anticipating insect activity take up feeding stations shortly prior to aquatic hatches. One morning when *Tricorythodes* were late, Doug Swisher pumped up a sizable bankside brown with one of the realistic no-hackle mayfly duns he and Carl Richards had developed. The fly represented another, but sparse, hatch on the river. That episode years ago cued me to attractor-fishing with highly imitative patterns of small mayflies. Some of my more memorable catches since that day have been trout that rose to a #14–20 dry when angling was slow. During many periods, only a few mayflies can be expected to hatch, but trout have a taste for *Ephemerella* that can give the angler a larger fish along the stream edge. Numerous small mayflies will emerge from often slower border waters, including the common *Baetis* species.

Edge-dwelling insects may be sampled widely by sweeping a tightly meshed net or more carefully by picking through streambank cover. Two aquatic hatches that reside as adults in streambank cover can give banner action during dispersal flights or when expected egg-laying flights are sparse. The caddises and particularly the larger stone flies produce angling similar to fishing a grasshopper along edges. One of my favorite western stone fly hatches, *Acroneuria*, occurs concurrently with the salmon fly (*Pteronarcys californica*) but peaks in the weeks afterward on a swift mountain stream. Now, in snowmelt waters dropping daily and flowing clearly, affording easier wading with gripping soles, these inch-long plecopterans congregate on scattered debris and foliage like bees around a hive. In lieu of an expected egg-laying flight, trout often engulf a floating imitation.

Streamside sampling is helpful in locating concentrations of *Acroneuria* stone flies, which are most numerous along scattered reaches of stream. While probing woody edges one day, I also turned up varieties of smaller stone flies; stones as small as ⅜-inch *Alloperla* species became palatable later.

A knowledge of the edge-dwelling varieties is valuable even in the case of terrestrials along a meadow stream. For instance, crickets become fidgety earlier in the day than grasshoppers, which must dry their wings of early dew. Hoppers jump when the day warms a bit. Certain overhanging tree leaves may be laden with a particular beetle, and the trout there dine on pelletlike naturals that fall. Terrestrials encompass the greatest variety of all insects. Common terrestrials change in abundance from one year to the next, and sampling also frequently shows a new or rare one that presently has hatched in greater-than-usual numbers.

Sampling and observing streamside cover may be a prelude to screening current along the bank in order to come up with a taking fly. The brown in particular shows a sometimes confounding selectivity to a certain insect—the "odd" fly. As one example, trout along the edges will concentrate on an early, sometimes brief, side dish of edge-dwelling mayfly spinners. Whether or not the spinner fall burgeons, the preference in feeding on a newly appearing insect is not unusual. With mayflies this can contradict the lore that a trout along a streambank teeming with terrestrials feeds endlessly on them. Though sparse numbers of little *Baetis* spinners flutter low along a grassy border, sipping trout feed sporadically, turning their appetites to the few spent mayflies adrift from farther upstream.

The elusive crane fly is another example of the odd fly that one trout will leap for. The adult is a terrestrial edge-dweller. Though a favorite Montana stream hatches crane flies in numbers, these spidery hatches, which resemble giant mosquitoes, seldom are easy prey. Highly realistic, spindly look-alike imitations lack realism *on the water*. The best imitation I've found is a stiff-hackled variant with a long tail of a few fibers of stiff elk hair. A trout will take it on a lofty drift, but this fly is often fetching when skimmed like an airfoil. One can be bounced over the water by snapping up the rod tip and forcefully making a strip of line. Doing this has twice lured a big brown to take the fly in midair. This hatch well exemplifies a bit of philosophy the late Dan Bailey once gave me: that realism to our eye can be but a starting point in finding a productive fly.

The Impressionistic Approach

Particularly bankside trout, because they see a variety of naturals, are not immune to patterns that exude realism but don't match any one insect. One I developed in the mid-1970s from related patterns, my No-Hackle Hairwing, is deadly as an impressionistic silhouette. It's effective in sizes ranging from a #10, 2X-long hook down to a #22 and in colors to match various hatches, both aquatic and terrestrial. A few anglers I've shared it with have scored heavily with slender ties on rising trout in hatches from midges up to large mayflies.

My No-Hackle Hairwing dry fly

This balanced fly, tied of elk or deer hair, floats upright for a proficient caster. The sloped-back single hairwing angles at 45 degrees over a no-hackle Goofus-type pod abdomen with dubbed underbody and tail fibers.

I developed the fly to raise bankside browns on flat water in spring creeks during quiet hours when patterns I had been using were no longer effective. Starting with my initial tie back then, it continues to attract larger trout. Even when a trout has come up and nosed a hackled fly, a quick change has brought a confident rise and take of the No-Hackle of the same size and color. Variations in the pattern for various terrestrials have a chunkier abdomen, and quill legs imitate leg-kicking varieties, sans tail.

Niches and Ledges

Before fishing, I look for two stream-edge dimensions. One is the true bankside niche; the other is the instream ledge. A trout will lair in an undercut bank or beneath overhanging cover that seems a

Rich Hansen, a 2-weight enthusiast, coaxes a Wisconsin trout away from the undercut.

double-edged streambank

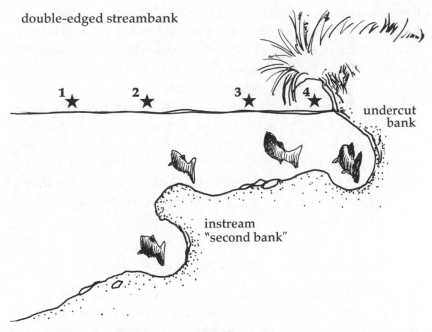

undercut bank

instream "second bank"

Diagram A. (1) A dry fly presented on the deep side is highly visible along the instream "second bank." (2) A dry presented parallel along the seam of the surface current over a ledge, where trout expect naturals to appear. (3) A feeding station where trout lurk tightly along the bank. (4) A trout in the undercut of a bank. A greased dry can be bounced on the surface at the border and skipped underneath the "roof." (Artwork by Sue Hunt, based on an original sketch by T. Wendelburg; reproduced with permission)

tight fit, though its sanctuary may be deeper than the adjacent stream bottom. Look first to the shallow edges skirting a stream-bank lie, for a trout will snug sometimes hidden while lurking for food under shifting, mildly eddying current. A fly presented 6 inches from the bank or along cover may not be taken, but one brushing along the edge cover attracts a trout.

Streams often display both bankside cover and, a yard or more into the water, an instream ledge, or "second bank." Also look for an instream ledge along a streambank that is barren and shallow. Trout lurking against the ledge will move onto the bankside flats when seeking food. An instream ledge may be only knee deep or may be several feet deep (like the long linear ledge harboring the quartet of trout related earlier). An instream ledge hems some pools, though many of these trout magnets are only a few yards in length.

A linear current seam on the surface and subsurface shadow are signs of a second bank ledge paralleling the current, which is illustrated in diagram A. Through your Polaroids you'll see the current seam, well-defined over an undercurrent that shelves mildly along the instream ledge. This seam is a food line carrying floating insects and a hotspot for the dry fly. Under a markedly broken surface or, conversely, flat water, the surface seam may not be well defined, but look for a slight contrast in subsurface coloration to mark the ledge. In an enriched stream, a bed of vegetation can mark the shallow edge of the ledge.

Tilting the Cast and Bouncing the Bank

Tips and techniques on fishing bankside drifts and cover could fill a book, but I've often combined the basic with the unusual to take trout in tight spots. Foremost, accuracy is the keynote in presentation. A tightly looped line naturally improves accuracy to set up a fly's drift on a narrow bankside feeding lane or to drop a fly tightly against cover. A high-speed cast arrows a fly to an edge or beneath overhanging cover.

To tilt the straight-line cycle forward, make a correspondingly higher back cast and lower forward cast. The tilted cast is ideal to drop a dry with impact before the tippet, an alerting bankside delivery that imitates a terrestrial, a stone fly, or another fallen bug. And a sidearmed, tightly looped cast slides a fly under a roof of overhanging cover. In this manner I once drifted a fly to a trout I could hear rising well beneath an undercut.

Bouncing the fly off a preferably solid bankside edge allows the tippet to pile. "Bouncing the bank" thus gives the fly a natural drift ahead of the unfurling slack. This is a simulation of a tumbling insect, but I've used it as well with a delicate mayfly imitation while duns funneled along a narrow bankside slick for a picky trout rising tightly to the edge.

Probing woody and brushy overhangs is especially profitable

when edge-dwelling insects cling to overhead cover. The prevalent caddises or stone flies, as well as moths and inchworms, among other terrestrials, have trout looking up for naturals to fly, tumble, and drop solidly. Each kind of insect behaves differently on water in the nooks and crannies, whether hopping, fluttering, skittering, kicking, or worming.

The larger, broadly overhanging willows and branches of other foliage offer a roomy, shaded bankside sanctuary. Such haunts may show snags from the stream as well as above. A dry with a palmered, stiff hackle greased for buoyancy can be teased gently across snags, a fetching method as trout respond to an insect reaching for safety or one suddenly awash.

I'll look for a low-hanging branch along the edge, or even well beneath an overhanging canopy, for special presentation. The cast drapes the leader (or fly line) across the branch. Often, when I'm fishing at an angle across current to a hang-up inside a canopy of slower water, no rod manipulation is needed to make the dry fly "come alive." It may drift away, but soon the nearby faster water pulls the line along, suddenly skating the dry; it'll often whip over the limb. Large trout have cartwheeled for the fly's brief flight as a careening insect on the wing.

But anglers generally pass up bouncy, shallow water under low overhanging foliage. Fishing from the stream, look for openings in the lengthy row of the lowest foliage. They're not apparent, but big trout fin under these tight canopies. On an across cast, using a side-arm, tightly looped, high-speed delivery, I snap my wrist down hard, as if I were skipping a stone across water, ending up pointing the rod tip directly at my target. This technique bounces the greased fly at the border, skipping it well under the overhanging roof.

Executing the Reach Cast and Curve Cast

Doug Swisher, who developed the reach cast, best describes the proper rod motion as painting the line on the water. I execute my usual reach by casting straight, and when the fly hangs in air over the target spot, I reach, extending the rod tip and swinging the rod horizontally, thus mending the line in the air before the fly alights. A reach can be directed as needed, even to sail a line in air over a bankside obstruction to drop the fly just upstream or downstream. Simply reach with a little overhand arcing loop in the rod wrist (as in forming a normal full mend of line on the water). On a cast in any direction, the reach lays the leader aside the fly, away from the trout's direct line of vision. When casting at an angle across current, the reach positions the line on a pendulum extending the fly's natural drift. For a short reach cast, I'll reach quickly to compensate for less line weight in the air. And a sidearm cast with an easy reach motion also bows a curve in the leader.

A tippet a tad light for the air resistance of the fly not only gives a dry a less hampered, buoyant float but also makes it easier to form a curve cast. Examples include a 6X tippet with a #16 dry or a 4X tippet with a #8 Bucktail Caddis type. I've often used a widely bowed line with a shallow curve to show the tantalizing broadside silhouette of a dry to a bankside trout facing upstream. For the trout in bankside water significantly slower than the main flow, a curve cast hooks the line farther upstream of the fly than any other cast and gives the longest float. Full-loop curves (the candy-cane shape) can be formed narrowly or widely, to adapt to various currents.

When the angler can't move a few steps to another location, knowledge of casting mechanics helps. The fly rod can be manipulated and line cast in variations of specific casts. And a cast can be presented differently from what is customary. In the two following examples, note that I'm a lefty.

I needed a negative curve to the outside of my casting arm for the rising trout in diagram B. Now only my vertical back cast cleared tall grasses. Not gripping the rod too tightly is a help in letting the line form correctly, and more so in this foliage-pinched, multicurrented situation, where only a slowly unfurling cast could give enough time to transform the line's plane and open the curve widely enough to drop the fly on target. By stalling the forward cast while canting the rod with a turn of my wrist to the outside, I tilted and began widening the loop as it slid by the willow, transforming it onto a horizontal plane. Lowering the rod tip farther, I waggled

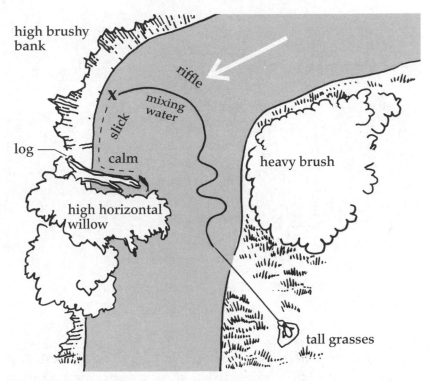

Diagram B (Artwork by Sue Hunt, based on an original sketch by T. Wendelburg; reproduced with permission)

a few shallow **S** curves down the straight portion of the cast as a final guard against early drag. The fly alit first, drifted down the slick edge, and curled back across the front of the log, a buffer of flat water. Divergent currents had nearly straightened the drifting curve as the brown's snout peeked, siphoning the fly.

In diagram C, I braced against a swift, choppy stream, a wadable foothold at a steep angle below an overhanging bush. Here I used a positive curve cast formed in reverse of the streamflow, but I faced the bank to help in forming the unusual line configuration. I cast across my body, whipping the line upstream, halting the rod at a right angle to the current. By reaching to extend the rod tip angling just below the horizontal, I bowed a curve only in the fly line near the rod. The bowed portion of fly line on a buffering shallow shoals

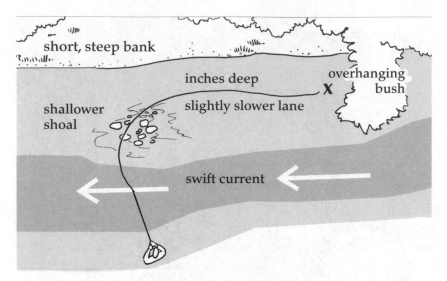

Diagram C (Artwork by Sue Hunt, based on an original sketch by T. Wendelburg; reproduced with permission)

created a backup effect along the line, thus permitting the fly to float jauntily into place for a protracted moment where the water lapped the overhanging leaves. Just when it cocked before dragging, the trout took it in a splash.

Give a Fly Pause

The two catches described above were the result of presenting a dry on quiet water buffers tight to overhanging cover. Larger wedges of quiet flat water and circling eddies that settle along the bank, often forming below a jut of land that diverts current, offer an opportunity to drift a dry at a snail's pace or at rest for a longer time. Insects collect on calm edges, where trout hold on station or cruise, rising to select morsels. Casting from slack water or from a low bank is often ideal. From the bank, line can be draped on shore, only the leader falling across water. Watchful trout may swim in any direction to take a realistic fly that's slowly adrift or motionless. With a long hairline tippet, my small dry wove here and there, not unnaturally, pausing to a stop near shore. A minute later a brown glided a couple of yards to take it.

The "different" presentation can be deadly on a buffer. I draped a leader across broad surface vegetation, and the rising trout nosed its slow drift. On instinct, I let it drift on and hang tightly along the matted roof a couple of feet below, anchored by the leader upstream. It had never actually dragged. I felt sheepish about the hanging presentation for only about 10 seconds, when open jaws that could have taken an apple surged under the flotsam, engulfing the fly from behind. But on an open area I've seen trout turn for a fly gone by and, if the fly is facing away, not bother to circle on below, as in this instance. The larger brown seems to have pride in not missing on its rise to an easily captured insect and often gets a bead on a leg-kicking terrestrial or a caddis from behind. With the trout's blind-side approach, a mobile insect is less likely to escape.

Who among fly rodders isn't prone to the enjoyment of watching a dry raft the water? As unseasonable as the pattern or presentation might seem, here are a few of the unusual times and places sizable trout have come up to my dry: a rainbow in March to a grasshopper, from behind a stream-edge flat rock; a brown at midday in summer to the same pattern, from under a lone railroad tie angled into sunny shallows along a long barren reach I was hiking; a brown in November to a Royal Wulff, brushing a shallow ice shelf at the tail of a pool; a 'bow in late winter, lifting from the door cavity of a junker vehicle tumbled from bankside riprap. Each can be explained logically: the presence of sparse winter stone flies the size of the hopper; a brown's summer retreat to a sometimes isolated shallow lair or feeding station for terrestrials; a brown's penchant for a dry while in shallows and attendant to spawning-time boldness; and the winter hatches and rising trout just upstream of the sunken junker.

Trout along the edges seldom fail to surprise me with their size and willingness to feed on floating insects. Even when naturals are sparse, the trout's taste for an insect will attract it to the top. Because of the nature of the wary larger trout, this is often an optimum time for the angler, too. Look bankward.

Terrestrial Strategies

A VERITABLE BUFFET of land-based insects provides a large portion of a trout's food intake, and numerous varieties are on the menu from early spring well into autumn. As terrestrial hatches burgeon, trout look for them, and to the delight of the angler, at this time a terrestrial imitation may be deadlier than trying to match tiny mayflies. An ant, for instance, is often readily accepted by a large brown as it sips from a smattering of many kinds of naturals, a situation known to anglers who have had the experience and who have rediscovered the trout's liking for terrestrials.

Ants

Ants in #16–22, both hackled and winged varieties, are deadly as the summer deepens. I have a system for their use based on color, and my basic threesome includes tan, black, and dark reddish dubbed-fur patterns. I'll opt for a dark ant on a dark day and a light ant on a sunny day, a strategy that usually takes trout, unless a particular ant is on the water in numbers and matching them brings results.

While September's great hatches of flying ants are a long-awaited event for me, a Flying Ant can do wonders prior to hatch days. For the wings, I like shiny, dry-fly quality hackle tips in lighter shades of gray. The natural translucence and luster catches the eye

A #22 flying red ant enticed this 21-inch Wisconsin brown to take on 7X tippet.

of a trout. On some blackish ants, I use grizzly-tip wings for a natural "buzz" and excellent visibility.

A wet will often take trout when they are most difficult. Some years ago, Roy Swanson gave me a couple of neatly tied, hard-bodied tiny ants with lacquered, wrapped thread body and thread legs. Drifted just under the surface, when trout actually were feeding on a smorgasbord of both aquatic and terrestrial minutiae, those dark red, lustrous ants brought a sipping rise from every trout I cast to.

While the smaller ants may be most abundant, hatches of large ants can be matched with comparative mouthfuls for a trout—#14 and #12. Carpenter ants and some others will attract beefy trout.

Finding the Hatch

Sampling the streamside foliage is one way to learn about terrestrials. Many insects are sensitive to bright light and cling only on the shady side of trees and bushes. Such insects are often busiest during overcast hours or amid heavily shaded cover. A hazy day will often give excellent angling.

Terrestrial hatches can vary greatly from year to year. I have experienced profuse emergences of tiny beetles one year but not witnessed the same abundant hatch the next season. Their natural life cycles and the effects of various agricultural insecticides on the land play a part in the presence of any species of this largest group of the insects—the terrestrials.

Screening the current can help to identify insects afloat in the film, as well as immersed terrestrials. More sunken terrestrials are taken by trout than most anglers realize. A late-summer sampling of a trout's stomach contents generally shows a great number and variety of terrestrials.

Knowledge of the trout's terrestrial preferences can lead to tying a taking fly pattern. Trout will key on silhouette, definitely, but also on color, so tie any new patterns to match the *size and color* of the naturals.

Beetle Tactics

Beetles colonize on overhanging willows in such numbers that their domelike shells speckle the leaves. Numerous beetles inevitably fall into the water, and it is their misfortune that gives anglers a good terrestrial opportunity.

I recall once finding a trout feeding on beetles as they dropped from an overhanging tree. Drifts with a #18 beetle resulted only in refusals, so I decided to change tactics. I added 30 inches of tippet to my leader and cast so the leader draped over a branch and the fly dropped down but then drifted naturally. That same reluctant trout now took it readily.

Trout under a broad overhanging tree will spread around to rise for insects that fall from the fan of limbs. Pelletlike insects fall from a height, and many become immersed in the surface film or sink. If you don't look closely you might not see these tiny terrestrials on the water. Sampling the stream with a screen might not catch any beetles, but trout take them selectively over other scattered tiny insects. In midday, gentle breezes promote a steady but sparse fall of beetles.

Greased leader methods can be successful for presenting a wet terrestrial, just as they are with drifting aquatic insect imitations along at a fixed depth. By greasing the leader, you can control the drift depth of the fly.

Terrestrial Strategies

Terrestrials of all types and sizes may be most numerous in the water on windy days. One of the deadliest presentations is casting an imitation of any terrestrial so that it falls before the leader with a natural impact. By observing the natural insects, I've matched the fall of beetles, little grasshoppers, and tinier leafhoppers or aphids, thus attracting shy trout that respond only to the realism of the impact. This is a finer version of the presentation often used with imitations of larger, bulkier terrestrials such as crickets and big grasshoppers.

Years ago, I floated the Au Sable in Michigan on a windy day with the late Jim Wakely, of Grayling. The angling guide suggested we use his imitation of inchworms. These little caterpillars were on foliage along the river's famed "sweepers," aged trees hanging low over the river. The fly was yellow deer hair spun tightly on a long-shank hook and clipped to a bullet shape. Dropping the buoyant bug hard onto the water beneath foliage lured browns instantly. Though especially effective on a wind-rippled surface, this delivery can be just as alluring on a flat surface, even when you pinpoint the drop within an inch of the trout's snout.

Simulating the struggles of a particular leg-kicking insect can signal trout that the food is on the table. Little aphids move in short but quick darts on springy legs; grasshoppers alternately drift and kick; and cumbersome crickets kick feebly and even flounder. A morsel that appears to be legging along in search of dry land may not always be as appealing to trout as one that seems injured.

Such natural, imitative action can be effective while the fly is yet some distance upstream of the trout but also anywhere within the

My cricket-beetle pattern, suggestive of two naturals

fish's sensory range, indicating a "hidden" terrestrial. Sound can suggest the freshly fallen terrestrial and, properly used, is an ally during the summer for fishing to the wariest of trout that will spook under a dragging leader or ignore a fly that does not meet its fancy.

During one outing I spotted a brown holding ahead of a small branch angling low over the stream edge. I drifted a #10 hopper past him, but the trout only rippled its fins. The fly then drifted around a small platter of vegetation anchored by twigs from the branch, and it curled in behind the flotsam. With my fly rod pointed low, I quickly stripped in a foot of line that pulled the hopper under with a soft "blurp." The trout pivoted, streaked downstream beneath the platter, and engulfed the waterlogged fly.

Summer rains can spruce up a stream by washing in terrestrials and adding needed oxygen to the water. At these times trout tend to feed. However, it is discouraging to find a stream flowing murkily. But the techniques utilizing impact and leg-kicking imitations can alert larger trout that will feed freely in tinged waters during the day, especially browns.

One memorable afternoon occurred along a meadow stream in which I could not see my feet when wading hip deep. I fished a hackled Joe's Hopper dry in likely lairs, but sometimes wet and deep, taking nice browns as I went. In recent years there hasn't been a good hopper hatch along that same stream. And over a few summers, this stream has been all but scoured by repeated prolonged rains. It is a small stream and settles sooner than most rivers, yet many of the natural foods, including smaller terrestrials, have been washed away—except for tenacious ants. Trout here will cruise calm patches picking the ants from trailing grasses along the edges.

Sow Bugs

The sow bug is a burrowing crustacean that survived these rainy conditions and remained present in numbers, especially along rooty pockets of tree stumps forming undercut banks. The sow bug burrows in soils and debris and is a hidden but common insect, especially along spring creeks. It crawls into crevices of woody matter and is also highly abundant along exposed soil banks edging gentler current. I've found trout with their stomachs full of these crustaceans, both in and out of the water.

The sow bug is a chunky critter. Its general coloration is dark brown on top, with its chitinous shell segmented like a loaf of sliced bread; its underbelly is lighter and lined with tiny legs. One has the shape of a half peanut, so the weighted fly I tie in #14–18 to represent it is dubbed the Peanut Fly. This tie also resembles various beetles.

Using the greased leader method, I like to drift the Peanut in shallows, down to water 3 feet deep, along a bank or in sluggish current around debris. It is most effective near the bottom, but hungry trout, with their usual foods diminished, will rise for one presented shallowly. Even in tinged water a drifting sow bug is taken gently.

The search for an effective fly will lead you to discover more about terrestrials, a varied, fascinating world of insects.

Grasshoppers Only

DRY-FLY FISHING at high noon on a bright summer day may surprise purists, but using a fly nearly 2 inches long would shock them.

Anyway, I had the Clark Fork River to myself as I waded in blue jeans across from the business district in Missoula, Montana. I tossed a big #4 quill-winged hopper upstream, never farther out from the grassy bank than I thought a grasshopper could jump. Then I heard a voice say, "Do you always float a fly so close to the bank?"

I turned around and saw a man behind me on a bridge spanning the nearly 200-foot-wide river. He must have been on a lunch break.

Glancing over the river, he asked, "What about all the trout out there on bottom?"

"Most brown trout hold along brushy banks," I answered. "Grasshoppers are everywhere on the banks, and the fish are looking up for an easy meal next to grassy undercuts. Unless you're working to a rising fish, there's little point in casting randomly over the acres of flat water on this river."

A minute after he left, a heavy brown splashed, taking my hopper when it brushed the grasses trailing along a rooty bank in the gentle flow. The fish jumped twice and then thumped downstream along bottom. When the hopper-fattened trout came in tired, I steadied it with one hand over its thick shoulders.

A locust-sized hopper really magnetizes Clark Fork brownies, I

My bullethead grasshopper passes for the real thing.

thought. The pattern has paired turkey-quill wings tied down longer than a 2X-long shank hook. If my angling on a bright, summer midday had raised the eyebrows of purists, that near finger-long dry fly in the jaw of the trout I now admired would have convinced them.

Another day while my car was being serviced, I walked down to the river in downtown Missoula and caught more browns, along with a large rainbow, on an outsized hopper dry. I was thinking over what the bill on my car would be when a 4-pound brown rolled up to the fly upstream from the Russell Street Bridge. All those trout hit a big hopper afloat next to the bank.

Grasshoppers spring or are blown by gusts onto the water. They become large and plentiful enough along meadow and agricultural streams so that trout on the bottom will rise and smash them hard. The expectant fish will hit a hopper made in a fly-tying vise just as eagerly.

Around haying time on agricultural streams like the Clark Fork, machinery working in the fields stirs up thousands of hoppers.

Large numbers of the insect careen onto the stream, and the trout may feed wildly on top. Anytime that you might shoo a few grasshoppers into a likely bankside drift, note the spot where a trout takes them and float a dry fly over the fish.

So, each summer and into autumn the allure of hopper fishing draws me to the meadow waters. When I was living in Montana, frequent windy days in the West tumbled hoppers into streams, exciting trout into feeding frenzies. The fish would fin a yard or farther from the bank, often hovering just below the surface, to be in place for the careening insects. In some instances trout actually lined up along a grassy stream edge, taking hoppers with slashing rises, creating silvery wedges of spray that scattered into droplets. Fishing from the bank with a low line beat the problems of the winds, but when casting was practical, a hard-driving low toss under gusts that dropped the dry fly solidly onto wind-rippled water attracted trout. Fishing with the usual upstream approach for the dry fly on one such day, I caught three bunched rainbows, red-sided fish of 1½, 1¾, and nearly 3 pounds.

Even when the meal is a large grasshopper, an individual trout can be as fussy as a gourmet. One little trick often turns this fish into a gourmand. A brown had come up repeatedly but shied from my hopper, whether it was drifted or twitched in enticing kicks over its lie. So I simply soaked the fly at my waders and then delivered it on a just-sunken drift, convincing the recalcitrant 3½-pounder to take it.

Large Hopper patterns are not only for western trout, though. Big Wisconsin trout have taken my Hopper during midday temperatures as hot as 101 degrees, and my friend Larry Nassau has floated long-winged sleek hoppers I tied to attract shy, larger trout as well.

Once trout are on the lookout for grasshoppers as summer deepens, these substantial morsels may be on the menu any hour. At dusk on a quiet western stream my outsized hopper drifted down the middle of a choppy-topped pool and attracted a lunker rainbow, and farther down the pool, a weighty brown. Notable? Two days later that twilight episode was repeated exactly on the same pool. And don't discount the hopper for nocturnal angling, particularly for a wily trout that has seen just about all other offerings. I'm reminded of several big native browns that succumbed to my hoppers in recent years along Wisconsin waters.

Hoppers lure hefty trout to feed on top, and prospects for a larger fish are likely in a stream skirting a roadside as well as in a wilderness meadow creek. In late summer a small stream lacing its way through the grasses beckons a fisherman just for the solitude, and the cool upper sections of the water can be gems of Hopper fishing.

Trout will rise readily to hoppers in flows of 60–66 degrees, though the presence of these largest insects of the season will occasionally induce trout to feed in warmer waters too. The adaptable brown thrives in waters warmer than those that delicate brookies enjoy. Yet late each summer, browns migrate into food-rich waters so chilly that on very hot days I'll fish from the bank or don wading gear instead of merely going in with blue jeans and shoes. In my experience, browns turn on to feed more dependably in hot weather than other trout do. On days with the early afternoon air at 100 degrees, they have leaped on my line and dashed around with vigor.

At noon one day last summer I slid into a narrow tributary whose water registered 54 degrees several hundred yards below the creek's source—a spring that pours in nearly 3,000 gallons of water per minute. Kneeling in shin-deep shallows, I kept a low, hidden profile to fish upstream between steeply sloped meadow banks.

Despite my low vantage I couldn't have begun to count the hoppers along this creek. They clung on overhanging stalks a foot above the water. They sat atop leafy watercress and on instream weed beds matting the surface and lining both banks. Some perched at the waterline, their antennae mirrored on the surface. Wherever hoppers are found, from alpine tundra to lowland meadows, the insects forage on grass and herbs and come down to the creek for the cooling effect of evaporation from the water. It's one reason why hoppers are numerous in creek bottoms during warm weather and on quiet dry-air days.

After knotting a hopper fly onto my tippet, with my fingertip I spread a thin coating of filmy paste on the fly as a flotant. I waited a

I admire a brown that took my realistic hopper imitation.

while, but not a hopper fell onto the surface. So I made my toss 30 feet up-current, the fly alighting on flat, gin-clear water in mid-creek. A trout in a moss bed on the bottom turned and swam downstream behind the drifting fly. Browns do that often. Through my polarized sunglasses I could see the head-on approach of a beautiful trout, thick through the middle.

Another trout, spotting the first or perhaps the hopper, swam from beneath the bank. The duo unhurriedly glided ever closer to the lone insect. The smaller of the two, which had angled from the undercut, sped up and took the fly about 10 feet beyond my rod tip. After its feisty tussle, I cradled the trout with one hand under the belly. Chocolate brown on its back and close-cropped black spots on its shoulders, the fish shone like a bar of gold with its bronzed sides. The brownie weighed heavily, fattened on hoppers. I wiggled the hook out and released the fish.

While tarrying a few minutes to puff on a cigarette, I scanned the silent valley beneath rugged hills. The sun moved along its high path through a cloudless sky. Trout in cold creeks lurk for hoppers when the bright, warming rays are on the water. Maybe that first fish would rise again. I repeated my cast, and though I can't say positively that the brown that took my hopper this time was the one that had eyed the fly not long before, it appeared to be from the same mold.

The durable hairwing hopper I was fishing appears to be alive while it floats low in the silhouette of the real insect. After releasing a trout, I rinse the fly, cleansing it. I puff dry the wing fibers, made of the hollow body hair of deer, and the hairwing holds its shape and retains buoyancy.

Usually a hopper having a tannish gray to a dark brownish gray wing silhouette and a yellow body matches the most prevalent insects and catches trout. On a given day, one or another color may produce better, simply on the basis of matching a fly to lighting conditions. A hopper with a fluorescent-chartreuse yarn body, the pigments activated by sunlight, has attracted trout for me. While perusing the fly counter in a fly shop a few years ago, I saw some black-winged hoppers and purchased a few. I put one to good use on an overcast day when it was highly visible on the water, and trout took it readily. A hopper with coal-black, cricket-colored wings has taken trout under gray skies.

Frequently well into summer hoppers appear bleached, perhaps from weeks of sunlight, and trout prefer a pattern that matches them. When paler grasshoppers become so abundant that hundreds of them spring and fly ahead of my feet while walking a meadow, I use drys that match their hues, often a hopper with a pale yellowish to cream abdomen, light tannish wings, and a pale olive head. Such pastel-looking patterns attract trout that now often refuse or just rise errantly to the distinctly colored, darker hoppers.

While a big hopper may entice a lunker from cover, a dry fly about an inch in length produces the steadiest fishing on creeks. By late summer, when large naturals are common along hay meadows, pasture, and in clover, trout stuffed with hoppers, oddly, may prefer smaller ones.

Even though many sizes of hoppers abound along a stream, trout of late summer can have a selectivity for little ones tied on #14 or

#16 hooks. Even while I've prospected a creek, a change to a mere half-inch hopper has often saved the day for me during low, clear water.

Those are days trout can become leery of the surface glint from a floating tippet or of its shadow on light bottom. Applying leader sink may solve the problem. Nonetheless, some trout may rise snout-to-hackles and then back down from the hopper fly. When this happens, I drift hoppers with sparse or no hackle but with realistic legs, and the wary trout take them. Such flies are available from some suppliers of quality flies and from fly shops in many locales. I also tie my own sleeker patterns. Those highly realistic flies appear indistinguishable from naturals on the water, and the test of a pattern is when the larger trout concur.

Trout in meadow streams develop an appetite for grasshoppers that can be just as insatiable as is your desire to catch them.

Fish Soft

Hair Bugs and Drys for Top-Water Bass

WHENEVER BASS become a compelling top-water challenge, I fish with floating patterns of hair and feathers. These materials diffuse light and appear alive in imitations of bass food. Creations of hollow-fibered, buoyant hairs variously spun or otherwise tied on strong light hooks float well and give bass a softer impression of natural bait. When retrieved, these soft imitations also transmit sound waves throughout the water, deceptively signaling that a natural food item—frog, mouse, insect, or other fare—is on the water. Should bass have had enough of hard-bodied, noisier offerings, the less-alarming vibrations emitted by soft surface bugs and dry flies become highly alluring. Though the deadliness of soft flies is not limited to deep summer and later, when most bass have become all but inured to the usual lures, let me give two examples showing the attraction of the soft bug at rest and in motion.

One late afternoon *Baetis* duns hatched and floated along on a bay; occasionally a wide ring revealed a big-jawed bass with a fastidious taste. A little observation showed that the bass was cruising along, taking a natural or two. The obvious presentation would be to drop a floating imitation lightly and well ahead of the anticipated path of the fish. Not only did I not have any #16 matches, but I had no other small drys either. So I quickly knotted on a #4 bug of clipped deer hair for the head, with a hackle of soft marabou behind the molded head, plus a pair of flared outward saddle hackles. Drop-

A largemouth bass airborne with a bullethead long-tailed slider hooked in its jaw (Artwork by Richard Fendrick, based on an original sketch by T. Wendelburg; reproduced with permission)

ping one onto the placid water 10 feet ahead of the bass that had fed twice, I left it still on the mirrored, softly shaded surface. The 3-pounder simply engulfed the whole works. For that day and the hatches that followed in succeeding weeks, the big alluring bug gave me larger bass. Though far from matching a small hatch, the soft offering simply appeared too lifelike for the bass to resist.

During an hour when the surface was as quiet as the lake seemed silent, I knotted on a larger #1/0 bug of the same pattern, and cast it long beyond a weed bed that provided cover for my wading. After leaving it motionless for a time, with brief lifts of the rod tip and short strips of line, I jogged in the bug. Its leisurely pace emitted soft lapping sounds, and it spread a wide, mild V wake. What followed astounded me. A bass some 40 feet away sensed the sounds of a swimming prey and measured the pace of the retrieve; this hovering bass then closed the distance in a straight line, actually estimating the point where the lure would reach the weed bed in front of me. Like a homing torpedo, the bass humped the water and closed the distance to the prey.

When I let the big morsel rest tightly at the edge of the dense weed bed, the bulge over the stalking bass, now just a foot away, disappeared. In 10 seconds that mouthful for any bass was siphoned under with virtually no commotion. I lifted my strong 9-foot graphite rod for 6-weight line and hung on to Mr. Big. The tackle held, and I was able to wrestle the 5-pounder through the spinach and play it to hand.

As I hefted the catch by bending down its lower jaw with one hand, I thought how in the past I had used at least 8-weight glass rods for presenting offerings to bass in dense cover. But for some years now, lighter, stronger graphite rods had performed well. This bulky bug, and others like it, would usually be prescribed for heavier fly lines, but a 6-weight, weight-forward line flings them well and minimizes line splash.

Some of the other sleeker floating patterns I've developed—they feature long, webby saddle hackles tied flat behind bulletheads of long elk hair—resemble the dependable plastic worm lure. They represent giant leeches, snakes, eels, salamanders, and other such foods. Those tied with shorter split-tailed saddle hackle and appropriate coloration are slender versions of frogs; the impression of bulk is achieved with the spun marabou. Even the largest of such patterns cast easily and long with my 6-weight graphite outfit. And with the smaller of these flies, lighter tackle can be used. The bullethead of hair is waterproofed with Flexament, but even this hardened head emits a hollowly gurgling, muted sound different from similar cork-bodied slider patterns.

Properly presented, they are deadlier more often than the spun-hair-headed bugs, though both have their heydays in waters I fish frequently. However, bass can become wary of any artificial and the identifiable sound waves it emits. The frog can be fished in many productive manners, from leisurely kicks to a faster-kicking escape. A sink-tip line will pull a buoyant bug under water during the retrieve, and it will rise during a pause; the waterproofed bullethead in this situation is an advancement over spun-hair heads that can become soggy. I'm still taking bass on an experimental bullethead frog I wrapped five years ago. Those soft materials—marabou hackles and saddle-hackle tails—collapse when taken by fish; yet they are durable.

One of the deadliest searching techniques with the snaky version of the bullethead slider calls for long casts. Then a bug can often be retrieved more rapidly by waggling the low rod, pointed just above the horizontal, in combination with continual quick strips of line. With #6 and smaller spun-hair-headed patterns only 2 inches long, this steady bring-back can be just as deadly as it is with the longer bullethead flies. Once a loose-line retrieve that attracts bass is established, the action on moody, wary bass can be steady.

The lighter fly line reduces on-water drag and permits the featured bugs to perform their acts naturally when retrieved. A short, strong leader of 6 feet may be right for probing pockets in dense bass cover, while a leader of up to 11 feet will give natural presentations with the smaller of these bugs.

The soft flies can attract resounding, geyserlike sprays from hard-striking bass, even when left motionless on the water; the ethereal impression of billowy marabou and feathers often brings out the killer instinct in a bass to take a helpless prey. Yet quieter takes with the motionless, soft flies are common. Bass chomp down on a softer morsel, enhancing sure hooking. Even when I'm slithering my longest bullethead snake at a fast pace, the usual strike is a muffled one. This exciting earmark strike is a "whumpf" accompanied by a thin, high wedge of spray when the bass takes the 6-inch fast-swimming prey at the head. These flies show markedly that size, a factor in attracting the hungry bass, can be achieved with long, slender, top-water offerings. Certainly, the tastes of bass change as the season progresses, and when they've had enough of frogs for a time, other imitations are generally more effective.

The bass learn when a natural is likely to be abundant and forage heavily on the food. Often bass develop a liking for panfish and will invade shorelines for summer-spawning sunfish, as well as smaller late-summer bluegills. This lore has been documented in bass literature, and some of the best imitations for luring bass are those tied by Bob Pierce, a Wisconsin angling buddy. His ties are flattened, thin sunfish and bluegills in various colors to match those currently favored by local bass. Complete with realistic tail, the spun hair is trimmed thin and left sparse below a hidden hook.

Bob floats the spun-hair fly low, pancaked on the water. Sometimes he leaves it still, or he evenly retrieves it a yard or so to simulate an injured, struggling little fish. The bass he takes on panfish imitations fill a void in the fishing time when typical bass offerings aren't attractive.

A mouse may be on the menu, especially along meadows where furry rodents hole up. A mouse comes out at night to forage, and that is a time to drop one near the shoreline so a bass can hear the impact. The mouse flounders but then swims as best it can, so a retrieve of an imitation parallel to the shoreline is a natural presentation. A simple tapered, spun-hair mouse remains a deadly imitation, but I often use a softer version that is constructed rather than tied. With a cork base on the hook, I lay down and glue on strips of soft fur in the contours of the natural, compete with tail.

At times, smaller imitations of mice and frogs, #6 and #8, are preferred by bass. In these cases, I'll often opt for lighter tackle,

Favorite bass fly patterns include (clockwise from the top) long bullethead slider, spun-hair soft bug, light moth, hair and marabou bluegill, and mouse.

such as a 4-weight outfit. Part of the fun I derive each season comes when bassing with a 2-weight rod (often with 3-weight, weight-forward line) and leader tippets as light as 6X. With scaled-down tackle, I've had near 3-pounders empty my line and go into the backing before yielding.

The majority of surface foods, including many varieties of insects, display two common on-water actions. One is abbreviated motion. You can simulate that action with wiggles of the rod tip or with inch-long retrieves. The other is escape action, imitated with a speedier retrieve of the artificial. Cover prime spots by working the offering in key zones. Whenever there is a probability that a bass may be close, fishing the presentation all the way to your feet gets some surprise takes. Most anglers develop presentations that then become habit because they often work well. However, when a customary method is not producing, try varying the timing of pauses, the pace, and even the usual order of the retrieve.

Once when bass were cruising and rising to insects, a little hair bug cast to the rise and left motionless didn't interest a fish. Quivering the bug or teasing it along in inches didn't work either. Yet when I left the bug at rest, then suddenly wriggled it several inches to a stop, I had solid takes. Such a slight change in eye-catching motion can make the difference.

An encounter with another bass some years ago is memorable because I had to adapt to lighter tackle for the clear shallow water over sandy bottom during daylight and to come up with a taking pattern. Some bass, drawn to two natural foods, would cruise about, variously taking small minnows, while sometimes a fish would rise to the low-winging pale moths on or near the surface. One elusive bass, larger than the others, seemed to prefer the moths on the surface. I opted for a 12-foot leader tapered to a 4X tippet, 6-weight double-tapered floating line, and the longest, lightest rod I had back then—a sturdy but light 8½-foot fiberglass rod.

At the vise, I created a bug to match the moths. The #8 tapered bug had a blunt rounded head, and when I trimmed it to shape, I positioned the wings high on the thorax. Again I waded unobtrusively into place. In time that largest of the bass surfaced 40 feet away. Quickly I cast the bug on the spreading rings of its rise, left it still, then gyrated it in place to suggest the natural fidgety moths. Finally I retrieved it to suggest an injured minnow. In minutes I spied the bass finning hurriedly along the surface, so I arrowed a long cast, dropping the bug in its path before the leader alighted. The delicacy and concealment of the long leader with a light tippet gave a hidden presentation. At once, the bug was displaced in a small splash. After bulldogging tugs, the beauty leaped straight up, hanging and shaking over the mirrored water. That largemouth was the heftiest one I took on a floating fly that year from a little lake I fished frequently.

That same day other bass fed in a predictable manner, taking moths increasingly into the twilight. After dark they selected spent moths floating low. Leaving the bug motionless for as long as a minute or two brought a quiet rise from a bass.

That bug has been a steady producer in the years since. For the moth hatches that occur on many waters, I began tying in bundles

Big bass taken on ultralight tackle can be superior sport.

of hair and positioning the wings high on the thorax. On such a thick bug, this wing position allows the fly to wobble a bit when twitched on the water. On some bugs, the wings are flared at an upward, nearly 45-degree angle to simulate a fluttering natural, while wings tied horizontally and at a right angle to the hook imitate the spent insect. These distinctions are useful on other flat-floating hair imitations I tie, including slender hairwinged mayfly spinners and damselflies. Bass can become highly selective well after dark, when they'll concentrate on the most easily taken and abundant form of the insect.

One calm, late afternoon in summer, the bass seemed to be absent when my partner and I waded a shallow bottom on Ninepipes Reservoir in Montana. Hearing a resounding splash from a distance, I turned and saw his light trout rod bowed. He later lifted the 3-pound bass high out of the water. It had taken a #8 dry fly.

Sometimes, bass are looking for the lightly floated, high-winged dry fly. My friend's favorites are meaty, fluttering-wing silhouettes such as the Wulffs, Goofus Bugs, and Bucktail Caddises. For spindly naturals, the ethereal long-hackled spiders and long-tailed variants are a good choice. And on a light leader they can be skipped and skimmed along the water.

Bass will select terrestrials when they are present. Various beetles and ants are common naturals and, along with other terrestrials, are not only on shoreline waters. Flying terrestrials, including winged ants, will fall far onto a body of water, while others that are wind-blown and adrift become offshore bass foods. Trying the unusual, on a sunny day I let a grasshopper dry float motionless for minutes over a sloping drop-off before a fish came up and took it.

When an angler who said he likes to fish mostly dry flies for bass showed me his boxes one day, I mentioned that there were no real mouthfuls of feathered hooks there for bass. Good-sized bass often will show a preference for insects of sizes and varieties found in a box of #12 and smaller trout flies, especially during the absence of more substantial natural foods. And when numerous naturals are on the water, even if they are small, bass can feed with a high degree of selectivity. Recently at dusk, I watched bass dimpling the surface, taking tiny fare in the surface film well offshore. The successful fly was a #14 polywing mayfly spinner.

Regardless of the size of the naturals, matching the insects with a dry will often give great results. Our angling literature generally regards trout as the fish with the greatest selectivity in feeding. Just the same, matching the hatch for bass adds a new dimension to most anglers' pursuit of rising fish.

With the onset of dusk, it takes about an hour for bass to develop their acute night vision. So, well after dark the bass may feed avidly on the sometimes smaller, less noisy foods when insects are prevalent. At 10:30 P.M. one midsummer night at the beginning of the Solunar Period, I quietly approached within 30 feet of a small stubbly weed bed pocking an expanse of barren shallows. Earlier I had spied a bass chasing sunfish there. I waited. Not hearing a feeding bass in the stillness, I cast my floater to the outer edge of the weeds. It had hardly dropped onto the mere foot-deep water when the 2-pound bass took it solidly but with a barely audible rise.

The larger fish did not begin feeding until nearly midnight, and then the bass that had migrated to the shallow rim waters to forage were receptive to a floating bug. After casting it to the edge of shoreline cover, I left it motionless for a minute or so. Then I jiggled it along, inches at a time. This gently audible presentation attracted muffled takes rather than explosive strikes. On the hook, the bass thrashed upward in startling splashes, punctuating the quiet moonless night and giving me shivers in the balmy air.

Tackle matched to the various hair bugs and dry flies makes bassing all the more enjoyable, because a measure of the fun in fly-fishing is taking a spirited, crafty bass with light, sporty tackle.

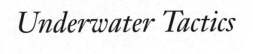

Underwater Tactics

Nymphing under the Hatch

I WETTED DOWN a lightly weighted Muskrat Nymph and cast it a few yards upstream of a trout swirling to take emerging mayfly nymphs just under the surface. The little fur fly drifted, ever-deepening, until suddenly my line tightened. When the trout tail-danced it looked to be larger than the one I had fished for.

Though duns were plentiful that chilly late afternoon, nearly all the visibly feeding trout took subsurface emergers. And the wide river looked rained on with the rises of trout. A closer description of the rises would be swirling or porpoising trout, slicing the mirrored darkening surface, which brushed aside drifting duns.

Often, fishing a nymph purposely beneath the rise has hooked larger trout, indicating that vertical feeding stratification is not uncommon. Whether or not drifting nymphs are more abundant than hatched flies on top, a sizable trout often holds at a deeper level and will take a nymph under the hatch.

Sometimes trout feeding under a hatch offer a complex situation. During a mayfly hatch the dun-feeding trout I was catching weren't as large as the fewer eye-poppers rolling underwater, raising bulges, their backs and dorsals occasionally knifing the surface. I switched to a mayfly emerger, drifted 6 inches deep. It caught nothing.

The only other likely bits of food in midstream near the surface at this time would be midges. My #20, tied dark of ⅔ black and ⅓ gray polypropylene built up near the hook eye, which could simu-

Cagey larger trout often dine on emergent forms of insects in stream, though hatches are on the surface. (Artwork by Richard Fendrick, based on an original sketch by T. Wendelburg; reproduced with permission)

late either nymph or pupa, didn't interest a trout on an upstream cast. So I fished from a new angle and drifted it downstream ahead of the 6X tippet. Simply, this presented a fly at a deeper level, about a foot under, and the first few casts took a large brown and a rainbow. Often catching trout goes beyond observation and insect sampling to a knowledge of trout-feeding characteristics and fishing a taking fly with a method that works at the time.

As I fished upstream, catching rising trout with a dry fly on the flat water of Poindexter Slough, a meadow stream near Dillon, Montana, I saw larger rainbows feeding in a shallow riffle ahead. A number of fish tailed, nose down with tail fin ruddering high, or bulged, turning swiftly in the ankle- to knee-deep fast water. These trout fed rapidly on the plentiful larder from the gravels. I cast up the riffle, and my lightly weighted mayfly emerger drifted downstream, ticking bottom to the nearest trout. It took with a swirl. An emerger bumping bottom on a natural drift took the remaining nose-down trout as well.

To hook trout that take flies suddenly, with slashing strikes to crush them, I keep the rod tip low, just above horizontal, and generally just let line slide through the thumb-forefinger grip of my rod hand as the reel sings out line. Rooting or bulging nymphers practically hook themselves.

Other nymphers feed delicately. A 3-plus-pound rainbow was feeding on little emerging olive mayflies along the stream edge. After taking one the trout would roll up. It porpoised at random in one direction and then another, making it impossible to determine when and where to place a drifting fly to its snout. When it humped broadside toward midstream, I quickly cast the fly some 40 feet so that it dropped in a couple of feet ahead, the leader safely to one side and giving me a hooking angle.

The weighted #16, with stubby ostrich herl for a vestige of emerging wings, sank and drifted a foot. The floating leader glinting on the flat surface twitched imperceptibly, and I merely tightened the line. The trout splashed head to tail, thrashing up a pile of water before heading to deeper water. I played the 19-incher to hand, and it seemed this hefty rainbow weighed as much as a bass the same size would.

Greasing the leader to within a selected distance of the fly adjusts depth of drift to the feeding zone of a trout. And the angler can see the floating leader pause when a trout inhales the fly. Polaroids are invaluable in the angler's nymphing equipment. Usually I fish a 10-foot or longer leader for nymphing trout in clear water and add a longer tippet when needed. A double tippet, 2 feet each of progressively finer "X" designations, such as 5–6X, and so forth, presents a fly naturally in the currents.

But matching a fly in the water is not always the taking ruse. Several kinds of mayflies hatched sporadically from a narrow pool on a Wisconsin spring creek, Black Earth Creek, near Madison. A lone brown swirled under water, bulging but not breaking the surface while taking the emerging nymphs. Because it fed rapidly, the trout almost had to be dining indiscriminately on the smorgasbord. A bright-bodied emerger, like one I tie with orange poly fibers, attracts trout in the same way as a dry fly such as Royal Coachman or

Wulff does in mixed or abundant hatches. My #16 emerger had a bulky wing pad of peacock herl to simulate the case when it's ready to split, or is splitting, prior to the wings emerging. This trout took it on its first sunken drift. A built-up wing case or a bit of stubby herl for emerging wings simulates those flies that don't leave the capsule until they have risen to the surface film or while the nymph is floating unhatched.

There was one fishing phenomenon regarding color that can't be explained scientifically, but it made all the difference to the trout. One year, while I fished three days each on two Montana meadow streams, a dark olive emerger took nymphing trout readily. The next year at the same time of season, with the identical fishing time on those waters, the taking emerger was the usual size and pattern but had a black body with a little gray mixed in. The only notable difference was that the second year most of the fishing was done under sunny skies, though even on the few cloudy occasions the blackish emerger produced, while the other didn't.

There's no doubt, though, that a fly matched to lighting conditions takes trout. In late day there's usually more red light from the sky, rendering reddish hues visible. Late one overcast afternoon a rainbow was taking the occasional nymph near a moss bed. There weren't many flies in the water. I drifted my orange emerger a foot deep and took the largest trout of the day. Another time pale midges hatched sparsely. Only now and then a trout took a pupa. However a fly tied with a copper-wire body and a tuft of gray ostrich herl spiraled around the head really cleaned up on the nice browns in this small midwestern limestone stream.

This shiny example using a more attractive color than the hatch was tied on a #18 Mustad #7948-A short-shank, heavy hook, creating a midge-sized offering with a larger hook gap for surer hooking qualities. And this visible little number took the evening's best brown on a blind drift edging a weed bed where I suspected a trout might be.

As an alternate method, presenting an emerger as one would normally fish a wet fly, across and down, can attract trout. There are two basic presentations I use to fish the "hot corner," where trout

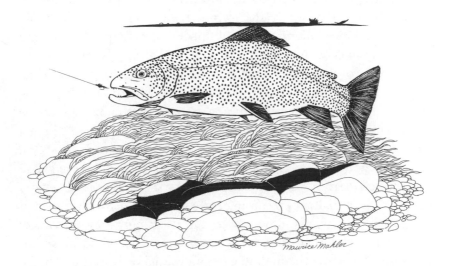

Nymphs presented downstream, with various techniques, are deadly. (Artwork by Maurice Mahler; reproduced with permission)

usually take the fly: Drift the fly naturally and then tighten the line so it turns to swing across in front of the trout. Or use a method I call quick nymphing, which involves casting across, angling down, and swimming the fly right away back across the current. This would seem to be a novice method, but there are still times when it is productive.

The first method was taking trout one day on the Firehole, in Yellowstone National Park, when another angler caught a 3¾-pound brown upstream a ways. Harry Mayo said it hadn't been rising, though trout all around were feeding. The beauty took the fly with the same method I was using. The fly had just turned the corner and was swimming across current near a mossy hummock. The fly in the trout's jaw, with the leader tippet snipped to avoid injury, had swept-back, gray, duck-quill wings lying back close to the body.

The yellow-floss abdomen was visible, and so was a peacock herl thorax. The tail and throat fibers were ginger hackle.

The #16, lightly weighted with fine wire, was tied to be a wet fly. It simulated an emerging mayfly, closely resembling patterns tied to be emergers with their feather wings lying back along the hook. Low-winged flies imitate those few species of mayflies that emerge underwater and swim to the surface, as well as awash varieties that emerge near or in the surface region. Harry added that patterns like this one for mayflies and a tiny winged midge he ties can be excellent when fished gently swimming across current inches under the surface around hatch times. I noted, "They can nail a little #24 pupa fished the same way."

Trout can be fooled by the reflections of emergers on the glassy underpane of rivers. In one such instance a trout slashed several times over my shallowly swinging little nymph and always returned to its visible lie in knee-deep water. The seemingly logical strategy would have been then to present the fly more deeply to its snout. But instead I swung the nymph even more shallowly, just under the flat surface where the trout had been swirling at the fly's previous reflection crossing the underpane. Ha! A hookup and a mighty satisfying catch—nymphing under a ghost of a "hatch" along the transparent shallows of the Firehole.

Sight Nymphing

SCOUTING AND SIGHT NYMPHING can pay off anytime of year. On one winter outing, my initial survey of a pool revealed nothing. I was about to move on when I spied a trout hovering in the middepths, slightly upstream of a tangle of overhanging branches. I threaded a small strike indicator, a half-inch piece of hollow orange fly line, onto the tippet and slid it into position over the leader-to-tippet knot. I knotted on a small weighted Hare's Ear Scud, one of my favorite patterns for between-the-hatches fishing, and checked the trout again. It was still on station, waiting for food to come its way.

A gentle sidearm cast dropped the little Scud far enough upstream for it to sink and reach the trout at eye level. In many sight-nymphing situations I rely on the indicator primarily as a guide to my presentation and watch the trout to detect the take. Sometimes the strike is obvious, but more often it's barely perceptible, a slight nod of the trout's head or the merest glimpse of white when the fish opens its mouth.

The trout swerved to one side a few inches, and, confined by dense streamside brush, I tightened my line by giving a sharp downward pull with my line hand and flicking my rod tip a few inches to the side. I guessed right, the fish didn't, and several minutes later I cradled 23 inches of glistening, chunky brown in my hands.

Fooling larger fish requires attention to detail in your approach, presentation, and terminal tackle. Over the years, I've worked out a system for sight nymphing. Polarized glasses and a wide-brimmed hat are the first two essential pieces of equipment. Approach the water slowly, with quiet steps, and keep well back from the edge as you begin your search. If possible, use brush or other vegetation as a visual barrier between you and the fish you haven't spotted yet. Scan the water carefully; don't expect fish to betray their locations by darting after prey, especially in winter when there's less for them to chase.

Look for the usual visual clues—shadows, patches of color that don't quite match the surrounding bottom, dark shapes, the tiny movement of a fin or tail. Calm water, naturally, is easier to see through than broken water, although investing the time to study a choppy flow will often reveal trout holding where there's shelter from the current. Let your gaze wander over the water, but examine each particular spot at least a couple of times before moving on.

Once you spot a lunker trout, it's time to begin planning your presentation. Matching a trout's feeding level is essential; a fly that's too high or too low in the water column is likely to drift by a fish unnoticed. It's hard to overemphasize the importance of presenting a fly at precisely the level at which a trout is holding, and estimating the sink rate and drift characteristics of a nymph makes sight nymphing an exercise in three-dimensional geometry. You'll need to move your indicator to match each situation, as well as adjust the amount of weight on your tippet.

Using a slightly lighter fly than you would when blind casting and placing it well upstream of the fish will produce a long, horizontal drift. While a shorter drift—a couple of yards or less—can present a fly accurately in broken water or along tricky current seams, dropping your fly farther ahead of the trout avoids alarming it if the water is placid. A light tippet sinks more readily than a heavier one and allows the fly to behave more naturally; I use 6X for nearly all my sight nymphing opportunities in low, clear water.

The lunker often chooses calmer, more open water to lurk in wait for prey; this is especially true of browns, which are often the dominant fish in a stream. Flat water, of course, presents a challenge that requires an unobtrusive presentation. A cast that keeps your line low and well away from the fish is advisable, as is a long, level drift and, ideally, a fly-first presentation. Along wider streams or when a fish is holding in midstream or near the far bank, I prefer to make an across-and-down presentation whenever possible, so the fly is the first thing the trout sees. Whenever you believe a trout might spy you, opt for a cast across and just slightly upstream.

Big trout often lurk near current edges or seams, and dropping your line and fly into flows moving at different speeds will do nasty things to your presentation. Your nymph can be pulled out of the target zone, or it can end up riding high in the current and over the head of a fish. As in dry-fly fishing, slack-line casts will lengthen the drift. But you frequently need to do more than simply drop your line onto the water in a series of S curves, especially if you're fishing upstream; "lining" a big trout turns all your careful watching and stalking into a waste of time.

When a straight cast won't give you the right drift or risks spooking the fish, a curve cast will set up a drag-free presentation while keeping your line away from the fish. Even a slight curve is an extremely useful presentation tool, and if you haven't yet learned how to execute a reach cast, do so very soon. Throwing exactly the right amount of curve or slack is, for the most part, learned only through practice, but it's a critical skill; too much slack in your line makes it harder to hook a fish.

In upstream sight nymphing, you can avoid lining a trout by also choosing a position that's not directly below the fish. Move off to one side a little; your angle of approach combined with a slight curve in your line will put both fly and fly line where you want them to be. Don't choose your position randomly; study the water and, if possible, move to the side that presents you with the least complicated currents.

Keeping your line off to one side can be tricky enough, but making sure the indicator is outside the trout's circle of vision can, at times, be nearly impossible. As handy as an indicator is to help guide a presentation, there are situations, such as in clear shallow water, when even the smallest indicator can let a large trout know that something's wrong. In such a case, it pays to remove the indicator

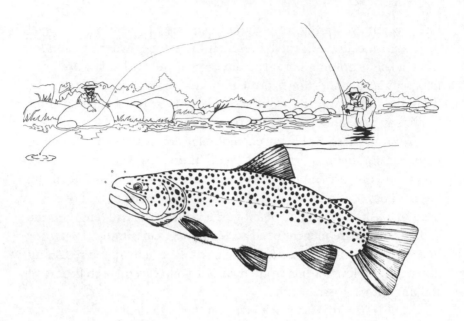

A buddy serving as a spotter can help the fly-fisher in placing accurate casts—sometimes when the angler cannot see the trout. (Artwork by Maurice Mahler; reproduced with permission)

and grease your leader to within a few feet of the nymph. The greased leader will help to control the depth of the drift and will provide you with something, however slight, to help you judge the presentation, but it's far less likely to spook the trout than a Day-Glo "bobber."

Although a trout taken on the first cast is the epitome of accuracy, with a light tippet and precise line control it's possible to fish to a sighted trout for quite some time. While I've known instant success on some of the spring creeks I frequent, I've also spent more than an hour working on a fish before convincing it to open its mouth. Spending that much time on a single fish without frightening it is nearly impossible without a light tippet, and that's one reason I rarely use tippet heavier than 6X. Fine terminal tackle also allows the fly to have a more natural, free drift. Any sudden movement of the nymph can spook a smart old trout, and I always let an untaken cast drift well beyond the fish before picking up my line.

Light tackle, in the 2–4-weight range, is an advantage when presenting a nymph to a sighted trout. A thin line casts less of a shadow and lands more gently than a heavier one, and a light rod provides you with a bit of cushion for the skinny tippet.

It's often a good idea to use a fly you can see in the water. While a #2 fluorescent orange Woolly Bugger is a bit extreme for sight fishing, a realistic pattern that differs from the color of the stream bottom by a shade or two will help you track your drift at close ranges. I sometimes use a Hare's Ear Scud in an orangy color; the fly combines a natural silhouette with a visible, but not entirely outlandish, color and has been responsible for quite a few trophies. Hunting a trophy will not only provide you with exceptionally satisfying angling; it will also keep your skills honed for when the mayflies start coming off again.

As a final tip, even with hatches in full swing and trout rising freely, scan the surrounding waters patiently. Quite often the largest trout of all is lurking motionless on a station, not rising, and just waiting for your offering to its snout.

Short-Line Nymphing

DRIFTING A NYMPH is a productive method throughout the year, and presenting nymphs on the shortest line that's practical will catch nearby trout, fish that are often overlooked and seldom presented a fly. Short-line nymphing has its advantages. Because there is less line on the water, the angler has more direct contact with the fly as it bounces along the stream bottom. Soft takes, which can go undetected when too much line is allowed to float on the water and absorb the ultralight taps of a finicky feeder, can be sensed more readily on a short line.

Since water tension on the line is greatly reduced or eliminated with the short-line technique, the all-important natural drift of the fly is easier to achieve. Currents with differing speeds present few problems to the short-line nymph fisher because elaborate casts and intricate mending are not needed to deal with line drag.

I pin the fly line under the rod handle with my forefinger and cast 15 feet of line quartering upstream. I drift the rod downstream on track over the short line, maintaining a nearly tight connection, while the slight sway of line gives a natural, deep drift of the nymph. The weighted nymph sculling along bottom transmits "ticks" to my rod hand. When the line hitches in its drift, I set the hook and the rod bows deeply against a bottom-hugging trout on the line.

Fishing with one hand gives balance to wielding the fly rod, like the balance exhibited by a skilled fencer, who grips his foil with one hand. When I start to fish and my rod arm is "cold," it's easiest to present a nymph this way.

Initially I saw this one-handed technique used by an angler who hooked one thumb on his belt when he began nymphing. After fishing out the drift, he raised the rod and swam the nymph to the surface. With an easy swing of the rod, he cast it angling up-current again. He didn't lift a hand to the line until playing a trout.

Whether or not you nymph with one hand, a short cast enhances accuracy. While a long rod is practical, any rod you like on a given stream can be effective. I've short-lined trout with a 5-foot rod.

On western streams that we fished in the fall, Jim Glenn, a Pennsylvanian, used an 8½-foot rod and often a line not much longer to drift a leaden stone fly nymph along the bottom of pools customarily fished with longer lines. Though he seldom cast as far as 30 feet, Jim took trout that often go overlooked in steadily fished rivers.

Holding the fly rod high, above the shoulder in a horizontal position, keeps most or all of the fly line above the surface. Thusly, a nymph can be presented in a nearly straight line in a single current, all but eliminating bows of slack or a dragging line. "Clothes lining" the fly line over faster intervening flows in this manner presents a nymph in the pillowed waters slowed by instream cover. A large rock or boulder, for instance, harbors trout in eddying waters or in the hole on its downstream side. A trout will often fin from this lair and hold aside or in front of the cover when lying in wait of food. Those up-front feeding stations frequently are small edges of softer water that are best nymphed with a short line.

While not always necessary, waiting a bit before fishing is a basic ploy. A bit of patience allows even the angler wading waist deep to become like part of the natural surroundings and definitely permits a cautious trout to settle down. It's time that enables you to read the water closely.

I've watched many a trout a short line away take my nymph. Doing experimental fishing, I've let a trout inhale a visible nymph (which doubles as a strike indicator), open and close its jaws tasting the morsel, and then I've set the hook. A visible sunken indicator on the leader gives closer detection of a trout's take, and using as short a leader as advisable results in more hooked trout. A leader of 7 feet is not too short in most instances, and a supple tippet will enhance presentations and increase the number of takes by trout.

Often trout lurk on the bottom waiting for a morsel of food to appear. Your nymphing should present the fly naturally. A final measure of the short-line technique's effectiveness is to fish the nymph nearly to you, by raising the rod. With stealth, you'll take hidden trout near the rod tip. And that's short-lining at its shortest.

One of the tricks to successful nymphing is achieving a natural, tension-free presentation while maintaining the line in a configuration and with the rod in position to hook a lightly biting trout. When nymphing upstream, raising the rod in an even draw as the fly drifts back in steady to swift water will enable you to sense the lightest take by a trout, even though a visible indicator (afloat or sunken) on the leader doesn't hesitate in the current.

A buoyant indicator on the leader is easiest to see but limits your possible presentations. Frequently I thread a hollowed half-inch piece of fly line up the tippet, snugging it over the blood knot. This unobtrusive indicator casts smoothly with light tackle and doubles as both a floating and a sunken marker. Greasing the indicator and the leader to the fly line allows a nymph a free drift and aids in setting the hook. But after a short 3–5-foot (often effective!) drift, a weighted heavier fly will sink the small piece of fly line and the leader. This is a different but fetching presentation with many imitations.

One of my deadliest techniques is to cast the nymph upstream into faster water and before the line falls make a sidearm horizontal reach with the rod to drop the indicator aside on slower water and put the fly first. The nymph tumbles down the faster water column, and the indicator curls in, trailing behind. Raising the rod lifts line off the surface if needed. With the nymph in swift water, this is important in keeping that sway of slack to enhance a natural drift with the fly while following with the rod in an angled position. In effect, the method I call the curl-in presents the fly ahead of the leader by using currents to create the same delivery of a fly as created by the

I handle a brown caught on a 6X tippet, a nymph, floating line, and a little strike indicator.

curve cast. In one instance a friend had finished taking trout in a pool when I showed him the difference a curl-in presentation can make. Using the identical nymph he had fished, I took four more nice browns simply by showing the fly in a new way in the same current drift—fly first, on a curl-in.

To fish a curl-in most effectively for that larger trout often lurking on bottom, let the fly sweep around and settle on the bottom, keeping the fly line well off to the side on slow water. The bright little indicator deep in a clear pool may dart short when a trout shovels in the motionless nymph. With experience, you'll be able to lift the rod, angled to the outside of the bowed line curled in at the right moment, and hook the trout. This technique has taken more large trout for me than any other when the stream seems absent of feeding trout and the better fish lurk deep in quieter waters. Effective for short-line nymphing, the curl-in is also productive on casts beyond 30 feet.

Nymphing during the Slack Hours

ECAUSE OF THEIR INSTINCT to seek habitat rich in food, their caginess, and their adaptability, browns of larger size inhabit flowing water regardless of the width of the stream. A lunker will enter a chilly tributary to feed on natural foods that may not be as common or as abundant in the main stream. The mouth of a tributary that appears narrow and sometimes shallow often belies a treasure of trouting upstream. The gentler pools on flat terrain near the confluence provide prime holding waters for larger trout.

One day, when a feeder stem I know did not yield a trout near its mouth, and minnows weren't darting about in the shallows as usual, I sensed that a big trout had been feeding there recently, and probably had moved on upstream. Sure enough. Later, in the middle of a pool, that fattened beauty appeared over the bottom, shaking its head, my #12 Hare's Ear Scud imitation in its jaw. Even the largely cannibalistic trout relishes the larger freshwater shrimp found in clean, enriched tributaries.

The stomach of one larger brown I caught in midday contained a 5-inch sculpin, a snail, and a fresh, creamy-tan shrimp. By sampling the natural foods in tributaries and small main streams that widen to 30 feet and by examining stomach contents, I learned a fishing pattern that consistently takes larger trout.

In streams of any size with 50–66-degree water, I found that sizable trout will feed actively during seemingly slack angling hours. They'll forage on easily captured crustaceans and other morsels such as leeches. Naturals other than aquatic insects supplement a trout's food intake, and during periods of the season when the more substantial hatches are lacking, these naturals may make up a greater source of sustenance than aquatic nymphs and larvae.

My early encounters with hefty trout that feed on crustaceans occurred in a freestone Montana stream 30-some years ago. I had found snails in crevices on the bottom and caught trout with marble-shaped lumps in their stomachs. My deadliest pattern became a version of the Renegade, a popular western fly. I tied it heavily weighted with wire under a bulky, lemon-shaped body of peacock herl to resemble the natural crustacean. During the apparent absence of midday feeding activity, a larger trout would take the snail fly. By drifting it deeply or rolling it along the bottom, I caught browns and rainbows averaging more than 3 pounds.

In the years since, the Renegade snail has been a deadly pattern for me when prospecting freestone streams. The snail also is a natural in a prolific limestone spring creek laden with a plethora of other subaquatic foods.

Trout such as this lunker brown lurk to feed on morsels other than aquatic insects.

The Girdle Bug, a rubber-legged attractor

The Girdle Bug, a rubber-legged creation, may be the most versatile of any pattern, for it can be presented in numerous ways to trigger a strike from a big fish during slack hours on the stream. I believe my article "Wild Flies That Catch Trout" (*True's Fishing Yearbook*, 1974) was the christening national piece featuring this pattern many anglers doubt even today. Although knowing that Girdle Bugs produce big trout consistently, I, too, wouldn't use one for the first few years that I fished in southwest Montana. "They're too weird," I surmised. Then Hobart Sneed, a Dillon tackle dealer who said he sold more Girdle Bugs than any other fly, gave me some to try. Presented on a natural drift, the outlandish fly took a sizable brown on my first cast.

Subsequently, a Girdle Bug took larger fish for me in just about any way a nymph, traditional wet or streamer, would. At times it seemed a Girdle Bug was the only fly that would work, and those times occur to this day more often than with any other pattern I use to prospect seemingly quiet streams for larger trout. The Girdle Bugs available in Montana shops in the 1960s were larger flies, not too practical for light tackle, with selections from long-shank #2 down to #6, with a few #8, dominating fly bins in the counter. But Sneed's gratuities started me on a tying venture, and I eventually toted a range of Girdle Bugs in #10 through #16.

Those smaller Girdle Bugs, scaled for use with light tackle, consistently produce great results, even in limpid spring creeks. Angling friends and I continue to try to justify what foodstuffs they represent, whether the fish are attracted to the larvalike chenille abdomen or mesmerized by the rubber legs and tails. Sure, when fished with action, the fly's elastic appendages sweep back and spring straight during a pause, and the fly is fetching when skittered dry on a pocket or twitched shallowly through a trout's window. But a most productive presentation, like the first cast I made with one nearly 30 years ago, is the natural drift. I believe the rubber legs are taken as a gaggle of larvae, as many natural caddises and other larvae and nymphs will moor, attached to a flotsam.

Why does the quiet stream give up large trout during the day? A lunker trout with a roomy belly to fill often feeds deeply after an insect hatch. It'll move into position to forage when it casts little or no shadow, and its dominance urges lesser trout to give it plenty of space. Dissolved oxygen levels decrease as water temperature rises; the larger trout needs to pump more oxygen through its system when feeding actively for any length of time. In streams with water temperatures cool enough for trout to feed actively during the day, higher dissolved oxygen levels ease the trout's effort when holding in even mild current. Finally, a trout may have been hooked a number of times during steadily fished hours, and it instinctively adapts to feeding during midday hours.

The chilly, gently flowing meadow creeks I fish most often harbor heavily fished browns that grow to the dimensions of footballs largely on an abundance of forage minnows. Yet they take imitations of comparatively smaller crustaceans and my All-Marabou Leech. During daylight such morsels are more palatable than elusive bait fish. Do nymphing methods take more large trout than streamers or bucktails in sluggish limestoners? I'd say so.

A light tippet sinks quickly, enhancing a deep drift with a

weighted fly. A slender tippet also gives the ultimate natural drift. I use a gossamer tippet of 30–40 inches or longer, even in tinged or chalky waters. In a limestoner, the larger brown can be as wary about a natural presentation in waters of reduced visibility as it is in clear water.

I'll drift a sunken fly as large as a sleek #8, 3X-long Leech on 6X tippet. And a #10 Hare's Ear Scud on 7X has convinced some of the warier, larger browns. Weighted flies on #8–12 hooks would seem large for a 5X or lighter tippet, but the flies and natural drift methods I use actually ease hooking trout while I'm fishing with a light-tipped fly rod. Hare's Ear Scuds, Marabou Leeches, and Girdle Bugs are examples of soft-textured impressions of various natural foods. A trout will inhale a malleable fly and hold it in the jaws while tasting the morsel, rather than instantly spit the fake, as is common with a small hard nymph in clear water. Even the Renegade snail is a harder pattern imitative of natural food that trout will take and crunch in the jaws. I once watched a 3½-pound brown mouth my #8 snail before I hooked it.

The hook need not, and should not, be set forcefully. A sidearm flick of the fly rod nudges the point into a heavy trout's hard jaw without snapping a light tippet. Always sidearm the rod in a direction that pulls the hook into the trout's jaw. When nymphing upstream, sidearm the rod either right or left, whichever angle transfers momentum the most quickly and doesn't pull the leader through a divergent current. When nymphing across or downstream, sidearm the rod downstream. This will naturally pull the hook into the trout's jaw.

Nymphing techniques for deep-feeding trout vary, but most big trout fall to a basic presentation, and that first cast to a wary fish is the deadliest. One summer Saturday afternoon, with the temperature in the 90s, I waded wet into the shallow tail of a familiar pool. I knew that in the afternoon a brown often drifts back to feed on the deep edge of the shallowing slope in the lower reach of a pool. I cast the fly 30 feet upstream into the chalky, placid water. It drifted deeply through a single lane of current aside the deep bank. Pointing the rod down the line with the tip slightly raised and stripping in line at the proper pace, I maintained a straight line to the naturally drifting morsel. The fly was only 20 feet upstream when that often indefinable pause in the drift led me to set the hook. Later, I lifted a shovel-nosed brown, the heaviest, thickest trout for its length I had caught in this stream. One such trophy, released, is memorable. When one big fish is lurking to feed, however, others will be on the prowl. Knowing this, I fished on upstream, and wasn't disappointed.

A larger fish will feed actively in the top half of a pool. A larger back-swinging eddy is easily observable. When fishing across the main current, elevate the rod high to lift the fly line over this current and drift a nymph naturally through the back eddy. Start the drift where the current curls aside and present the nymph on a continuing drift path through the back-swinging current.

When casting upstream to the top of a pool, drop the fly in the lower yard of the incoming shallows to start it on a deepening drift. Here are two tactics to present the nymph deeply into the pool: (1) Use a heavily weighted fly and let it drift in deeply, then raise the rod as the fly nears the bottom in order to ensure a straight-line connection. Doing this will also hook trout that take gently as the fly drifts deeply through a current slot. (2) Use a slack-line drift to tumble the fly quickly and deeply into a pool that drops steeply below the riffle. Raise the rod to lift the floating fly line and waggle it in horizontal sweeps while again lowering the tip. This method of laying a series of S's of fly line along the water will slow the drift, settling the fly deeply. When the nymph is on the bottom (often within seconds after forming the slack), again raise the rod tip while stripping in long hauls of line. The moment the line straightens, a trout is often fast on the hook.

The slack-line drift also gives a deep presentation with a lightly weighted fly. An artificial that is approximately the weight of the natural will drift buoyantly. An artificial deeply awash in the pool is especially effective. When you make the final long strip to straighten the line, the fly swims suddenly.

Adding motion to mimic the natural will alert a trout to take the fly. One day, for example, I met an angler on the stream who showed me a snapshot of a 5½-pound brown he had recently caught in a neighboring Wisconsin creek. He said the lunker took when he interrupted a Girdle Bug's drift with a wiggle.

When usual methods haven't produced a larger fish in a likely spot, present the fly dead still on the bottom. Let it settle naturally just behind (or aside) the current. The slack waters in the upper reach of a pool are particularly productive when this method is used. The presentation is often easiest to accomplish when fishing from the bank and casting the line into gentle edgewater. Should you wait up to several minutes, it's not unknown for a big trout to shovel in the motionless morsel. After a time, just ease the fly in a crawl, preferably across current.

This patient tactic also takes a trout that may be cruising along bottom under a calm area of stream. On occasion it also will tempt larger-than-average, lethargic fish queued in slack-water edging current. One bright midafternoon during the lowest water of the summer, I found browns bunched in the darkest, deepest patch of slack water below a gently welling current. When I hooked one, it seemed to excite another to take the fly. Yet the next trout took only after a fly was left motionless for at least 20 seconds and then crawled broadside toward shore.

The method is also deadly for a trout you can see holding on the bottom in quiet water. One bright noon hour while I waded up a little stream in Michigan's Upper Peninsula, I spied a pair of sizable brook trout holding on the bottom in crystal water below the panning, incoming shallows. Presenting the fly on a settling drift rested it 6 inches ahead of the duo. In less than a minute, one eased toward the fly, nosed down, and took it. The other wouldn't spook from its position. On a repeat presentation, this trout didn't take the fly until I crept it to a stop within an inch of its jaw.

A final tip for nymphing in evenly flowing to sluggish water: Rather than holding the rod higher, position the rod at waist height and horizontally or in a lower angle, to avoid slack between the rod tip and the water. The low rod points directly down the path of the fly line, in hooking position. In this way, the line naturally drifts slowly over the course of the nymph. To stay hidden from wary fish,

I'll sit along the edge of a pool. My fly rod then is even lower to the water. This restful angling method has taken larger trout not far beyond the rod tip.

Give the malleable flies that imitate morsels other than aquatic insects a try during the quiet hours. That's when larger trout are feeding.

Light-Tackle Streamers

MODERN GRAPHITE RODS cast with power and precision, and the wide range of fly lines available for various presentations has opened a new vista in trout angling. Now the angler who once relied on heavier tackle and often long casts to deliver streamer flies has increased opportunities to use light tackle for the same purpose. One key strategy for light-tackle streamer success is to seek waters flowing at a manageable level. Some streams, including limestoners and spring creeks, are less affected by freshets. During any season of the year, trout in these waters can develop a ravenous appetite for an accurately presented, swimming imitation of food, often a mouthful of a fly, which lends credence to the lore that a predatory fish prefers to consume a food item fully 10–20 percent its own size.

One of the deadlier impressions that trout also take for a swimming food is my All-Marabou Leech tied with a longer, fuller tail. One bright midafternoon last year I tarried along the shallow side of a pool on a moderately flowing Wisconsin limestoner, knotting a #8 Leech to a 6X tippet. The weighted, long-tailed fly of 2¾ inches swims seemingly unattached to the light leader and is often my choice for calm or clear water. On a 2-weight rod equipped with a 3-weight line, such unlikely combinations of large flies and light lines have served me well as matched tackle for larger trout. Sleek patterns such as my Leech, with its dubbed marabou body wrapped over weighting wire, can be cast smoothly with the light rod by

A long-tailed All-Marabou Leech enticed this brown, which tested a 2-weight outfit.

lengthening the casting stroke and taking advantage of, rather than fighting, the weight of the fly.

I knew, from previous years, that the pool held large trout, and I thought, "About this time of day one usually holds over there." I took two steps downstream for a direct across-stream cast to the deep opposite bank and let the fly sink. I left the fly dead still for a moment, moved it a foot to another stop, then retrieved the Leech with repeated 3-inch strips while vibrating the low rod tip from side to side; the fly bumped seductively along, ticking the bottom broadside across the current.

The strike came at midstream and might have snapped an even heavier tippet but for my raising of the rod horizontally and giving the heavyweight a slip-strike. My usual composure while parrying a bullish trout on light tackle soon turned to excitement when the fish ran upstream near the surface, its size exaggerated by the tricks water can play with light. Eventually the tired trout was herded, like a wallowing small pig, into the shallows and steadied with a tailing grasp. I snapped a close-up photo while the fish rested upright. A trophy trout can be revived and released without being lifted from the water; a precaution I often use is to wait until the fish is revived enough to balance upright before removing the hook with forceps.

Not all big trout on the prowl remain unseen, and even a cruising fish may be on the lookout for a meal in one bite. Near the mouth of a tributary I spied a 4-pounder downstream as it cruised the edge of a flat and disappeared into deeper water. I cast downstream beyond its estimated position and wriggled the slinky Leech back up-current along the bottom, and this fish had a deceptively gentle take for its heft.

How excited can a stream's big trout get over the prospect of a mouthful of food? Consider this: After taking a 23-incher from another known midstream lie of large trout, I switched to a small wet fly to probe the incoming riffle. A minnow of 4 inches took my fly, skittered across the top, and with a rush a big brown replaced it, almost magically. I expected the trout to eject the forage fish, but I soon realized that the #14 hook of the wet fly had somehow been transferred to the corner of the 22-inch brown's mouth, and I played it in. Definitely, the large trout wanted a full meal in the form of a *swimming* natural food.

To be successful, the light-tackle streamer fisherman who wants oversized trout needs to combine proper fly design and selection, a variety of presentations, and appropriate tackle to make those presentations work.

Fly Patterns and Adaptations

My Marabou Leech is a fly that gives trout the impression of various substantial natural foods when tied in appropriate colors and fished to mimic the real thing. The action of the long, wavy marabou tail is complemented by the dubbed-marabou body; the body is combed with a piece of Velcro glued to a stick, to create a "breathing" action in the teased-out fibers along the hook. Always tied weighted, this fly can be deadly when drifted, but its pulsing allure when fished in the innumerable ways streamers can be effective makes the pattern a good example of the need to show a fly that differs somewhat from the common bait-fish imitations.

A new look in a streamer will frequently take trout that have seen all the common patterns. Sometimes a new "killer" fly may simply be an adaptation of a known pattern. On a trip out West, I wrapped a short, stubby version of a Marabou Muddler on a #8, 2X-long hook. Thick golden-olive dubbing replaced the flash of tinsel chenille and blended nicely with the short yellow marabou wing; the little fly proved its worth in pools where typical patterns are larger and gaudier for Montana's browns and rainbows.

Another year, on the same waters, I resorted, with surprising success, to a little white streamer I had tied for crappie and bass. With a wing of wide hen hackle feathers flared outward over a red yarn tail, a white chenille body, and a white head with red eyes, the fly waved and fluttered in the water. On the retrieve, the little streamer's wing feathers pulsed together and "thinned down" considerably. Such comparative simplicity in a fly should not always be overlooked in favor of creating highly realistic matches of local forage species.

Every selection should include realistic patterns, of course, and one found in my fly boxes is a chubby, tapered, furry-textured sculpin with a lifelike flexible tail and broad pectoral fins. This pattern has taken large browns from my native Wisconsin meadow streams and Montana's rivers.

In tying up a new fly, you need to consider silhouette, action of materials, proportion (chubby versus thin), color, and the use of flash materials and often a "hotspot" bit of bright color. Size is a matter of bulk as well as length to the hungry trout, and color is usually the second most important factor. Anglers develop personal systems in the use of color; I doubt anyone has a monopoly on conclusiveness, and the wise angler remains flexible.

My own theories are based on those factors that have given me trout consistently. Under a bright sky I'll use an olive- or lighter-colored fly; under an overcast sky, a dark or black pattern. In discolored water, a bit of bright color is always an aid to visibility; on one western spring creek only a small streamer with a whisk of red in the wing and a red throat transformed chasing trout into solidly striking trout. Independent of conditions, two colors that remain effective are white and yellow.

Sleek patterns have received well-deserved praise for their success in clear water, and the concept can be applied to Muddlers. Trimming the bulky, clipped deer-hair head and thinning the wing gives a standard Muddler a quicker sink rate. Years ago, Harry Mayo of west Yellowstone supplied me with Marabou Muddlers tied with a single winging feather to accentuate marabou's natural breathing action; they took large trout that day and have done so ever since. I also fish a bullethead marabou streamer, created by tying the marabou feather on backward (i.e., projecting it out over the eye of the hook), dubbing marabou the length of the head, and then reversing the wing feather and binding it down at the rear of the head. This pattern sinks readily and has proven to be deadly.

Presentations

Let's not forget that basic methods with streamer flies still take trout. Once, while wading a riffle head and photographing my partner fishing upstream, I cradled my rod out to the side in the crook of my arm, its sinking line trailing downstream to the streamer hanging deeply in the current. Each time I flipped the film-advance lever, the rod tip twitched. After a few pictures, a trout responded to the streamer's sudden jogs, softly whacking the fly; a trout will often bat a food fish in an attempt to stun it. After another slight twitch of the rod tip (again, caused by flipping the film advance), the trout took solidly; with the rod handle pinned, I turned from the waist, hooking the beauty. "Hanging" a streamer—parking it out in the current and giving it some motion now and then—is a method that is as effective as it is easygoing.

Just as different variations in patterns produce, so will presenting a familiar fly in a previously unseen way; presentation can be another aspect of a new look in streamers. One example is a technique I employed on the upper Madison River in Yellowstone National

Park, where a long cross-current cast with a sinking-tip line allowed me to get the fly down deep while still permitting me to mend the floating portion of the line. As the Marabou Muddler drifted along, I repeatedly flipped additional short lengths of line out of the low rod tip, giving the fly a natural, deepening, straight drift well down the pool.

When the line angled below me and straightened, I raised the rod quickly; the fly turned sharply across the current, "trimming thin" for a yard. I immediately lowered the rod tip while jiggling another few feet of line out, again drifting the billowy fly directly downstream. As the current took up the short slack, the fly swung a second time in a small area and was taken with a strike that yanked my fly rod nearly to the water.

Casting across and down to swing a streamer broadside back across the current remains a deadly method when the fly is presented at the proper pace and depth. While helping a novice flyfisher, I started by advising him to cast and "just hang on." He turned to look my way, asking what to do next, just when a brown blasted his fly in midstream. After that, he gained confidence in the swinging fly.

Applying rod-tip action to a streamer swinging across current triggers strikes from otherwise recalcitrant trout. Tom Henderson, who introduced me to the upper Madison years ago, masterfully demonstrated brief, snapping twitches of the fly with rod-tip flicks as crisp as the squeezing of a hair trigger. Subsequently, I was able to help another angler with a different variation on imparted action; simply pumping the rod tip evenly just 6 inches every yard or so during the streamer's swing will sometimes persuade a reluctant trout. On smaller streams, a sharply angled downstream cast and a short swing of the fly across likely-looking water often makes the best presentation.

My favorite technique to cover the water is the "full delivery." This method is particularly effective in (but not confined to) the swifter incoming and deepening spill near the top of a pool. Fishing from the shallow side, cast upstream at an angle. Often a slack-line technique is needed to get the fly deep immediately; depending on water type between you and the fly's lane of drift, these include stack mending, easy upstream mends formed by simply lifting the rod and laying the line farther upstream, repeated circular upstream mends, and S casts. Hold the rod high and point it at the estimated position of the fly; keep mending line to allow the fly to drift naturally and tap along the bottom. Trout hunker in pockets beneath the deeper swift water, and a streamer presented as you would roll a nymph is deadly in rocky nooks and crannies.

When the line passes downstream at a 90-degree angle to the current, continue to move the rod tip to "target" the position of the drifting fly while twisting from the waist and reaching downstream with the rod. To lengthen the drift even more, lower the rod and wiggle short, slack S configurations of line onto the water; with proper timing, each added length of slack never interrupts the pace of the fly.

Be ready for a strike when the line tightens below you and the fly turns to swing cross-current—this is the first of two "hot corners" in the presentation and most often the deadliest. Swinging the streamer across the flow is the next leg of the presentation, and while a spirited trout may prefer to come up for a fly swimming above eye level, tapping the fly along the bottom during the swing is an especially effective trick. The second hot corner is at the end of the swing when the streamer turns up-current to hang directly below you.

The full delivery is also useful to deliver a fly unobtrusively to trout on the shallow side of the river below you. Look for a small area of bottom change, such as a deeper hole downstream surrounded by shallow bottom, and then "spoon feed" the trout by drifting in a teasing, hanging fly. One productive variation of the technique is to bring the fly upstream a few feet and then let it drift back to its original hanging spot; at times, trout want a fly jigged sharply and bounced along upstream. Always fish out a full delivery by retrieving the fly upstream; unseen trout lurking in the shallows amid rocks often turn their heads to snap in a jogging streamer.

Upstream streamer fishing is a seldom-used technique, and while it's especially useful on a narrow creek, I've also found it productive along the shallower edges of a river of any size. Drifting the fly back to you with easy 3-inch swims helps keep the line straight and presents the fly much as you would a nymph. A basic Muddler is hard to beat for this method.

If undisturbed, frequently overlooked larger trout will lurk in the shallows during the day, often near the shoreline; even in clear water, individual fish often cannot be spotted among the camouflage of bottom and current. Swift, bouncy waters, particularly over a dark bottom, can often be successfully fished with short casts up to 30 feet. But if the water is flat, I generally make longer casts to the shallows, using a simple swinging broadside presentation of the fly.

Another target often overlooked for streamer fishing is the swift, tumbling water over the shelf at the top of a pool, sometimes within just a few yards of the deepening trough of the pool. I pointed out one such apron to a friend on a sunny afternoon—about the last time when conventional stream lore would lead one to fish there. I made a long cross-current cast with a sinking-tip line and gave two quick, arm-long strips; a brown slammed the fly. My friend was just as surprised when a second brown lurking in the same small area solidly nailed the streaking fly at the moment of its pause between strips of line.

At times you will want to extend a streamer's drift, but very few anglers take advantage of the simplest way of doing so. Have you ever lengthened a fly's drift by walking or wading shallows downstream? This may seem a unique manner to achieve a long drift, but everything from a few steps to a 20-foot walk along a low bank has helped deliver a streamer perfectly to a productive spot.

Tackle

Most anglers tote both a floating line and one or more types of sinking lines on spare spools. Having just the right line to present the streamer properly is critical; let's note some of the differences in fishing a streamer on a floating line versus a sinking line.

At the outset I mentioned using a floating line on waters such as limestoners. I'll use a longer leader of 10 feet during the day to present a streamer at the feeding level of watchful trout in clear, calm flows; even with a weighted fly, an added bit of lead on the leader may be needed to get the fly deep enough. I've fished certain free-stone river pools where the same system is efficient. These waters generally enter a pool swiftly but settle to a moderate flow with depths to 5 feet. Probing bottom with a floating line and a weighted streamer fished slowly but with enticing swims avoids spooking the trout. Indeed, in one of my favorite pools, friends fishing sinking lines rarely take trout during daylight.

However, for waters that flow more deeply and swiftly, even if they are not wide, a sinking-tip line is needed to reach bottom-hugging trout. A range of sinking-tip lines offers sink rates for virtu-ally every type of water. Even with a sinking-tip line and short leader, which keeps the fly on that all-important level plane neces-sary for correct presentation and sure hooking, added weight can be required on the tippet in fast or deep water. I prefer lead that's quickly affixed and removed, such as twist-on lead strips.

Many anglers employ 30-foot sinking shooting heads to cover wide water, and with 7–9-weight outfits, routine casts of 100 feet or more are possible. Here's a way to sink a fly deeply into distant cur-rent without having to cast quite so far and without having to use relatively heavy tackle; the method still uses a shooting head. When the fly hangs downstream representing the length of your longest cast, hold the mono running line against the rod handle and strip line off the reel, forming a 5-foot loop trailing in the current. Pinch the loop in your mouth, strip more line from the reel to form a second loop, and hold it, too, in your mouth. Transfer the running line from your rod hand to your mouth, and as you retrieve keep forming loops which are held in your mouth. Make one back cast to line up the shooting head and make the forward cast across the river. After the cast lands, feed the extra loops out of the rod; this allows your fly to sink to a depth downstream that normally would be achieved had you been able to cast the extra distance. The technique is not a substitute for distance casting, but it lets you swim a fly deeply in fast water otherwise unavailable. "Stored" extra loops re-leased in this manner do not impede a fly's natural course through the water, and the method also enables you to extend a deep presentation far downstream with a shorter cast and in swift, narrow rivers.

Be an Easygoing Diehard

Streamer fishing doesn't have to mean high waters and heavy lines, and the fly fisher who searches out and takes advantage of more moderate flows will have larger trout on lighter tackle as his reward. Make your streamer fishing techniques as varied and precise as your dry-fly and nymph angling, and I expect you'll enjoy the same excitement I know when that prized and previously elusive fish is taken and released.

Drop the Bomb Accurately for Larger Steelhead and Salmon

SPRING, SUMMER, OR FALL, when I think of steelhead, I simultaneously think of salmon—and I give thanks that my flies and my techniques with those flies take both. I watch with respect as the great salmonid fish—shimmering majesties in the water—journey upriver to spawn. They're easily the largest cold-water quarry found in great seasonal numbers in flowing water. Following winter's steelheading, various strains of steelhead enter rivers in staggered runs from spring well into autumn, providing a renewed angling experience we eagerly look forward to.

On the Wisconsin rivers that flow into the western side of Lake Michigan, unless steelhead are present, my attention focuses on the king salmon and rosy-sided, willing coho salmon of autumn. The kings, largest of river-run salmonids, remind me of submarines in their manner of gliding through calm water. And when they paddle on pectorals and ruddering tail, virtually running atop a long, shallow riffle on the way to spawning territory, they bestow a sight second only to the image of a 30-pounder tail-dancing across the river with my marabou fly hooked in its jaw.

The techniques I'll offer are effective whenever the various salmonids are in the rivers. In conjunction with these techniques, I find that marabou-tailed and winged flies not only have a knack of stirring a fish in familiar water but also are decidedly deadly when prospecting new water.

I lift a king salmon taken on a Lake Michigan tributary using a 4–5-wieght outfit.

Marabou for Simulating Prey, Intruders—and Eggs

The wavy marabou's natural billowy action on numerous patterns suggests minnows, crayfish, and other naturals that from time to time attract salmonids, whether stimulated by hunger or by the instinct to devour an intruder that's disturbing the immediate area, especially on a redd. And steelhead that have been in the river a considerable time will take nourishment; even the king salmon, regarded as a fish that disdains food intake after returning to the river to spawn, will move to snap in a swimming marabou, or one left dead still on bottom, or a naturally drifted fly.

Marabou appearance can also imitate a cluster of spawn. During spawning when eggs are adrift, the idea of presenting little round egg imitations of the spawners' own species doesn't much appeal to me. I'm not deprecating the effectiveness of egg flies, but that's one "hatch" I prefer to nod to with small marabou Woolly Bugger types and dubbed, marabou-bodied, puff-tailed flies.

Color can be the important variable in a taking fly, and the knowledgeable angler goes astream with a wide selection. I've given slide-illustrated talks on color effectiveness in wet patterns for various water conditions, times, and lighting, and I've written about the rainbow's magnetism to reds. A recent conversation with a steelheader who regularly fishes other Wisconsin rivers revealed our similar experience. In 1989, dark colors such as black, olive, and brown were steady, while in 1990 brightly colored flies dominated our fishing logs. We both ply some rivers that are often crystal in clarity, but much of our angling is on rivers whose flow is frequently tinged to murky. The visibility of bright and fluorescent colors, especially chartreuse, orange, and a bit of red, dependably gives catches in tinged water as well as clear water.

Egg-Sucking Leech—the Bomb

Woolly Bugger–type flies are probably the best-known fish catchers in recent years, and the version I tie and call the bomb is aptly described as an Egg-Sucking Flash-a-Bugger. It's just a gaudy-bright tie of the widely known Egg-Sucking Leech, originally an all-black fly with a red head. I began tying brightly colored bombs because of the deadliness of fluorescent chartreuse in a silt-tinged river I fish. From little (#8 and #10) versions to blockbusters on #4 and occasionally #2 long-shank hooks, these bombs take fish.

Straight-Line Presentation

The strangeness of new water is compelling, and on a Saturday trip last spring to two rivers unfamiliar to me, flowing crystalline under a bright sun, the chartreuse Bomb was one of two greenish marabou flies that took steelhead.

The first river led me to a large pool fed by a rambling white-water spill. An angler tarried along the bank near the top, and he remarked that the angling had slowed. His stringer trailed the morning's efforts, a brace of small 20-plus-inch male steelhead taken on a small streamer. I asked if I might toss one into the froth, and he urged me to take his place. A 3-plus-inch bushy-tailed fly on a #4, 4X-long hook underwrapped with 30 turns of 0.030 lead wire is a "secret" of getting down to deep fish without additional weight on the tippet. I cast it up-current into the tight corner of the white-water tumble, and it quickly settled beneath the champagnelike froth and drifted deeply through the calmer flow beneath. It drifted a yard or more on a straight line beyond my high-held light rod, and I pointed the tip on downstream over the estimated position of the fly.

The take, a steelhead's light tap, turned out to be a heavyweight that pounded deeply, not wanting to leave this shaded sanctuary. But in an eye-blink the line had sizzled, cutting water to midpool, and the steely leaped vertically, flashing mirror-bright.

The springy, 4-weight graphite rod gave me a sense of helplessness against the seemingly tireless swiftness of this beauty, but I know well the mechanics of a light rod's ability to parry larger fish. And while I'm ordinarily adamant about beaching my own fish, this time I welcomed my acquaintance's offer as he brandished his net. Eventually I led the she-fish back-flat over the lowered net. I ad-

I took this steelhead using a 4-weight rod and a 2X tippet.

mired the sleek but deep-bodied female, whose coloring was iridescent blue and tarpon silver with pink stripes. Chunky with eggs, she weighed 13 pounds. Looking up, I saw seven anglers gathered around the pool. I mused how a different fly can work on steadily fished salmonids.

The Nymphing Method

The second river flowed widely and shallowly over a light bottom, which imposed demanding conditions for the steelhead holding 40 feet upstream, belly on bottom, its dorsal nearly creasing the surface. I flopped open one of my marabou-laden fly books for a Marabou Leech. The pattern I developed, simply marabou tail and dubbed marabou body (which I tie extensively for trout), has been the ticket for river-run salmonids for a number of friends in regions as far north as Alaska. Now I chose a little #10 olive. My upstream cast dropped the wetted fly well above the fish, line aside, and it drifted, sculling bottom; the snout siphoned it in.

From fast-water prospecting to slow-water sight fishing, the nymphing method is a sound way to introduce a skilled trout hand to angling for steelhead and salmon. On one of those days when I was with a newcomer to steelheading, I spotted a fish for my partner, who was wading below. The steely's dark shape finned above bottom near the edge, ghostly in stained, gliding water. John Gray made the upstream cast and drifted a lightly weighted black Woolly Bugger; as I watched his indicator, set 30 inches above the fly, I told him, "The fish is a foot closer to shore." On the next presentation, he accurately corrected the drift, and I saw the steelhead delicately take the #6 as if it were a small nymph. Even so, it had turned downstream, soft fly firmly in mouth, before the indicator so much as paused on the flat surface. John set the hook, and that one ran the fly-line length of the pool more than once before he beached it.

Fish holding in place are prone to take a fly that's properly presented. Usually, a drifting artificial must be presented at a slow pace to an exact level. Whether the targeted fish is hovering high in the water or hunkering on the bottom, it may want the fly on a plane along eye level. While a floating indicator adjusts the depth of a fly, I often just drift a visible marabou a bit higher in the current to a hovering fish by changing the placement of my cast and fishing a high-rod presentation.

By holding the rod high and drawing it downstream to keep the leader and line on a plane parallel to and higher than the fly, I've also sensed the upstream-facing steelhead's light take. However you nymph, the strike indicator may be best for long drifts, but the float is not a substitute for a straight-line presentation and the knack to detect a sometimes imperceptible take.

Whether I'm fishing the water or sight nymphing, a highly visible fly has proven its worth, doubling as the indicator for instant hook setting on short casts and long, on hovering fish, and for fish on the bottom.

Short Subsurface Drifts

Occasionally a fish is spotted shouldering near the surface in fast water. Accurately placed, the slap of a bomb pattern a yard or two upstream alerts the fish in mixed current to the suddenly adrift, billowy marabou fly. With a high-held rod, even a heavily weighted marabou can be presented on a short drift near the surface; in fact, the weighted fly with the natural buoyancy of billowy marabou actually holds its straight line of drift better than an unweighted hook. The fly must be presented "between the fish's eyeballs" and often showing a broadside silhouette.

A weighted hook accentuates the natural action of a marabou tail differently from an unweighted hook. Fish go for different impressions, and variations can be produced with tails tied in different ways, from short and full to long and sparse. With a long-shank body of soft marabou dubbing or chenille, the lengthy fly is frequently taken by a large fish at the juncture of rigid body and billowy tail—right at the hook.

Fish initially attracted to a large or highly visible fly may nonetheless be convinced by a small bit of contrasting color or sparkle. Even on flies with strands of Flash-a-bou or Krystal Flash, a butt of an egg color or of tinsel chenille or a wisp of bright marabou under the shank and covering the hook will provide such attractor hotspots.

Weighting and the Direct Swing

A skilled fly fisherman I met on a river some years ago, Gary Nimmer also uses Woolly Bugger–type flies extensively. He prefers unweighted flies, adding split shot or a lead strip on the tippet as needed. This rigging gives the fly a buoyant, free drift. For a presentation along the bottom, he positions the weight against the hook eye to create a tail-up presentation of the marabou. Gary is adept at stalking steelhead lurking in shallow water and taking them on a naturally drifted Woolly Bugger. I once mentioned the deadliness of an orange marabou and tied Woolly Buggers to his specifications featuring a mixed yellow-orange tail. He pumped up his largest steelhead on an upstream cast to likely water by imparting short-jigging action to a #6.

With a properly weighted bomb and an accurate cast, a taking presentation on an angle across and down often need not require a lot of fancy line work. The direct-swing technique is one example of a deadly delivery. An across-and-down cast that is placed beyond and above a sighted fish allows an easy swing of the fly, swimming naturally back across and broadside to the fish's snout. The possibilities of casting angles and the distances involved include all the water downstream of your position. The key is allowing just a slight downstream bow in the nearly straight line, fly-to-rod tip, to swing the fly at the proper speed and depth; this is accomplished by leading with the rod at a downstream angle, tip slightly raised. You may need a long cast to swing the fly to the snout of a midstream fish; always fish out a swing, for a targeted fish that lets a properly paced fly swing across its lie will sometimes glide over and take it near the end of the swing.

Another use of the direct swing, and sometimes the full delivery, is to present a fly safely, without disturbance, into a hanging position directly below you and below a likely spot or a sighted fish. (Let only the leader swing in over a sighted fish.) Then, retrieve the fly directly upstream, edging past the fish's head; the sudden appearance of a marabou intruder within a jaw's snap brings out the territorial instinct in a salmonid.

The full delivery covers the most water, but each leg of this presentation can be effective. The full delivery may be helpful simply to swing the fly on a deeper course below you. An across-stream cast allows the fly to sink more deeply on a natural drift downstream; then start the deeper swing across current.

Line Control

Line control and rod manipulation hone this presentation. Adding slack to the opening drift to present a fly still more deeply can be done in several ways, and such methods are valuable in themselves to present the fly on a drift to a fish across stream and below. A curve cast naturally swings the fly in the air to drop in ahead of the leader to set up a deeper drift. On-water upstream line mends will hold a fly in a spot for a longer time and subsequently deepen the drift.

To enhance a downstream drift following an across-current cast, I keep the fly slightly ahead of the rod, moving the raised tip downstream at the fly's estimated position in the water but allowing just the slightest up-current sway in my straight-line presentation. Leading properly with the fly on a downstream drift produces the ideal impression of a free-drifting morsel, with the rod in hooking position.

When the fly drifts to the targeted location across and below, to either a visible fish or a suspected lie, I transfer the rod tip just ahead of the position of the fly. The direct line removes all tension and gives sensitive strike detection. Even when using this method just to set up a deep across-stream swing, be ready for a fish at the hot corner. Leading a bit with the rod turns the fly to start its direct swing across stream.

The Dead-Still Presentation

The natural drift also is useful to set up another presentation that's deadly with a marabou. It's accepted that a fish on bottom that refuses an eye-level drift may then take the same fly slowly tapping along the bottom. When this fails, presenting the fly dead still on bottom in front of the fish's snout is very rarely tried—and very enticing. This do-nothing technique is productive on a cast in any direction, but if possible, position yourself at an advantageous angle upstream, make your cast angling down, and swing the fly in below to settle accurately on the bottom.

In one unusual episode, my only angle was an across-current cast to drift a weighty small bomb to steelhead directly across stream, snug on a midstream bar under swift-rippling clear water. Even with a curve cast and repeated circular upstream mends that are kind of fun to do and normally hold a fly in one place, the fish disdained a fly at the snout. Yet when the fly snugged into a rubbly crevice under a slightly calmer edge flow, a fish would dart as far as 5 feet aside to snap it in. Over a period of time several of these fish in turn moved to a dead-still fly in shallows well aside their lies. These males took it for an egg, as eggs would be adrift from the redd upstream.

Though I prefer to use a floating line whenever it's productive, I always tote a spool with a sinking or a Wet Tip line in my vest. When currents run swiftly, a sinking line may be needed to settle a fly on the bottom, even in shallows.

More often, a fly crawled along the bottom onto a redd and left motionless will attract a watchful steelhead or salmon. Fish have swum 10 feet to scoop up my "intruder" on the redd. Dark-colored Woolly Buggers, with the front half of the hook weighted, are highly productive for me. Such patterns suggest native forage fish and crayfish, and the nose-down, high-tail silhouette mimics the crayfish's working chela and also imitates a small fish nosing down to eat eggs. Even in the slightest current, soft marabou billows on a dead-still fly, creating a pulsing impression of life.

The motionless fly on bottom is not only productive on spawning fish or on a redd; it will also attract fish that lurk in a pool, sometimes even as they appear and disappear, preparing to run up the riffle. One such fish repeatedly circled a small pool, tarrying at the incoming riffle. With a straight cast I dropped a heavily weighted bomb directly onto a flat at the riffle corner. When the fish came by on its established route, it nailed the dead-still fly.

Natural Drifts, Varied Retrieves

Similarly, the direct downstream cast with a weighted bomb left hanging deeply, but sometimes well above the bottom in the swifter water, can be as effective as any presentation. The natural current action ripples the marabou, suggesting a jockeying forage fish.

On most presentations I let the current activate the marabou, and when retrieving I present the fly at an easily captured pace. But imparting rapid action can draw these fish from a distance, as with other species. Unseen fish near a redd, for example, may not always respond to the fly crawled up onto the nest and left motionless. Then I've swung the fly in well below and, with a low rod tip and sudden long strips of line, veritably hopped the bomb along upstream. A red-and-black version was puffing up silt on each hop upstream, and as it bounced over the redd, a lunker dashed from its hidden lie to nail the fly settling on a hop 5 feet upstream of the redd.

To recap, while the various techniques mentioned take salmonids, the natural drift for steelhead is common if not widely used with Woolly Buggers and other long marabou flies. And on my introductory trip for salmon some years ago, the kings in autumn gently took my white Marabou Leech on upstream casts and natural drifts near bottom in a gin-clear, gliding creek. The day's last catch was an eyeful for one who had previously fished only inland trout streams—not only an eyeful, but also an armful on a 7½-foot, 4-weight rod. The 40-incher took a bullethead yellow Marabou Muddler, #6, drifted with 3-inch strips through middepth.

Last year I hooked kings in the 30-pound class, one of them exactly as described and on the same 3-plus-inch chartreuse bomb mentioned in the opening description of the steelhead that also snugged beneath fast water. While marabou flies are effective through the day, most anglers know that morning and late-day hours are the times when the fluffy, larger patterns prove the adage "large fly, large fish." My first cast last autumn produced a bronzed, barrel-shaped, male king in a favorite pool, and my conviction that it wouldn't happen again proved pleasantly incorrect a couple of weeks later. My loosening-up cast across a murky current pinch dropped the chartreuse bomb, tied with added new color, fluorescent orange-red mixed in the tail. I let it sink for a second, made two easy 10-inch broadside strips, and a hidden 20-pounder came up and took it. The silvery fresh king, bright as a steelhead, rambunctiously splashed the surface and soon all but beached itself. A quick catch in all respects, indeed, and a telling example of both the steelhead and the salmon sharing a propensity to take a marabou fly properly fished.

Tackle Considerations

While 7–9-weight outfits are popular along many rivers I fish, I'm currently attached to a St. Croix 9-foot graphite I use with 5- and 6-weight lines; the outfit displays parabolic action without sacrificing backbone. When fishing smaller flies, the lighter fly line gives a distinct advantage in gauging the presentation and is sensitive enough to transmit the taps of a fly along the bottom.

I like a leader butt of at least 2 feet of red Amnesia monofilament. For the 6-weight line, I use a longer section of 30-pound blood-knotted to 25-pound test; on the 5-weight line, I use sections of 25-pound and 20-pound test. This heavy butt provides a smooth transition to cast my weighted flies, and its high visibility provides a guideline. Amnesia straightens easily, a boon for heavy butt mono. To complete a basic 8-foot leader, shorten the butt of a 7½-foot knotless tapered leader to the diameter of the finer Amnesia. I cement all blood knots with Super Glue.

The 2X tippet I usually start with allows a weighted fly a naturally loose action. A finer tippet can be added for low, clear water and smaller flies, or the leader can be shortened to a heavier tippet in many instances, especially for murky water. For heavily weighted flies and big fish, loop the tippet twice through the hook eye before finishing the improved clinch knot.

At this moment I'm thinking of going steelheading. With the drag set on the reel, the bright steelhead won't overrun the spool though emptying the fly line in brief seconds in a series of somersaulting cartwheels, leaps, and headlong porpoises. Always keep the spool full of fresh nonstretch backing line.

If some of these techniques are new to you, give them a try when the situation presents itself. Use marabou. Its spectrum of colors and billowy action work magic on these valiant fish.

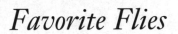

Favorite Flies

Early-Morning Eye Opener

THE EARLY-MORNING SUN shone through the trees, spotlighting four browns rising madly in a nearly head-to-tail diamond formation over a shin-deep riffle on Michigan's Au Sable River. I was fishing the river's North Branch east of Grayling in the Lower Peninsula, a sometimes overlooked part of the storied Au Sable river system.

The fish stuck their snouts out to take a tiny fly that I assumed to be a midge. So I tied on a #24 Adams. Staying back for a 40 foot cast, I tossed out the fly and a 12-incher took it. That fish splashed wildly and spooked the other trout back under the bank.

At the tail of the next pool, a half-dozen trout dimpled the wrong-way flat surface of a tough-to-reach backwater eddy ahead of a downed tree. I fished to them but subdued them all with the midge, so I took a closer look at the flies on the water, and the flat surface of the pool gave me a better picture than the sun-sparkled choppy riffle had. I scooped one of them up in my hand. Those flies on the water were not midges at all but bona fide mayflies not much larger than a match head, with wings that would extend not far beyond the perimeter of a pea.

"It must be the Tricos," I thought. Local anglers had told me about the prolific late-season hatch of the tiny *Tricorythodes* mayfly, due any day around July. I had never even seen one of the miniscule mayflies with the tongue-twister name, but the one in my hand looked like the artificials I had bought. Quickly I snipped the midge

185

off my 5X tippet, and with tweezers I picked a #24 white-wing, black-bodied Trico from my fly box. It was no easy task to knot on the little fly, since the pool ahead had become alive with rising browns.

The pool was a beautiful sight, flat and dark as an old iron frying pan and shaded by trees over the deep side. For 90 feet up to the incoming riffle, several dozen fish rose to take the little mayflies, which had become as abundant as freckles on the surface. I spotted some barely perceptible, saucer-sized rings and knew they likely marked large trout. As I moved slowly into position to angle a cast up and across to the nearest trout, I saw it outlined golden in a shaft of sunlight as it came up and sipped in a *Tricorythodes*.

I dropped a light cast and the fly alighted 3 feet ahead of the fish. I leaned low to the water for a better angle to pick out my artificial. Drifting along amid all those look-alike flies, it was about as hard to see as a speck of dust on a pane of glass.

Well, to be brief, I ended up putting down nearly every fish in the pool. It was humbling. I caught one fine brown by drifting a #22 emergent Trico nymph just under the surface, but that's not what the trout wanted. They were taking the dry fly, but not mine.

A half hour later I stood in midstream in the riffle ahead of the flat pool. Trout rose steadily along the broken water, and they had to be easier pickings than the fish in the mirrored pool, I kept telling myself. But past fishing experience saved some face for me. With a nail clipper I trimmed off the ends of the spent-wings and the tails of my #24 fly. I had been showing the trout the right pattern all along, but the slightly trimmed, smaller fly matched those on the water for size. I caught six trout in the next 10 minutes.

Then the parade of *Tricorythodes* flies was over, and most of the trout stopped rising. About an hour and a half had passed since I spotted those four fish I thought were taking midges in the riffle, and now I knew I had a lot to learn about the fishing in this hatch.

Back at the car I opened my copy of *Selective Trout*, coauthored by Doug Swisher and Carl Richards. This book had most of the major fly hatches, and under "The Late Season" I found the *Tricory-thodes*. Various Trico species are only 3–6 millimeters long, and trout holding near the surface, their cone of vision focused on a small, narrow feeding lane, are able to reject a fly just a millimeter or two out of proportion. My trimmed fly had fooled a few good fish, but it obviously wasn't as effective as a fly properly tied to the size of natural insects on the water. The authors had warned, "For the angler equipped with the right pattern in the right size, this hatch provides the ultimate in small-fly, fine-tackle fishing."

I had been fishing with Doug and Carl just a few days before, and they had told me the *Tricorythodes* hatch occurs daily from early July into September. After the morning's fishing I had to return to Wisconsin. I called Doug, who had said he would be at his cabin near Grayling and could fish in the mornings. "I've fished the hatch of white-wing blacks the past thirteen summers on the Au Sable, and it's really exciting with light tackle," Doug told me.

Three weeks passed until I could return to Michigan. Now it was early morning, and Doug and I waded the main branch of the Au Sable. A brown trout nosed up and sipped in my dry fly. The 1-pounder jumped, fins flared, then tail-danced its way off the hook. Just then I heard the high-pitched clicking of a reel drag, and I looked out on the river. Doug held his fly rod high and horizontal with the tip bowed toward a trout running out line. In the time it took Doug to play in and release his larger fish, I made several casts and hooked another brown. Even as it somersaulted on the end of my tippet, I heard Doug yell, "Hey!" Again I glanced up his way as he hooked our fourth trout in a matter of minutes.

That flurry of takes to our flies was the action that you hope for with a river full of rising trout. But the past hour the furtive browns had fed steadily though carefully on the *Tricorythodes* flies, and they had been hard to coax up to an artificial. "With so many rising trout," Doug explained, "I seldom make more than five or six casts to any one fish, unless it's a big one. Since the rise of fish to Tricos lasts an hour to an hour and a half each morning, you'll usually do best by showing the fly to as many trout as possible."

By midmorning the mass rise of browns turned off like a leaky faucet; a few fish still rose to other types of mayflies, which hatched sporadically. As we walked back on a trail to our cars parked at one

Doug Swisher plays a brown during a morning fall of Tricorythodes *mayfly spinners on Michigan's Au Sable River.*

of the public access sites on the river, Doug told me more about the *Tricorythodes* hatch.

"Along these fly-fishing-only waters in the upper reaches of the Au Sable, you can count on great numbers of trout to rise each morning when Tricos are on. To me the fishing in this hatch is the most enjoyable all season, and that's saying a lot, because the upper river offers fly hatches from opening day in late April through the extended fly-fishing-only season running through October. What's more, the spring-fed main Au Sable almost always is in shape for fly-fishing. Rains seldom muddy the river or cause it to rise more than a few inches.

"But I've also had good fishing in Trico hatches on trout streams in the East and West. Some of the better fishing has been on the Battenkill in Vermont, the Beaverkill in New York, and the Henry's Fork of the Snake River and Silver Creek in Idaho."

Doug gave several reasons why this productive mayfly hatch, which occurs on streams around the country, is relatively unknown. (1) *Tricorythodes* species produce a prolific hatch later in the season after significant mayfly hatches are thought to be over. (2) Few mayfly hatches that attract so many trout to feed on top occur in the early morning, as this one does. (3) The emergence and egg-laying cycle of the *Tricorythodes* occurs in a few hours and therefore may go unnoticed by anglers.

After hatching, most other mayflies fly away to bushes on the bank, where they molt. A day or longer after hatching, they return over the water to lay their eggs. Then they fall onto the water. When great numbers of the flies, now in the spinner stage, return to the water in what is commonly called a blanket spinner fall, the trout may rise in great numbers to them. But an angler must know the hatch and be able to expect when a spinner fall may occur. With a sudden shift in weather, a spinner fall may become scattered, or the flies won't return when you are ready to fish. Still, spinner falls of mayflies, which often occur in late afternoons and evenings, are the fare for some outstanding dry-fly fishing to rising trout.

But with *Tricorythodes*, there's little of this uncertainty once you locate a stream section with silty backwaters where the nymphs

hatch in abundance or a reach of river below the hatch sites to which
the spinners will float down. Except for a downpour or a strong
wind, you can expect these spinner falls, which raise up large numbers of trout to feed on top on the Au Sable, just about every morning for two months. This is because, after the *Tricorythodes* hatch
(usually from 5:00 A.M. to 7:00 A.M.), the mating flights begin almost
immediately over the waters. Then the flies lay their eggs and fall
onto the water, usually in a blanket spinner fall. A *Tricorythodes*
hatching, mating, and egg-laying cycle is simply an instant-coffee
version of most mayfly hatches, and it woke me up to some great
fishing.

Because hackled flies weren't catching many fish for Doug and
Carl some years back during periods of high selectivity, the two
anglers began experimenting with better fish-catching flies. Most
readers know by now that they introduced the no-hackle dry fly that
turned the tables on selective trout. Their initial book, *Selective
Trout*, was the result of five years of study in entomology, and it
offers a classification of trout-stream insects around the country
along with matching flies. Today, some three decades later, *Selective
Trout* remains in print and is considered a classic fly-fishing work of
all time.

On one of the subsequent mornings of fishing the *Tricorythodes*
hatch, Doug and I arrived at 7:00 A.M. to find the river without a fly
to speak of on the water. "We had a cool night, and the hatch will
start later when the waters warm enough," he related. "After cold
nights in late August or in September the hatch may not be until
later in the morning. This is often the situation on western streams
where nights are cold."

When the *Tricorythodes* hatched that morning, Doug continued
educating me. The first flies danced in shafts of morning sunlight,
the flashes of their whitish wings looking like fireflies. In a few minutes, the hatch became thick as a fine snowfall, with thousands of
the flies sparkling against the deep green pines up to the treetops.

Later, flakes of white, which looked like shavings of wax, began
appearing on the surface. Doug explained, "Those flakes are the
whitish wing skins the flies have shed in the air. When you see them

drifting downstream and collecting on eddies, that's a sign the flies will be mating soon. After mating is over, the flies will fall like confetti onto the surface. As the spinner fall reaches its peak, trout will be rising all over."

We were wading at the edge of a long riffle with sunny waters like crinkled tin foil. More trout began rising as the flies dropped out of the sky. In a few minutes, a dozen browns fed on top within a 40-foot cast. The best fish we saw humped out its back as it rolled up to inhale a *Tricorythodes*. That 2-pounder worked over gravel along the opposite bank.

Doug cast a line across stream, reaching out his rod to let the fly line drop up- current from the leader to float the fly down ahead of the tippet. He showed the fly over the fish a dozen times while it continued to spike naturals floating inches away. Finally the trout sipped in Doug's number. He raised the rod tip to nudge the tiny barbless hook into the trout's mouth. The brownie was on, and it splashed. "Ah hah!" Doug exclaimed. "I hook many more trout now than I used to with small flies simply by offsetting the bend. That

Natural Tricorythodes *mayfly spinner showing clear wings after shedding skins*

throws the hook point out of line with the shank and allows a greater angle for hooking."

When *Tricorythodes* species shed their whitish wing skins, the wings on the flies become crystal clear. Soon the clear-winged spinners piled up on eddies off the main flow, where the heads of trout popped up to take them. Often it took a slack-line cast or a curve cast to float the artificial naturally and drag-free on the trout-filled slower waters off the main current.

Just after I had fished to trout working in such an eddy pool with only one rise to my fly, I expressed my disappointment in a few choice words. Doug said, "Just as a spinner falls onto the water it might float with the wings half-cocked in a wide V or flat. Later, it settles flush in the surface film as it drifts downstream. Some of the trout are so particular at times that they'll prefer one of those presentations."

On the last morning we were to fish together, when *Tricorythodes* flies were done, we waded past a feeder creek, and Doug remarked, "A few years back I caught a 19-inch brown near that inlet. The

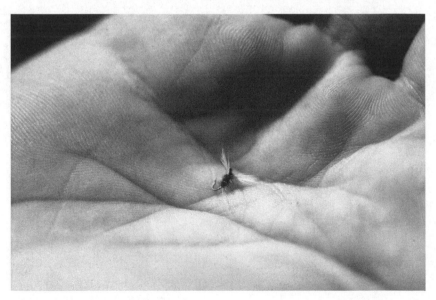

A Tricorythodes *hen-wing spinner, #24*

big trout kept on rising to other flies after the Trico spinner fall was over."

The next morning would be my last fling this summer on the Au Sable, and, like my first time in a *Tricorythodes* hatch, I would be alone. By 8:30 A.M. not a *Tricorythodes* had hatched on a wide, slow stretch. So I drove downstream on the South Down River Road, which parallels the main Au Sable east of Grayling. In a few miles I turned in on one of the side roads leading to the many public-access sites on the river. Here the meandering bends along walls of pines created patches of sunlight and shade on the water. Old snags, locally called sweepers, hung on the banks out over the water's edge or in the river, providing trout cover. The waters were already studded with trout rising to *Tricorythodes* spinners. Behind the sweepers, along downed logs in deep bends and in riffles and pockets, trout queued up head-to-tail, the dimples of their rises overlapping. Individual fish left the cover and fed on shallow bars.

I worked on upstream, catching and releasing trout from every group of six to a dozen fish I cast over. I would start with the lower-most fish first, and then work to the next one ahead. Soon I was passing up 12-inch trout for larger fish. When I couldn't coax one 14-incher to strike, I drifted the #24 fly just under the surface, and that trout nailed it, swapped head-to-tail a few times, and dove for the bank. My light rod turned the fish, and it thrashed on top. Just ahead, along the near bank, a big fish worked in only a foot of water. My first cast floated the fly only a few inches aside, but the trout turned and took the fly.

In all, I landed and released a dozen browns, and raised twice as many to the fly. Finally, I had a morning in which the trout took my fly avidly in the *Tricorythodes* hatch, and my only discontent was that I had to leave again. I had learned much from a master angler about selective trout in a little-known mayfly hatch. This is fishing so fussy that one angler won't bother with it, while another calls it the most exciting dry-fly fishing ever with small flies.

Mayfly Emergers

OBSERVATION IS ONE of the great teachers in fly-fishing. This was never more evident to me than it was one pleasant morning 15 years ago when I stood motionless on a bridge over an evenly flowing, clear creek. Upstream of the bridge, I could see a trout finning near the bottom in midstream. It inhaled an insect I couldn't see, then began finning or swimming within a 5-foot-wide pie-wedge fan to intercept morsels a bit higher in the current. After taking each insect, the trout returned to its original feeding station.

This eager trout covered a substantial area, feeding from near the bottom to about middepth. With a little closer observation, I found it was taking emerging mayflies. Even when hatched flies began floating on the water, the trout continued to take five or six nymphs subsurface for each insect it took on top.

My observations that morning showed me that trout often prefer nymphs under a hatch. While this is common prior to the hatch and at its onset, nymphs and floating emergent forms of mayflies often are favored by discerning trout throughout a hatch, particularly in heavily fished waters.

I carry a rolled-up, fine mesh seine in the back pocket of my fishing vest and use it to pan a sample of the nymphs from a stream. Then not only can I present a matching pattern, but also I can fish it at the level where trout are concentrating on nymphs. Trout learn to expect hatch times and will hold in a feeding niche below the

This rainbow was fooled by one of my small Baetis *emergers.*

source of a hatch. Knowledge of hatches and how the current will drift nymphs to feeding stations of trout leads to successful fishing.

Sometimes hatches do not appear at the anticipated time or in the numbers we expect. Still, a few, and often many, nymphs will be present. During these "false" hatches, which often occur for a definite span of time, a match of the nymph will be readily accepted by trout.

One dark day I did well with an imitation of a tan olive *Baetis* nymph during the hours when the hatch normally occurs. The few duns that hatched did not interest the trout, but an emergent pattern, drifted through feeding slots, did. The trout were dining avidly, some secretively, deeper in the stream. The #16 had a dark wing case, simulating mayfly nymphs prior to emerging. This false hatch was no myth; it lasted about two hours, and when the nymphs diminished in numbers the trout stopped feeding on them. Such migrations of nymphs are not uncommon, whether or not the hatch develops.

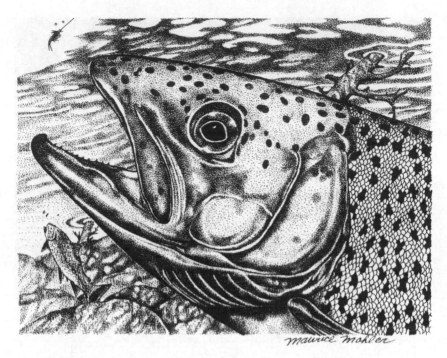

When emergent mayfly nymphs hang in an ascending posture adrift near the surface, matching nymphs tied with a bit of light wire in the abdomen simulate the natural insect's behavior. (Artwork by Maurice Mahler; reproduced with permission)

Trout see ascending nymphs against the backlighting of the sky. When you look into the water, the fare is almost always invisible. Doug Swisher advises placing white sheeting deep in the water so you can observe the naturals over a light background.

Although trout generally feed at a level where food is concentrated, a larger fish will frequently take emergent forms of mayflies even while numerous duns are sedately afloat. A cagey streamside brown trout, for example, may feed quietly on nymphs while rainbows at a riffle edge are bulging in sharp turns for nymphs freshly adrift and plentiful near the source of the hatch.

Consider two details I've learned in tying a productive subsurface emergent mayfly nymph. First, a loose wing pad that undulates under water, such as one of ostrich herl tied down only in front at the head, is a deadly impression of realism. Selective trout key on this. Second, I've observed *Baetis* nymphs adrift near the surface while hanging at a slight angle. To simulate this posture in my nymph, I rear-weight the pattern with a few turns of fine, light wire under the abdomen near the hook bend. These points are important in matching the behavior of the smallest of mayfly nymphs. Greasing the leader to within a selected distance of the nymph gives it a natural drift through the trout's feeding level.

Isolated hatches are not unusual and may appear in the insect's small area of habitat. One morning before the main hatch of larger mayflies appeared in currents, I spotted a sizable trout feeding inches deep beneath mayflies along the gentle stream edge. I selected an emergent nymph showing an olive cast. That trout about 40 feet upstream took it when I drifted the emerger just inches below the placid surface. As I learned in subsequent fishing, an early-morning hatch of little mayflies may last only a brief time. Trout apparently sense this and feed along the edges where these flies emerge at scattered locations.

When the day's main hatch of mayflies is short and sparse, the emergent nymph may be the taking fly even after the number of nymphs has dwindled. One day mayflies emerged for only 20 minutes. The trout fed avidly. I could see the fish flashing beneath the surface to emergers, well under the rapid-hatching duns, which quickly flew into the air. Though a drifting imitation produced, another presentation mimicked the swimming emergers. I allowed the nymph to sink, then raised it with wiggles of the rod tip. It attracted trout with an eye for the natural action. The imitative pattern continued to take fish for more than an hour after the hatch, a usual duration for this species to emerge.

To me, the most exciting angling with an emergent pattern occurs when trout are rising to floating naturals. There are several basic forms of emergers, and trout can be partial to the silhouette that is predominant on the water. The majority of the mayfly nymphs drift in the surface region, and they will often drift a considerable distance before the shuck splits and the winged adult emerges. Recognizing when trout are sipping these low silhouettes will help you catch some of the warier trout. If high-winged duns are not being taken, lean low and close to the water to see if trout are feeding in the film. It is not unusual for a trout taking floating nymphs to rock a nearby drifting dun. While trout may be selective to floating nymphs when the fish start feeding topside early in a hatch, an imitative pattern frequently will work throughout the emergence period.

Patterns that imitate floating nymphs may be as simple as a hook of dubbed fur or poly fibers. These are easy flies to tie and are effective for simulating the smaller mayflies. Highly realistic floating nymph imitations have two or three individual tails, an abdomen of a material matching the natural (such as quill or dubbing), a well-developed wing pad, and legs of feather fibers or hackle points. Hackle barbules extend horizontally beyond each side of the wing case. A floating nymph presented dead drift on a greased leader is the standard method. The natural wriggle of a mayfly in its attempt to emerge from the shuck can be duplicated with a twitch or jiggle of the rod tip in most instances and will often trigger a strike.

A trout's selectivity of the most abundant form of emergers on the water can be remarkable. Consecutive days on the same water with the same hatches of small *Baetis* nymphs notably showed this. On the first day a simple floating nymph of dubbed fur readily took the rising trout, but in seemingly the same situation on the next day this pattern was ignored by the numerous rising trout. Leaning low for an angle to see along the surface, I noticed that otherwise imperceptible little triangular forms of emergent gray wings sprouted from drifting emergers. I concluded these were just the hind wings, which are shorter than the main wings that were still stuck in the nymphal shucks of the *Baetis* nymphs. With the weather just a few degrees warmer than yesterday at the same hour, the prolific hatches had developed in this manner. I knotted on an emerger having very short, stubby, divided winglets of hen-hackle tips and began catching trout regularly.

As a hatch develops, flies may appear with their wings sloped back low over the abdomen. In my experience, trout feed selectively on these mayflies. Patterns developed by Doug Swisher and Carl Richards effectively imitate these flies. Patterns may also represent

Two low-winged emergent mayfly duns, one trailing its nymphal shuck

mayflies that simply are slow to emerge, as well as stillborns. The wings may appear humped as if they are still caught in the trailing nymphal shuck. A related silhouette matches the mayfly's wings free of the shuck and sloped back, the hatching dun still dragging its nymphal casing. Even when entirely sprouted low wings are visible, sampling may show whether the fly is attached to the nymphal shuck or has emerged and should be matched with the shorter body and color of the dun.

On cool days when the hatch burgeons at a steady pace, mayfly emergers with their full wings back have given me outstanding fishing for a half hour or longer. When low-winged emergers are somewhat abundant on the water, larger trout have provided rising targets. Eye-opening trout are apt to rise to the surface to feed when and where emergent forms are present.

In chilly or damp conditions and in any weather when the duns take longer to raise their wings, backwing mayflies may be the form of insect on the surface for the duration of a hatch. A no-hackle with wings of realistic texture and color matches the naturals. A fly tied with its wings flared outward aside the abdomen is usually appealing to trout. Quill wings, coated with vinyl if desired for added durability, are used on many patterns. For delicate wing impressions, I like wide hen-hackle tips. When you are on the water and see the back-lighted wings of the naturals, dress the wings lightly with a grease, such as Dilly Wax, which renders a natural sheen. Simulating the natural appearance of the mayfly can be important.

One breezy, sunny late morning, hatching mayflies, with their wings back, slid along the shifty currents. Some fluttered broadside across the current in gusts. There, a larger brown cruised up and downstream atop a shallow, mossy ledge paralleling the opposite bank. The elusive trout would appear anywhere under the 50-foot-long masked glide and rise to feed. I tied on a #16 matching Pale Morning Dun, with shaped back hen-hackle wings and the three tails of the natural. I had tied the pattern for this very opportunity.

When the trout rose to near the top of the pool, I angled a widely bowed cast upstream of its mark. As the fly drifted nearly to the fish, the current in midstream evenly pulled the line and the fly turned, its no-hackle, shiny silhouette sliding slowly broadside across the trout's window. That gaping jaw appeared underneath and quietly siphoned in the Pale Morning Dun.

After playing the hefty trout on a willowy little rod and 6X tippet, I cradled it with two widespread hands, one under the belly behind the gills, the other wrapped in front of its tail. I gently eased it forward and backward a few inches at a time, pumping oxygen back into its system. When released, the beauty weaved back into the pool.

The Duns of Autumn

L ATE SEASON breathes new life into a stream. September and October angling is for trout that have been fished all season and are not easily fooled, though they feed spiritedly with the resurgence of daylight mayfly hatches.

Species of the group commonly known as blue-winged olives (of the genera *Baetis*, #16–24, and *Pseudocloeon*, #22 and #24) are stirred to hatch on typical, comfortably cool autumn days when the sun peeks in and out of the clouds. Autumn duns characteristically drift a long way while drying their wings, and in chilly or damp air they may float seemingly endless distances. Even the veteran secretive trout, sensing the easily captured flies, fins on station, tipping up to feed as if relishing each mayfly.

Rivers offer deceptively concentrated autumn-hatch fishing. You will see hatches on big rivers such as the Clark Fork below Missoula, Montana, in riffles near the heads of pools, and in eddies in which queued trout roll and boil beneath these confetti-like hatches. Such eddies often give way to deep water and are fishable from shallows above with a downstream dry fly.

However, autumn hatches I've known on rivers can go all but unnoticed. Long-drifting duns will funnel down-current tightly along the river edge. Additional *Baetis* duns emerge from edgewaters the length of pools carrying just the right current. Often larger trout rise only in a long, narrow bankside line, feeding in dimples. During low autumn waters this scenario has given me fishing similar

On a glorious autumn day in the West, a trout leaps on my line.

to working up a narrow creek but on a vast, quiet river pool much larger than the dimensions of an aircraft carrier deck.

Prolific hatches also occur on spring creeks. Water temperatures of these enriched streams are cool and stable, seldom varying 10 degrees on any day. These delightful waters maintain temperatures in the 50s, and with a rise of only a few degrees mayflies may emerge any day. In such stable temperatures it is the change that triggers hatches, and it may be of only academic note but mayflies emerge on the prolific, warmer Firehole, in Yellowstone National Park, even after trout season closes in the park at the end of October. If you care to hazard November weather and fish the colder Armstrong or Nelson's spring creeks near Livingston, Montana, they have hatches, too. It wasn't too many years ago that I could fish in solitude, with perhaps another angler or two, on those popular meadow streams in October.

All spring creeks are not as well preserved as the Armstrong and Nelson's. Some that I fish in south-central to western Wisconsin are subject to high, sometimes muddied, waters. A few of the numerous spring creeks in this region of top brown trout streams are pristine, always clear and low in their runs through natural meadows. These roadside spring creeks are among my favorites, including one only 15 feet across that I consider the best brown trout creek of its size I have ever fished. Despite changes wrought by man, the ability of mayfly nymphs to exist in this fertile little creek is remarkable. Wisconsin's September *Baetis* hatches may not be as dependable as those found on western spring creeks, but on the right day fishing to Wisconsin's duns of autumn ranks as the best of the season.

Baetis

In late September, shortly before the season closes at the end of the month, Wisconsin *Baetis* duns emerge as early as noon and appear until late in the day. Typical of the species, the duns hatch initially in swifter riffles or edges, from the quieter nooks of buffering submerged vegetation.

One day when the first *Baetis hiemalis* dun rafted along the border of a shelved weed bed, a 12-inch brown quickly angled up from beneath an awning of vegetation only 10 feet in front of me and took it. Even while that one splashed loudly on my line, a larger trout began rising from its niche along a streamlined weed bed in a short riffle only a few yards beyond. When the *Baetis* hatch switches on, the trout don't delay.

When the hatch develops, I like long reaches of slow-moving, smooth water flowing over moss and weed beds on narrow creeks. On a chilly day along such a glide, protected from strong, gusting winds, the duns drift long. When they flutter up, meeting the gusts, they invariably alight again.

On this day a natural, sampled with an aquarium hand-net, showed a light-gray underbody with a hint of brown on the abdomen and a faint olive cast. Its wings were light gray, as its two split tails were. Under overcast skies, the dun in hand as well as those on the water showed dominantly light gray overall. In a fly box I found some #18 drys with divided wood duck wings, sparse light-gray hackle, peacock-quill bodies, and light-gray tails. A hackled imitation would be the thing to match the naturals that drifted, often high on their legs.

There were never enough naturals for a fish to feed with a rise rhythm, yet each brown remained on station and took nearly every dun that appeared in the lane of drift overhead. I took trout by showing the dry fly within 10 seconds after a trout had taken a natural, but I had to bowl the strike lane—the browns would not move aside to the fly.

Another day on another creek, in a misty haze and intermittent fine drizzle, *Baetis* duns floated seemingly forever, with their wings clasped tightly together as one. A no-hackle dry matched their "frozen" silhouettes. As many as four nice browns fed on station around each mossy hummock in one of the greatest trout rises I've witnessed on a 20-foot-wide creek. The hatch that day blanketed the small stream.

When autumn duns hatch, trout often become highly selective. The more closely the fly imitates the size, silhouette, and color of the natural insect the trout are taking at the time, the more effective the pattern will be.

Tiny #24 all-gray, hackled drys with hackle-tip wings have given excellent fishing during heavy hatches of *Pseudocloeon* on western spring creeks when I did not have quality no-hackle duns of the proper size. One October day on Nelson's the naturals were floating high, and the trout picked the artificials lacking an olive body but of realistic size and silhouette. Perhaps ironically, the largest trout I've ever taken during hatches of autumn duns, a hulking brown, sipped a *Pseudocloeon* imitation, the smallest of the late-season mayflies.

Doug Swisher and Carl Richards, in *Selective Trout*, point out that features and coloration of the many blue-winged olives are so similar that in many instances identification at the species level can be determined only by an entomologist. They suggest drys with light-gray wings and olive bodies for light species and patterns with medium-gray wings and olive-brown bodies for darker species.

"For the angler who wants to keep his *Baetis* patterns to a mini-

A #22 gray Pseudocloeon *dun in the jaw of a big brown*

mum," the authors write, "the best approach would be to carry duns with olive-brown bodies and medium-gray wings. . . . If this approach is followed, use two parts of medium-olive fur to one part of medium brown. . . . A wing that is too dark normally works much better than one that is too light."

The No-Hackle Solution

Excerpts of postseason letters from two anglers with whom I fished in the West recount typical experiences in main hatches of the day during autumn on western spring creeks. Jim Glenn wrote: "We went to the Firehole and caught an excellent hatch about noon. For about two hours the mayflies blanketed the water with trout everywhere, dorsal fins sticking out of the water, sipping duns. A #20 or #22 <u>no-hackle</u> [Glenn's emphasis] with light-olive bodies would take them." Another angler visiting a Montana spring creek wrote: "The weather was terrible, cold raw and windy. It looked so miserable I thought it would put down the fish but was I in for a surprise. In the morning I did fairly well but I got caught without any no-hackles when the hatch started. I tried tying some no-hackles during the hatch. The flies I managed to complete looked like hell and did not work any better than the standard drys had. Getting caught once without any no-hackles was enough."

I became convinced of the value of no-hackles on a bright September day more than a decade ago, when I first met Doug Swisher on Armstrong Spring Creek. The hatch that day was *Ephemerella infrequens*, a pale morning dun that is always the prime September mayfly, appearing sporadically until the end of October. The duns are matched with #16 and #18 drys having light-gray wings tinted yellow, pale-yellow bodies with a bit of light olive mixed in, and three light-olive tails.

In turn, Doug and I alternately fished to five nearby rising trout. A few rose to the hackled fly on my tippet without taking, but Doug's no-hackle then was taken confidently by each one. (I have since repeated such experiments on my own, with similar results in pale morning dun and *Baetis* hatches, during midday feeding. When hatches are heaviest the trout become highly selective.)

After my introduction to no-hackles, in the succeeding years that I fished Armstrong in autumn, *Baetis* species seemed to increase in abundance. They would begin to appear in greater numbers in October, and on some days #18 and #20 dark olives shortly followed brief late-morning emergences of gray-yellows. Hatch cycles of one insect species or another may vary from year to year, but the *Baetis* species are predominant hatches as autumn lengthens.

There are wonderfully long October days when several over-lapping *Baetis* hatches provide angling from late morning until late afternoon on western spring creeks. They have, in my experience, occurred most often on shallow, moderately flowing, weedy streams, such as Nelson's and the similar meadow reaches of the Firehole. The first emergence is matched with #20 and #22 olive-bodied, medium-gray-winged no-hackles; the main hatch of the day that follows is #16 and #18 duns (*Ephemerella infrequens* and/or a *Baetis* species, such as *tricaudatus*). The trailing hatch, usually in midafternoon, is a #24 *Pseudocloeon*.

Just which hatch I have chosen to call the main hatch of the day may vary, but it is from late morning to early afternoon, or sometimes starting around noon in chilly weather, that the most and frequently larger trout rise to duns for two hours or longer. Often this period is filled by the larger mayflies of autumn.

Observation some years ago revealed that when trout started taking newly emerged, full-winged mayflies at the onset of a hatch, many species drifted a long way with their wings sloped back lower than usual over the abdomen. A no-hackle tied with divided duck-quill wings, nearly horizontal and full length, matches them. However, I didn't have any my first day on the Firehole late one October, and after tying them at night, my results improved on following days of the trip. The full-length wings are the essential difference from emergent patterns tied to be floated.

To simulate most naturals, I tie mine with the quill wings close together, tips spread naturally. These sleek flies are less air-resistant than high-winged no-hackles. A #16, tied properly, can be snapped out there on a 6X tippet with a tight loop. They are most effective near the source of hatches, generally providing an hour or more of fishing as hatch-matching imitations in chilly weather. Mayflies emerging from broken water can raise their wings sooner after surfacing, and they struggle to do so for balance. Flies hatching on small, gentler riffles and on smoother water having a tenacious meniscus typical of spring creeks are slower to raise their wings. When low-winged mayflies are the most abundant form on the water, trout feed heavily on them.

Larger hummocks of vegetation form pallets on the surface, and such vegetation hummocks interspersed along gravelly runs are prime areas harboring sizable trout laired near an abundance of mayfly nymphs. Trout feed to newly emerged mayflies on flat water behind the vegetation, on slicks alongside it, and on the cushion of slow water that forms in front of the hummock. A curve cast works best, yet a loose-line presentation is also effective with the fly accurately placed so that it will drift only a yard or two to the fish. Particularly on the patch of slow water ahead of a moss bed, dropping the dry fly onto the spot of the rise, lightly, has yielded some fine trout.

Fishing upstream among a maze of moss beds enables you to have the optimum angle to play a good trout on light line. The fish generally runs in a linear up or down route and thus it can be coaxed along the open slots between moss beds. Staying downstream of a mired trout also is an advantage when easing it from stringy vegetation. When a nice one gets below you and noses into vegetation, give a little slack, and often the trout will dart into the open again. If not, gentle line tightening with the rod pointed directly at the "snag" has a magical way of easing the fish free, so you don't have to shorten the line and go after the fish with your boot.

Fishing fine-and-far isn't always desirable in such cover. When you keep a low silhouette, especially on cloudy days, a leader as short as 8½ feet, including the long tippet, can be effective with presentations to 35 or 40 feet. In open water 10–13-foot leaders, and occasionally longer, are helpful, and they make for easy long drifts of the fly.

Most of the duns adrift on the water for very long show upright wings, and a standard no-hackle dry matches their high silhouettes. Slow eddies that face to still water and the inside elbows below sharp bends are areas of flat water where sailboat-winged mayflies are eddied together into small "regattas." You can float a dry fly with nearly no motion on some of these trout windows or let the fly meander and drift a minute or longer on others. An extra-long tippet and a light slack-line cast are advisable, as is fishing on still water or the very slow current. A good brown will hold at a deeper level than other trout hovering near the surface, occasionally rising to one of the duns. Should it take your dry, this patient fishing is mighty rewarding.

When you get the drift of the duns, the fishing is as rewarding for the angler as the mayflies are for the trout. Can it be that fish that have been in the stream for years develop a memory that anticipates the time of year when the duns of autumn drift long?

Small Stream Caddis Bonanza

STREAMS AS NARROW AS a country road furnish blue-ribbon angling at caddis time. Caddises are so common that it is rare for a stream not to have hatches, and certain delicate species indigenous to clean, cool headwaters and tributaries emerge in abundance. Angling amid a treasure of a hatch can require special techniques tailored to small stream confines. And realistic fly patterns that work when trout are "keyed" on a particular, abundant caddis are convincing as well to wary spring creek trout in a sparse hatch.

A bonus in the compact stream environment is that caddises are handily close by, offering knowledge through observation and sampling. While different species emerge from specific larders, even one species displays so many trout-luring actions that observation is a guideline to angling, helping to reveal what fly and presentation the sighted trout will take. But coming up with a taking pattern is often best accomplished by sampling a fresh natural.

Most of the prolific hatches I've encountered fall into a size range matched on #14–20 hooks, with timely emergences of tiny #22 caddises, though fewer larger varieties. Sampling elusive naturals can be difficult. Use a small screening or hand net to trap emergent forms and hatched winged flies most obtainable near the source of hatches, frequently on moderate to swift flats or riffle edges. Some caddises, too, tend to drift a long way on chilly spring creeks, making them easily available to trout—and to sampling.

After a hatch has been in progress for a number of days, look closely for the adults along streamside cover. The sunny side of grassy or woody debris may show nary a clinging caddis, while the shaded undersurfaces are liberally populated with them. Samples can be cupped in a clear container, such as a 35-millimeter film canister. When subsequent egg laying occurs, observation should be followed by sampling for a closer look at caddises bearing an egg sack.

Most periods of activity for a single species are lengthy, emergences and egg-laying episodes occurring over two to three weeks or longer. Thus the angler can glean the fine points of the specific hatch that are unique, because the insect is confined to a certain water quality and not found on other reaches of the same stream.

Hatches of delicate caddises attain greatest abundance in oxygenated waters, generally with temperatures in the mid- to upper 50s, flowing over varied bottoms having plentiful stony to gravelly mixes. Stable spring creeks that seldom vary significantly in flow and temperature over the year provide optimum conditions for larvae to develop, and such streams harbor the best of these hatches.

Hatches for All Seasons

Let me detail one example of a delicate caddis that thrives in clean habitat and how water temperature and quality have affected the hatch on several streams I fish in southerly Wisconsin. Species of these little black caddises, *Chimarra*, are widespread and afford excellent angling in other regions of the nation; they burgeoned in a Montana freestoner I fish following improvement in an upstream waste facility. On one spring creek, the little blacks emerge below an incoming crystal spring, its upwelling waters always in the 40s, and along bottom habitat just described and as far downstream as a sewage-treatment plant. Since the treatment was improved, isolated emergences of *Chimarra* have occurred on downstream waters. They appear from late May into early June. But subtle changes in upstream water quality have diminished once cloudlike hatches. On a neighboring spring creek that always flows cooler into June, *Chimarra* activity continues longer, a week or more into the month.

Caddises such at these have the longest hatch durations on waters offering ideal conditions. They have surprised me by emerging in February on a full-blown tiny spring creek that gushes from a fissure; over the year, I've never recorded its temperature more than a few degrees either side of 50. The hatches often peak in July. The creek shortly enters a meadow limestoner that is as cold as the 40s during the winter, ranging to the upper 50s in August; on most days water temperature varies by less than 5 degrees. In recent years, with a reduction of extensive grazing farther upstream, little black caddises that have dispersed from the tributary (including larvae perhaps carried by a beaver that took up residence in the tributary and swam down the main creek almost daily) have burgeoned along the wider main creek. They emerge on downstream to the junction of a tributary that empties in at that point, often silty and in summer several degrees warmer. This riffling, gliding meadow limestoner has produced the longest seasonal *Chimarra* hatches I've known, from peak emergences well into May continuing sporadically in dry, warm years into deep summer.

Anatomy of a Hatch

Caddises often present befuddling situations. The following are capsuled insights into some of the secrets of hatches and approaches to the small stream.

On a pleasant sunny morning I stalked at a right angle to overlook the head of a pool along a 15-foot-wide brushy stream. The *Brachycentrus* hatch beyond my hidden vantage revealed a textbook scene, an anatomy of a caddis emergence. Fed by a deepening, swift riffle, the curving pool flowed steadily, with more than a dozen browns strung in a line along its 25-foot crescent. Innumerable little flashing caddis wings glinted whitish in the sunlight when these otherwise drab, grayish naturals with translucent wings fluttered along and short-hopped downstream. The larger trout hunkered deeply

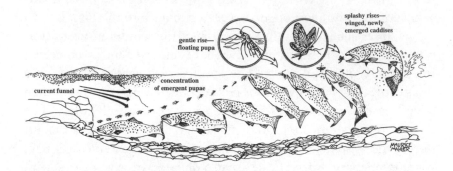

Anatomy of an emergence of caddis flies (Artwork by Maurice Mahler, based on an original sketch by T. Wendelburg; reproduced with permission)

behind the turbulence at the top of the pool. This pecking order by size, with individual fish trailing in an ascending slant downstream, corresponded to the upward path of the emergent, rising pupae.

In the ideal light I could detect the ghostlike little pupae ascending in a long-drifting manner through the crystal water. Now in abundance, the pupae made easy pickings, permitting trout to hold and feed ravenously. The lead fish, easily the largest, consumed only the pupae near bottom in its feeding lane. It became my target. I knotted a pupa on 6X tippet, wetted the waspish-looking fly with low-slung wing pads, and with a few angling upstream casts it washed deeply and directly to the waiting trout. Weighted with lead only on the rear of the hook, the pattern drifted in an ascending posture, matching the naturals. A little bright indicator on the tippet is advisable, but in this instance I wouldn't have needed it. When the trout's mouth opened white, I tightened the line, hooking it. Later I slid down the short embankment with my light rod bucking over the brown, which was walloping the eddy that encircled me, its surface flecked with countless shed pupal husks, translucent and shiny. When I released the trout, I knew it would feed again soon— an earmark of a concentrated caddis hatch. From the bank I watched the trout regroup without delay and resume feeding as steadily as before.

A right-angle approach to a small stream gives you a window to the hatch, and it's a way to select a larger trout. Along a close-cropped low meadow bank, I'll keep low and fish from a distance, casting along the ground, with the leader and fly falling onto water at an angle that presents a fly effectively. Even if you choose another angle to fish, one of the delights of a caddis hatch is that, unlike in the example above, a larger trout often rises to feed on the surface with the appearance of the first few naturals. Watch closely. The early-rising trout may or may not be taking the fully hatched, winged caddises.

Floating Emergent Caddises

It's not unusual in caddis hatches for trout to rise but spurn any full-winged dry fly. Trout often key on emergent forms, just under or afloat. Such selectivity is typical at the beginning of a hatch, especially near a source, whenever emergers are more abundant than freshly hatched flies. Trout will select emergers even though winged

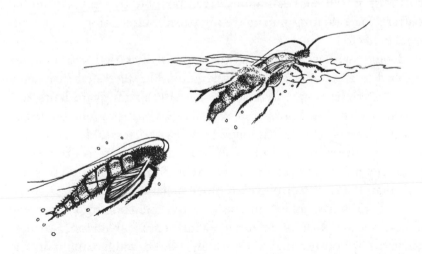

Trout can be highly selective to emergent caddis pupae in the surface region during hatches. (Artwork by Maurice Mahler; reproduced with permission)

adults are on the water or fluttering in the air. Many species of caddises drift a considerable distance in the surface zone before emerging; they become easy pickings on which trout may feed.

On gliding waters typical of spring creeks, trout may stay on emergers throughout a daily hatch; then the naturals float a long way, more or less trapped in the tenacious meniscus, the surface zone or film. Thus the natural drift with an imitation is notably productive on chilly streams.

There are exceptions, of course. "Rocket" caddises are instant-hatching caddises, which have the ability to emerge and fly quickly. The wings of caddises remain waterproof inside the casing, allowing for the different actions a species may display upon emerging. Nonetheless, with the exception of these rocketing caddises, water temperature and atmospheric conditions influence the time required for a winged adult to emerge.

I've observed larger pupae of rocket caddises in a lengthy, drifting, and spurting ascension through a pool while the normally secretive browns intercepted them at the surface with explosive splashes. One time when the hatch was sparse, I sat down on the bank and followed up each spray-tossing rise by casting a #14 pupa to the spot. Though sampling was impossible that time, a simple pattern for a floating pupa gave me paced but exciting action with sizable trout.

Doug Swisher told me of these pupal flies tied solely of fur dubbed in a cylinder shape on the hook. He suggested that many caddises are hairy-textured, so a pupa with liberal guard hairs emphasizes a shaggy impression and also gives maximum buoyancy when skittered. (Often the pupa surfaces and scrambles along the water, usually shoreward.) However, I match numerous little pupae with only finely textured fur, no guard hairs, and tie them to be slimmer than the chubbier pupae of other species.

The stillborn caddis, an adult partly emerged from the pupal shuck, is also a form of emergent caddis that trout key on. Swisher-Richards stillborns, tied with widely bowed wings caught in the trailing shuck, represent a notable advance in angling. Those I tied

My caddis emerger, trailing a pupal husk, with wings just bursting

for *Chimarra* readily took otherwise unwilling trout that February day mentioned earlier and on many other occasions.

An emergent floating caddis pattern I developed represents a natural insect's next step in hatching, with the wings just burst free but tied short. It has taken more trout for me during hatches of grayish *Brachycentrus* caddises than any other emergent dry and can be tied to match other hatches as well. The trailing shuck is usually soft Antron fibers, the abdomen a mix of hare's ear with another color predominant of the natural. The wings are quill feathers, such as mallard, tied at an angle or flat, and slanted outward and short but swept back. The head is dubbed fur of a finer texture than the abdomen but matching the natural in color.

Highly selective feeding to emergent caddises temporarily stymied me 25 years ago on the Henry's Fork of the Snake River, in Idaho. Observing at close hand the caddises that trout selected from mixed hatches, I finally snipped the tail off a small, slender Goofus Bug dry. The makeshift Emerger simulated the wings just burst from the shuck, and on water the fly's slanted float accentuated its visibility. Any trout that rose with snout to drifting fly but hesitated was convinced with a bare nudge of the imitation.

"We got skunked," an angler commented, speaking for his partner and himself after the rise was over.

"I took more than thirty," I answered.

Judging from experiences ever since that day, the importance of emergent caddis imitations cannot be emphasized enough.

Better Dry Flies

Compared with the array of established, commercially available patterns for classified mayflies, Caddis drys have not been developed to cover anything approaching the vast range of naturals. The excellent angling attainable with those caddises that are available may be one reason, but the angler who also ties patterns realistic to the trout will discover increased success.

Sampling natural insects provides detail beyond stream observation in tying a caddis dry for selective trout. On waters I fish frequently, for example, the broad-winged black *Chimarra* caddis appears most often in three distinct sizes. Sampling showed the actual wing lengths to be 10 millimeters (#16), 9 millimeters (#18), and 8 millimeters (#20). Although the differences are slight, trout will be selective to just one size of natural; they often key on the most abundant size present.

Because of *Chimarra*'s high visibility, the size difference among the trio appears greater than it is. To the trained eye, observation shows which one the trout are taking. A tad larger black caddis is not uncommon, and a #16 with a longer wing, the fly totaling 13 millimeters, stands out markedly. A millimeter gauge is handy, too, to measure abdomen length in tying caddises.

Sampling frequently shows differences in color shading and size among caddises that appear alike from a distance. Trout taking blackish-winged naturals, for instance, may discern abdomen coloration as subtle as brown or dark gray. Species coloration varies not only with region but also over time; late sampling has shown coloration differences not apparent in earlier hatches. And as a rule, many caddises that have resided for a time amid streamside cover darken in hue.

Tying caddises with respect to wing position is one of the keys to choosing a pattern, especially for larger trout observed feeding on specific naturals. I tote drys for each known caddis in at least two distinct wing textures. The durable hairwing sloped back over the hook may be positioned low or at an angle, flared as high as 45 degrees above the hook.

But a quill-winged caddis creates a realistic impression for microscope-eyed trout. A caddis with wings closed at rest, forming the pup-tent silhouette, is matched with a folded quill, trailing edge clipped at a slant and longer border on bottom. A pattern tied with individual quill wings slightly spread and raised simulates a fly on the water, about to hop or fly. Quill wings tied broadly split (delta style) suggest a fluttering caddis and, when tied lower, simulate both a drowned fly well into a hatch and a spent caddis at egg-laying time. Match the female egg-laying caddis with an egg sack.

While sparsely hackled patterns add "bugginess" and create a higher float, wary trout often ignore or splash at this silhouette, no matter how small the fly. The deadliest of my patterns in #14–22 are no-hackles. Hairwing and quill-winged drys tied with various materials for the abdomen create a buoyant no-hackle. For example, a fur with guard hairs (such as hare's mask) creates a buggy abdomen; a fur or synthetic dubbing or a wrapped quill stem with four turns of palmered hackle (sheared on top, clipped short on the sides, and squared on bottom) creates a slender abdomen with a hairy impression.

A finely textured fur or dubbing matches the smoother, slender abdomen of numerous #16 and smaller caddises but will float under a properly tied wing. Just a fur head and fine fur abdomen will jauntily float #18–22 quill-winged no-hackles. A pair of split antennae are a visible aspect of realism on a no-hackle.

Caddis-gnashing trout can exhibit an ability to slice the tippet, and 5X is not too stout for most creek caddis angling. My caddis drys are delicately balanced, tied on strong, light-wire hooks, and they float lifelike on 6X or 7X if needed, with smallest sizes for wary trout. I've found the realistic dry is taken in the manner in which the trout has been consuming naturals, minimizing the chance of a broken tippet.

Natural Drift, High or Low Float

A realistic caddis dry opens a new world of success with the natural drift. It's my steadiest presentation, and not only because naturals tend to drift for a longer time on a chilly, smooth surface. A dry that appears to be a natural and is easily taken attracts even trout that are feeding on fidgety naturals. And individual trout, often larger fish, will feed quietly, always awaiting a fly that's easy pickings, even though other trout are feeding splashily.

Whether the dry of the moment is a hackled or no-hackle imitation that floats on the abdomen, a greased fly that rides high on the water is highly visible and often the difference in the angling. Dilly Wax flotant adds a luster without gumming up a delicate caddis dry.

On the other hand, close observation is a cue to the times when a no-hackle presented lower in the surface film is the taking dry. Even with caddises adrift, fidgeting and fluttering, caddis-conditioned trout have shown selectivity to just low-floating naturals. Present a dry sans flotant, with the wing barely visible on the surface. A hair-wing, such as a pattern I tie with a few underfibers of light-colored fine deer or elk overlaid with thinner, dark mink fibers, traps minute bubbles in the film. A quill wing tied flat is another effective silhouette. The low float is often the ticket near the end of a surface-feeding period, whether the activity is a stream-born emergence or a spinner fall. Sizable trout have then raced 10 feet to solidly take a mere #18 long adrift and nearly awash.

The Lively Floating Caddis

Inching the floating imitation to alert a trout is even deadlier with a realistic pattern. But matching antics of the natural at the time often requires innovation. Some caddises inch along with pauses, while other species (both pupae and winged adults) scurry shoreward.

To match caddises on the move, cast upstream, laying the line near the lee bank and letting the current swing the fly around toward midstream (often the opposite bank). The current naturally forms a widely bowed curve cast; on the hemmed small stream it often isn't possible to cast such a broad in-air mend. When the drifting fly reaches a spot with the leader extending across current, keep the rod tip low and inch the line in with the rod hand. The fly is thus retrieved at a right angle toward the tip of the fly line. Trout feeding selectively take a no-hackle that matches the broadside jog and pace of the naturals crossing a flat, wide eddy.

When caddises display fidgety actions on the water, trout congregating near hatch sources can be taken from a deeper eddy patch. With a brief wait between upstream casts, a progression of methods that always gave the same dry a new look took trout for me on just a few square yards of surface. The variations went this way:

1. a natural drift on a loosely cast straight line that presented the fly head first
2. a yard-wide negative curve cast, drifting the fly rear-end first ahead of the leader
3. a curve cast to set up the drift and then a single twitch of the fly broadside to current
4. the same as number 3, but then inching the fly two or three times broadside
5. a slighter curve dropped a bit farther upstream, so when the fly drifted over the hotspot, short rod-tip twitches inched it at a new angle back upstream

Sudden Impact

The sudden impact of a dry on the water before the tippet falls is deadly whenever a natural would drop similarly near a trout's snout. The technique is not only for a recalcitrant sighted trout but also for the times when only a few caddises appear in a flurry. When the rare caddis appears and is taken, delivering the dry within seconds attracts the trout to take it as a reflexive feeding response.

Since not all hatches are prolific, and several caddis species may hatch at the same time of the season, I hook alternate dry patterns on the sheep's-wool patch of my vest. Some caddises, frequently larger ones, tend to hatch suddenly but in sparse numbers, so having a match handy for those instances allows a quick fly change. As I tarried in a pool, a larger #14 emerged on the riffle upstream and hopped along downstream onto flat water; near midpool, a brown zoomed up and took it splashily the instant it dropped again. Soon the trout captured a second long-hopping caddis, and now I was ready. The split-winged quill-wing match dropped with an impact mimicking the natural's drop onto the spot of the rise, hooking my largest trout from that pool. Only a half dozen of those large, meaty caddises hatched.

Skimming the Caddis

Almost any change in atmospherics may trigger caddis activity, but one day when a steady drizzle began, the naturals and the rising trout waned. I greased the leader and fished the water with a no-hackle hairwing. Simply raising the rod to draw the fly along the surface attracted trout to rise and take it.

An across-stream cast dropped the fly tightly beneath a grassy bank, and a lunker brown showed in a yard-long swim to the fly that was skimming away, merely nipping it. I tried to stir the fly with a variation of a method known as snapping the water. With care, a dry can be cast onto the water near a visible trout and snapped away, with the leader never falling. Doing this on a patch of water alerts the trout to a number of caddises. Finally, the dry is presented directly to the trout.

But now, over several minutes, I created various caddis actions some 5 feet upstream of the hidden trout's niche, in the process hooking a small trout that splashed wildly on the flat water. Later, when I repeated the same presentation as before, skimming the fly

Hatched caddis flies and larger trout congregate around overhanging foliage.

broadside from the undercut but a bit more slowly, the bigger brown—hanging deeper, snug to a ledge—ascended and engulfed it. Gotcha!

The skimming caddis generally is very natural-looking to a trout after a week or more of emergences, when adults clinging to bankside cover have become numerous. Trout eye the bank edges, knowing caddises may appear. In the absence of a hatch from the stream and sometimes prior to a hatch that day, trout poise for an early caddis along the stream edge.

Caddises will flutter along the stream in dispersal flights, and, in my observations, despite their haphazard appearance in the air, they are adept fliers compared with the bumbling larger stone flies. The caddis has rounded, tapered, trailing edges on its two pairs of wings. The wings are mounted in a triangular position. This wing design and posture create an airfoil feature that promotes lift, stability, and maneuverability in the brief space during flight. Few caddises fall errantly, but the trout are expectant.

Swarming Caddises

Displays by various caddis species include naturals fluttering in swarms like popcorn in the popper or in tight-weaving figure eight–like formations low over the water. Swarming often precedes egg laying. Frequently, trout can be seen hovering high in the water or in shallow water beneath swarms, and some will leap to snatch caddises in the air. One enterprising brown that I watched repeatedly somersaulted, slapping its tail through a thick swarm and against a bush laden with naturals in an attempt to bat flies onto the water.

No single technique is a panacea for taking trout when caddises are thick over (or on) the water, but an alerting presentation, a contrasting presentation, or a high-floating ethereal dry gets the attention of preoccupied fish. A Bivisible and a sparse-hackled variant with a long, stiff tail and distinct quill wings that appear to hover are two patterns that take trout on such occasions.

Egg-Laying Caddises

Some caddis species mate in the air, and I've seen caddises clinging in pairs (even threes) adrift and fidgeting on the stream. Certain caddises bounce up and down, while others float to wash eggs in the water. A few species dive and deposit their eggs beneath the surface. Observing the manner of ovipositing cues a presentation. It's not unusual for just a few caddises to drop and lay eggs under swarming naturals, and not all showy swarms result in substantial spinner falls, nor do all egg-laying caddises drop from a group of swarming naturals. Egg laying usually occurs in late afternoon or evening, but I've encountered it earlier in the day. Look for the egg sack on the female's abdomen.

The fortunate angler will witness multiple, overlapping caddis activity—emergence, swarming, and egg laying. Numbers of caddises and the varied feeding ways of trout often complicate an angler's attempt to identify the stage of the hatch that's attracting the better trout. I try to focus on a taking fly, techniques, and a trout.

One cool sunny day, I watched as caddises emerged along a creek

Enterprising trout will vault for caddises fluttering over the water. (Artwork by Maurice Mahler; reproduced with permission)

seldom more than knee deep and drifted along in the pup-tent form. Well into the hatch, kaleidoscopic little clouds of previously hatched caddises shrouded overhanging foliage; trout fed in every describable way, and many of the techniques mentioned took individual fish. Yet through this confusing activity, the most productive tactic was a natural drift with a no-hackle to trout rising quietly across the middle two-thirds of the 20-foot-wide creek. Wading this stream, I often kneeled for a hidden profile and also for a low angle to arrow a tightly looped cast to bankside edges. My short (5-foot) fly rod gave me additional space to control configurations of casts.

Creating Caddis Action

Caddises are excitable insects, and even during slack times this behavioral trait will give catches and anecdotes worth sharing. A small trout splashing on the line triggers a lone caddis to hatch just upstream and flutter along briefly until taken by a nearby, hidden 2-pounder—yet another instance when a quick delivery of the dry counts. One angler expertly slaps his fly line across a riffle, spurring a caddis to emerge and bounce along, attracting a trout, with a partner in position ready with a matching dry. In the absence of an expected hatch, a pupa raised from bottom and twitched shallowly through a pool takes a number of trout, and then a deep, natural drift hooks the aroused larger trout on bottom. It works both ways—the insects turning the trout on to feed, and conversely the actions of trout exciting insects to hatch and other trout to feed.

Does any other hatch permit the angler to *create* action, using dry or wet patterns, with the same degree of success as when caddises are expected? A small stream caddis bonanza is a treasure of trouting.

More on Caddis Drys—the No-Hackle

W HEN A TROUT takes a dry fly that appears to be a natural in the eyes of an angler as well, it's a wonderful meeting of the "minds." Various no-hackle caddis dry flies are examples of these kinds of realistic patterns because they are accurate in the perceptions of selective trout and the angler. The patterns are easy to tie in comparison with no-hackle matches of other insects, and they're useful for a wide variety of angling situations. No-hackles can make the difference during caddis hatches— emergences as well as egg-laying time.

Caddis patterns are also useful when you are not trying to match a hatch. Trout recognize a caddis as a natural food, for this large group of insects offers species common on all streams and through most of the year. The no-hackles are effective on trout that are highly selective over another hatch. Trout simply show a liking for caddis, and a realistic pattern can be the deadliest of all.

From my experience primarily on heavily fished waters, and mostly with browns, I've learned that selectivity in a trout's manner of feeding is not always attributable to a large number of naturals being on the water, causing the fish to feed exclusively on the abundant food. Selectivity can be a result of natural wariness and of the trout's perception of a fly, especially in low, clear water. The so-called selective trout need not be rising but may be lurking, whether or not it's waiting at a feeding station. In this respect, the no-hackle caddis is effective in fishing the water.

A no-hackle caddis imitation

A split-wing no-hackle caddis imitation

A simple version of a no-hackle caddis is as effective today as when it was developed several decades ago. It has a dubbed-fur abdomen under a hairwing flared backward over the hook shank. A typical hairwing no-hackle pattern has a sparse wing of a hollow, buoyant hair, such as elk or deer hair.

Some small varieties of caddis naturals have slender abdomens, and these are best imitated with a finely textured dubbing. Other naturals are chubbier, so fur with guard hairs suggestive of a larger hairy natural works and also helps float the fly. Synthetic dubbing that gives a sparkle or translucence is now used on some no-hackle caddis drys.

On one expedition, trout sharply taking naturals virtually "untied" an already well-used hairwing pattern. The episode showed me the effectiveness of an impressionistic, hairy-textured caddis sans hackle. The gradual shearing of the fly caused it to match stages of a dry caddis on the water. The elk-hair wing became chewed short, rendering the fly an emerger. When only the body of hare's-ear dubbing remained, the fly resembled a floating pupa.

The malleable bundle of a hair wing can easily be raised so that the wing flares at a higher angle from the hook, giving you a pattern with a high-winged silhouette. It's a small adjustment, but the high wing of a fluttering caddis on the water, unencumbered by the buzz of hackle, is lifelike. The fluttering-wing version, of course, can also be tied at your vise with the hair wing flared at or above a 45-degree angle. The high-winged hairwing caddis works both during hatches when naturals are fluttering and when you're fishing the water and trout are holding deeply or along the bottom.

Trout taking full-winged caddises on placid spring creeks had been baffling to me, until I fed them a no-hackle on a natural drift. Observation has often shown that selective rising trout choose a fly that is at rest, wings closed in a pup-tent silhouette.

One realistic hairwing pattern I tie has a smooth-textured fur (or Fly-Rite) abdomen, not relying on bulk or guard hairs for flotation. The underwing is a few fibers of light-colored buoyant elk or thin deer hair. The top of the wing is a fine darker hair, such as mink, which naturally mixes in. In #16 and #18 complete with antennae, this two-tone wing pattern has given me many sessions of great angling. Properly greased, it floats jauntily with the downwing low but over the water. It is even deadlier when it floats low, sometimes awash in the film, and thus it is impressionistic of an emerging caddis, as well as an egg-laying adult, and, finally, a spent caddis.

Such a hairwing pattern is practical; it naturally hangs awash, even in broken water. It's always incredible when supposedly wary trout, sometimes appearing unexpectedly, chase through clear, placid water to capture this Caddis presented on a long drift in the surface film. The action often occurs toward the end of surface feeding, whether during an emergence or a spinner fall.

When trout begin to recognize a hairwing caddis as a fake, a pattern tied with a trim, neat quill wing is the best choice. The quill-wing dry, tied closed or narrowly split and slightly raised, is the ultimate for matching a caddis afloat with its wings closed in the tent form or slightly open. While the quill-wing caddises are important on placid or clear waters such as spring creeks, trout under rippling water and in quickly flowing freestone streams will also scrutinize a wing silhouette. Such realistic patterns are deadly on a natural drift or when presented in a lively manner.

Caddises show many actions on the water, but whenever I believe a trout is wary, I choose a quill-wing no-hackle caddis. I've cast one to mimic the "sudden caddis" that drops solidly onto the water, floats briefly, and then flutters away.

Even amid the flurry of varied forms of rising that accompany caddis time, with some fish leaping airborne for fluttering insects, an individual fish may be sipping caddises. Watch for such quietly feeding trout, for they are usually large.

An earmark of caddis fishing is that a taking technique is cued by observing the way a trout is taking naturals. The natural little twitch as the drifting fly nears a trout's snout can be even more convincing with a no-hackle caddis. I've also had to float a quill-wing no-hackle on a widely bowed slack line and inch it quietly with pauses in pace with the naturals that trout were taking as the tent-winged flies made their way across current on flat water.

Because of their effectiveness, #18–22 quill-wing no-hackle microcaddises may someday become popular as standard dry patterns. I tote both light and dark versions. A fur body with a fine texture and a fur head floats the smallest Caddis. The miniatures match many midges. They're excellent as chironomid imitations, so your tying is not only for small caddises to microcaddises.

Many of us have encountered mayfly hatches and have not had the right patterns to catch trout. I've had instances when no-hackle mayflies were too light to interest trout rising to darker mayflies. But a no-hackle caddis has done well even in such instances. A no-hackle caddis may be taken as a welcome change and a familiar, tasty morsel. I've also had success with no-hackle caddises that simply matched the size and color of the problem hatch.

The caddis silhouette is generally impressionistic of so many insects, both aquatic and terrestrial, that these drys are universally used for fishing the water. No-hackles have worked regularly for me. When caddises have been hatching, residing on streamside cover, and returning to lay eggs, a match of the natural is often deadliest. Trout are often poised for fluttering caddises, flying caddises, and in anticipation of egg-laying caddises.

A specific caddis hatch is generally lengthy and drawn out, spanning two weeks or longer. I usually tie both hairwing and quill-wing flies for a specific hatch. In some instances the durable hairwing flies are all that is needed to catch trout. But the discerning trout might show only to the quill-wing dry along the quiet stream, especially in clear water or on a placid surface. Thus, a pattern tied for selective rising trout also has a place in strategically fishing the water. Such catches, perhaps of previously sighted trout, show the value of the differences between hairwing and quill-wing silhouettes.

There are more than 1,000 species of caddises. Several species of these tasty naturals hatch throughout the season. Common colorations include white, cream, tan, brown, olive, gray, and black. Matching the body color of the naturals is often critical to imitating a natural; your choice of wing can be just as important. If you don't have the exact color needed, tie your flies with a light or dark shade of a similar color to suggest the natural as closely as possible.

Here are some hints to help you sample naturals. Use an aquarium hand net to scoop flies off the water. When you are gathering egg-laying caddises on the surface, note that the egg sack should be matched for color. Previously hatched flies that cling to the shady side of streamside grasses can be cupped uninjured in a 35-millimeter film canister. When you are sampling caddises along the bank, be aware that some varieties darken significantly after hatching.

The Unknown Fly That Turns On Trout

T HE NEWCOMER couldn't have been at a better place and at a more likely time to tie into a trophy trout on a dry fly. The fellow said he was new to fly-fishing, and this was his first outing on a mountain stream. Maybe my confidence sounded like bragging, but I offered to show him some of the fastest dry-fly fishing in the West, and right now. Conditions were perfect, the July afternoon warm and sunny as we headed for a place I had in mind. After a short hike we came to a gravel bar that sloped into the stream. He could wade out in hip boots and cast over trout splashing at inch-long flies on the water.

"What are those bugs?" he asked predictably.

"Golden stone flies," I answered. "We'll have good fishing."

It wasn't only the trout slashing up wedges of spray that had my acquaintance's eyes wide open. The sight of a western stone fly flight at its peak makes it easy to forget you have a fly rod—for a moment anyway. The flies were over the water in the hundreds. Their blurred, fluttering wings caught the sunlight, and they looked like small lights playing against the dark cliff on the opposite side of the stream. They gyrated around the bushes overhanging the water like bees at a hive. Clumsy fliers, some careened onto the water and fluttered downstream to float by female stone flies just skimming the surface and heading upstream, the tips of their abdomens dipping below the water to wash off eggs. It would be easy to drop a fly over the nearest splashing trout.

"Nothing wrong with casting to a rising fish," I said. "But many wary, larger trout are on the bottom. With all this activity they're aroused, and they'll take a natural insect. So fish all the water. You don't need a delicate delivery. Try dropping a fly down hard the way a real stone fly falls."

As he waded in cautiously, I headed downstream to a deep pool, hoping to do just as I advised him, for I knew where some big trout were likely to be in a spot he couldn't reach. Even in my chest-high waders with felt soles, it took some tricky wading to cross to the far bank at the tail of the pool.

Now I edged upstream along the cliff, wading waist deep. With a short line, I dropped a #8 hairwing dry stone fly upstream onto a deep pocket. The fly floated tantalizingly, almost at rest on a sheet of water eddying gently behind a ledge. A bottom-hugging trout charged up and tossed spray as it nailed my larger-than-life dry fly. This trout didn't want to leave its deep-water area, and I gave and took line while it made runs to the edges of the pool. When I had the trout close to my outstretched net, it suddenly splashed, screeched line off the reel, and jumped, but soon a 2-pound brown lay in the net.

A few casts later, a rainbow holding deeply on the rocks gulped in the outsized dry fly on the tabletop eddy. That would have been enough for me, but I decided to drop a few casts a yard ahead of where those fish had hit. This time a 3-pound brown smashed the now-soggy fly. Man alive! The sudden strikes and the size of the fish had turned me on, as pumping up several hefty fish did. The stone fly–laden bushes overhanging the water had a lot to do with their eagerness.

When I returned to the fellow I'd left on the gravel bar, he was beaching a brown trout even larger than the last one I'd caught. No doubt that fantastic afternoon made a dedicated fly-fisher of him, for the action continued as long as the sunlight kept the stone flies dancing.

Most stone flies have the same silhouette—four wax-papery, veined wings folded over the back and usually extended beyond the long, slender abdomen. When the fly is at rest on foliage or a rock,

A golden stone fly next to its hairwing imitation

these wings lie flat. Most stone flies have two tails. There are some 400 species in North America, with bodies as short as ⅛ inch and as long as 2 inches. There's no mistaking them for that common insect, the caddis, whose wings sit like a pup tent over its back, or for an upright-winged mayfly.

Wherever you fish on western rivers, stone flies may be on the trout's menu. They're commonly found along the rocks and brush that edge swift, clean, rocky-bottomed runs but also along smooth-flowing rivers that have rubbly and stony bottoms. In their aquatic stage as nymphs, most stone flies found in the West need rough bottoms where they can cling under rocks and cool water with high oxygen content. Most of the western species that are active during the day hatch in the warming waters of spring through midsummer.

There are more stone flies along streams than many anglers realize, and most are small, from under ¼ inch to about ¾ inch. Only a few stone flies are an inch or slightly longer. When those larger, meaty insects are out they attract big trout. In my estimation the 1-inch class produces the steadiest of the good dry-fly fishing to be had with the stone flies, despite the publicity surrounding the largest in the West, the 2-inch whopper commonly called the salmon fly.

There are many uncertainties about the salmon fly hatch occurring in late spring or early summer, when the waters often run swollen with snowmelt runoff. Dry-fly fishing then can be somewhat impractical, restricting the walking angler to shallow spots and bank fishing. Early-season periods of cold weather may turn off the hatch, or the trout become so stuffed with salmon flies that most will take only a weighted nymph drifted on bottom. The salmon flies hatch a few miles farther up a river each day, and the angler must locate the head of the hatch for best dry-fly action. I have seen more disappointed men who have traveled thousands of miles for the fabled salmon fly hatches come away fishless because of a combination of these difficulties.

I had been among them one year, and when the salmon fly hatch was ending in the upper reaches of a river, I encountered by chance some 1-inch golden stone flies. I had then only sampled western stream fishing. The first half of July I found 1-inchers along scattered stretches, and *I didn't have to follow this hatch*. The trout took a dry fly well wherever stone flies clung on overhanging branches. Along one short stretch, I took six trout from 15 to nearly 22 inches in a week, and since have found that such catches can be made in a much briefer time. This introduction to 1-inch stone flies occurred on Rock Creek near Missoula, Montana. Other larger rivers nearby— the upper Clark Fork, Big Blackfoot, and the Bitterroot—also have 1-inchers. The enjoyment of wading a stream and seeing tremendous flights of 1-inch stone flies and the expectation that the next cast will bring up a 2-pounder beat all the hoopla about the salmon fly.

In the case of most 1-inch stone flies, the angling is *not* to a hatch, which usually goes unnoticed in the evening, after dark, or in early morning. The nymphs leave the undersides of rocks and crawl out of the water, perhaps onto a midstream boulder but mostly onto the shore. The softened shell splits open along the top of the back, and the winged adult works free. The adults cling to the over-hanging brush, and the trout lie waiting below. When a summer day has heated up the air and the insects begin flying over the stream— some not too successfully—it's well worth being there.

One early afternoon I waded into a swift shallow stretch of Mon-tana's Big Blackfoot, and out of the corner of my eye saw a stone fly tumble from a bush on the near bank. It fluttered its wings as it bounced down the choppy water, then—splash!—it was gone. Brac-ing against the force of the water, I quickly stripped out line in false casts and dropped a hairwing dry fly behind the bush. It floated quickly away and a butterscotch-sided cutthroat chased it down-stream and hit hard. The plump 12-incher tugged and jumped in the clear mountain air. "Only the beginning," I told myself, and I wasn't disappointed.

The trout weren't rising often to the naturals, but it seemed that every time I dropped the fly onto a pocket one would rush up and take it. It didn't matter if I used my then favorite #10 or #12 Bucktail Caddis or a King's River Caddis, two dry flies which are near imita-tions of inch-long stone flies, or if I used a Goofus Bug, its upright divided deer-hair wings resembling a struggling stone fly. When I reached a place that seemed to offer a big fish, I switched to a larger #8 dry fly, somewhat bulkier than the real insects, yet a taker of my largest trout when I cast to a spot.

The downstream approach offers more than easy wading along swift waters. I recall many times working upstream and not being able to get a worthwhile presentation with a dry fly onto pockets that I was sure held trout, and even subduing risers. I often head back downstream and pick up some mighty fine fish I did not inter-est earlier.

The downstream cast helps one slide a fly into openings along brushy banks and put the fly over hiding trout that can't be reached any other way. On open waters as well, a downstream cast shows the fly ahead of the leader and allows the fly to float naturally on a quiet pocket for fully a couple of seconds. Many a trout that wanted extra time to look over a stone fly has smashed my artificial, rocking me back on my heels.

That's the charm in fishing on top with stone flies—the strikes tend to be splashy and sure, and you pray that this magic will last forever.

Midges

Tiny Dynamite for Trout

MIDGES, THOSE MINI-MINI-FLIES only 5 millimeters or so in size, are the smallest aquatic insects on
which trout feed, but they offer rising trout to the angler
more often throughout the year than any other aquatic hatch. While
most other hatches are couched in annual time slots and may be
more abundant one year than another, the midge hatches are comparatively dependable.

Midges are usually the first hatch of the day, but whatever hour
they dot the water, they often precede the appearance of larger insects, thus trout rising to midges are often receptive to a realistic
pattern of a somewhat larger insect. For example, on streams where
caddises are awaited by the trout, my own #14–20 no-hackle imitations can be delightfully effective. In recent years, most of the 16-
inch and larger browns I've seen rising during daylight on favorite,
small spring creeks were up to midges on flat water. These trout
took a low-floating little caddis dry.

You can decide for yourself if the trout are selective to the hatch
or to a quality dry presented naturally on a light tippet. While trout
can be highly selective to the proper midge tie, it is not carelessness
which causes the fish to take an intruder fly; an insect that is familiar
and tasty supplements the diet.

Matching the midge hatch, nonetheless, gives the most consistent results. A few species of midges attain 10 millimeters in length.
Even others a bit smaller, tied on #20 hooks, seem in the minority

to smaller chironomids. The tiniest flies are difficult, if not impossible, to match. You can develop tunnel vision over midge hatches that range a couple hash marks either side of 5 millimeters. After squinting at #28s for a time, a hatch of #24s becomes welcome to the eyes.

Recognizing the stage of the midge on which trout are feeding and presenting a similar pattern are the key to success. Trout will feed subsurface on the slender, wormlike larva, the pupa ascending and drifting, the pupa dangling vertically to the underpane of the surface film, the emergent pupa low on the meniscus, and the stillborn adult. These forms are naturally longer, by as much as a few millimeters, than the same hatched, winged adult. Imitations of the adult, in silhouettes representing the fly at rest, fluttering, and spent, complete a basic assortment of midges.

Midges hatch on almost every river and creek. Though gentle-flowing sections and flat water beckon the midge angler, I've marveled at how trout several feet deep will rise to midges on a bouncing current during summer mornings.

The larvae are unique in their adaptability to a variety of instream habitat. They will cling in crevices along hard bottom from gravel to rubble and in debris. They'll burrow into silt and are notably abundant in vegetation. The tiny insects are hardy, capable of thriving despite temporary and long-term changes in the stream habitat and water quality.

In my correspondence with fly-fishers, one angler wrote me that unusually high water early in the season had reduced the mayfly hatches, but the midge hatches were super. I had similar experiences when midging was the panacea in the search for rising trout. Another angler wrote that he had recently taken a 6-pound trout on a #16 dry fly in a midge hatch along a placid reach of a large river on the edge of a city. He explained, "We were yards upstream of a sewage treatment plant, its effluent of discolored water fanning into the border of the river. Some trout dimpled in that darkened lane of mild current, though many others in inviting waters along the clear river were hovering near the top and gently ringing the surface to the prolific midge hatch."

This reminded me of a similar situation along a narrow spring creek—one that I alluded to earlier in "Small Stream Caddis Bonanza." Miles downstream of a municipal treatment plant's conduit pipe, the species of mayflies that trout fed on had waned as increasing civilization burdened the facility. During this time, midge hatches flourished. Recently, treatment methods were updated, and some of the delicate varieties of mayflies have returned. Others, including a few of my favorite hatches, are greatly diminished or gone. The insect life also has been subject to siltation and chemical treatments on farm fields bordering the country creek. Some terrestrial hatches have suffered. However, throughout the last decade, the midges have remained abundant.

Midges attain remarkable abundance in enriched waters; in limestone streams there may be up to several thousand larvae per square foot of habitat. During hatches, a sizable trout will lie near the surface and consume perhaps hundreds of midges in an hour.

The first time I fished one Montana spring creek, clouds scudded low, and gusts swept away most of the hatched flies. The trout fed on emerging pupae. Not having any such patterns with me, I knotted a #24 Adams on a 6X tippet. I scissored the hackle to a stubble so the fly would resemble a pupa and drift low like the natural. A dimpling trout, hidden beneath the surface glare, sipped it, barely ringing the water. I tightened the line, and my fly rod bowed into a deep, throbbing arc. For a while it seemed a muskrat was hunkering on the bottom. I reeled in some line as I waded ahead and stomped on the bottom, urging my quarry to swim. Line began to click steadily off the reel. Well upstream the fish surfaced, heading broadside across current. Later, I clamped my hand over its head, pinning the gills, and hefted a heavyweight rainbow. The tiny hook, a tight gap even for the wire loop on the rod butt, had securely notched into the fish's snout.

Landing a larger trout on a midge and a light leader is a memorable experience. You have to meet considerable odds. In most streams, larger-than-average trout for the water feed on midges often enough to add allure to the small-fly, light-line angling.

On windy days, trout concentrate on pupae whenever they are

more abundant than hatched flies on the surface. One of those times is at the onset of a midge hatch. One pleasant morning in early spring I waded slowly and quietly into position to fish upstream in a long, placid shallows of a meadow stream in southwest Wisconsin. My leader was adapted to ply this challenging knee-deep water where the hatch was beginning, and a few trout rolled to feed. The length of my permanent leader butt, the Fly-Rite, hot-yellow, knotless tapered leader, with a long, clear 6X tippet, measured 14 feet.

Trout were taking pupae inches under the surface. I lightly greased the leader to within 6 inches of the fly so it would hang naturally below the surface and glide smoothly and slowly. The #18 imitation of dubbed fur had throat fibers of soft partridge for a pupa's low-slung wing case.

I watched a large trout swirl. On a 50-foot upstream cast, I dropped the fly 5 feet above the trout; the leader settled as wispily as a spider's silk ahead of the 4-weight fly line. The pupa drifted to the trout, and the swirl repeated. I flipped the low rod sideways, an automatic hooking technique, then carefully played the fish. I soon eased in a deep-bodied 15-inch brown.

The shallow flats hadn't been overly disturbed, and I waited again. Then, a few yards ahead of the hold where the initial trout had fed, another beauty rolled. That one I unhooked with tweezers. It was an inch longer than the first. Releasing that pair of fine trout was the culmination of sport I had enjoyed by matching the tackle to the angling and presenting a pupa to the feeding level of the fish.

While a trout feeding visibly near or on the surface during hatches is a readily sighted target, a larger denizen often feeds secretively below the surface on larvae and pupae. There are times when only smaller fish are surfacing, and then you might consider making presentations to strategic lanes of drift, at the edges of moss beds. Wearing polarized sunglasses, you often can spot a beauty finning in place, sometimes in shallow water near the source of hatches where pupae drift in numbers. Greasing the leader to within a selected distance of a lightly weighted pattern allows the proper presentation for the depth.

Various simple patterns to suggest pupae and larvae are effective.

By sampling the larder with a screen held across current, you can determine the color of the insects, then use the appropriate pattern. Trout often develop selectivity to the color of the naturals. One pattern which has given me delightful fishing for some years is simply fine copper wire wrapped tightly along the hook, with a tuft of herl such as gray ostrich or peacock for the head. As with other attractor flies, this shiny miniature has days when it outproduces somber patterns.

Although drifting a sunken imitation is often successful, trout may be partial to a pupa fished in an ascending manner. With the fly deep, raising the rod tip while evenly stripping in line simulates the insect rising through the water.

At the top, a pupa clings to the underside of the meniscus. One way to present a dangling pupa is to knot a short length of leader material of the next finest diameter or "X" designation on the end of the main tippet. Apply grease on the leader nearly to the fly.

A basic pupa pattern is a hook of dubbed fur tied to be slender, with a bulkier fur thorax. It is productive beneath the surface and floating low on the water. When presented in the surface film, it simulates the midge prior to emergence of the winged adult. Trout generally will await the drifting pupa. When this fails, nudging it or wriggling it along will attract their attention.

The stillborn midges, developed by Doug Swisher and Carl Richards, are outstanding for emergent, floating flies. They imitate naturals that are slow to emerge or never hatch and can be indispensable for highly selective trout. When the fish seem to have microscopes for eyes, a no-hackle stillborn is deadly. The phenomenon of the stillborn midge, a partly emerged adult trailing its pupal shuck, actually is quite common, and trout will pick them during heavy hatches.

On a day when hatches were abundant, I found that an adaptation of a humpy midge attracted trout. It had hackle tied full circle in front of the small pod, as on a Goofus Bug dry. With both slender midges and bulkier blackish-brown gnats emerging, trout were partial to the pudgier dipterans. The little #28 matched the latter closely and was designed for buoyancy and skimming.

Trout dimpled steadily behind large moss beds, sources of the hatches on flat water of the Firehole, in Yellowstone National Park. Though I always begin with a natural drift to a feeding trout, it gave few takes. Then, on a slack-line across-stream cast, I drifted the fly nearly to a hovering trout. Simply holding the line then permitted the currents, which appeared smooth but were deceptively varied, to activate the little spec. It would skim up, then back downstream, or it would ski across current. When the fly glided slowly in front of a trout's snout, the rise was a gentle sip, in the manner the fish had been taking naturals.

The first trout I played in was a 2-pound brown. Larger trout were rising on that overcast autumn afternoon; the air was a few degrees above freezing shortly after a snowfall. The hairline tippet could not hold the biggest rainbow I've ever hooked on a dry—a lunker on a #28! However, the 40-inch, double tippet (equal lengths of 6X and 7X), which allowed the currents to present the fly so appealingly to the feeding trout, produced memorable fishing. Though fluttering naturals speckled the air, the fish weren't taking them, but they did take the little artificial at their snouts.

When trout are taking full-winged adults, the basic hackle-only Midge dry still produces. While sparse hackle suggests a fluttering insect, the barbules penetrating the water more closely represent the insect's six long legs.

Often trout become selective to a realistic wing silhouette of the naturals; midges have one pair of wings. On one recent trip, trout wouldn't take my hackle-only midge. The first presentation with the same pattern having upright, divided wings of grizzly hackle tips, simulating a drifting insect fluttering its wings, brought a sure rise.

One of the winged versions is easy to tie. A section of soft feather (such as wood duck or mallard) is used for both tail and wings. Position the bundled fibers on the hook for the tail. A soft fiber tail allows the fly to wiggle a bit as it drifts—a little motion to impart life. Then bind the dubbed thread forward for the abdomen. Bend the feather up and tie it as divided wings. Clip the wing tips in proportion to the fly. A turn or two of hackle fits in nicely. You can

From a snowy bank on the famed Firehole River in Yellowstone country, I caught this brown on a midge tied to a 7X tippet.

place eight #24s within the perimeter of a penny, and these quick-to-tie midges are handy to have, for trout generally prefer a fresh fly.

Trout perceive wing form in finite detail. One time, when my fluttering-winged midge floated unheeded by a feeding trout, I put down my fly rod and crawled close to the stream, not 2 yards from the brown. Peeking through tall grasses I saw the trout was selective to midges that drifted at rest, their wings flat back over the abdomen.

Impressionistic patterns may be tied with a pinch of fine-fibered hair. A highly realistic tie has paired hackle-tip wings, tied flat, low over the hook. Hackle is flared under the hook because the natural at rest balances on its legs while adrift.

A consistently successful dry is a no-hackle with wings of hen-hackle tips. I tie these in the above-mentioned silhouettes, as well as horizontally spread for flush-floating spinners. One still summer morning, trout fed steadily on fallen midges, plentiful on flat water.

In the profusion of insects, the fly that most attracted trout was a no-hackle that appeared to be minutely different—one wing sticking up, the other flat or immersed.

Though white-to-cream midges and blackish midges are common, they may be of numerous other colors, including shades of gray. When trout are selective to any particular hatch, color can make the difference. Some years ago on Michigan's Au Sable, Bill Monohan was catching trout at a steady pace. "They're taking olive midges," Bill pointed out. He gave me some #24s, and I joined in on the action.

Trout will develop a taste for midges, and then a dry fished to a likely feeding area can attract the occasional, large, nonrising trout, especially during low, clear water. It has happened for me during late winter on the lower Bitterroot in Montana, as well as on limpid streams during warmer seasons.

One episode showed me that the nature of a trout may not be readily apparent. I spied a brown lazing 3 feet deep on the bottom, under a steady parade of naturals on the surface. It wasn't rising to them. I had a #24 gray midge on the 6X tippet for other trout surface-feeding nearby, and I drifted it along a lane directly between this larger trout's eyes. The beauty tilted up swiftly, as though in response to a large terrestrial, and took the midge deftly. It was autumn, which is when spawning-bound browns will chase and strike, but such a take in this circumstance seemed unusual. That 3-pound brown lumbered around, splashed, and leaped before tiring. A sizable trout uses considerable energy against a light tippet and rod, and I patiently revived it for release.

For midging, a limber rod with a sensitive tip has two distinct attributes. It delivers a feather-light presentation, and it has delicacy when tightening a light line to notch the small hook into a trout's jaw. I prefer playing the midge game with a light, short rod and 2–4-weight line.

For roll casting on foliage-hemmed creeks, a leader as short as 7 feet may be advisable. In most instances, a 10–12-foot leader is fine; the 14–16-footer is often helpful in low, clear water. A light tippet is of immeasurable importance. Tippets of 5X down to 8X are standard for the midger.

In midging, a rising trout of any size can take on the appearance of a trophy. A 9-incher may feed with wiles worthy of the fly rodder's best efforts. A sprite, pan-sized trout may never really end its splashing and tugging when played in. Just the same, release it very gently. The sport of light-line fly-fishing may well have its brightest future with these smallest of abundant aquatic hatches.

Wire Nymphs

HAVING WIRE NYMPHS in your fly box is the fly-fishing equivalent of the baseball manager who has great relief pitchers in the bullpen. Really good relief pitchers come through when called on to pitch out of a jam, and wire nymphs can help when you're in a tough situation on stream.

Small wire nymphs can take wary, midge-feeding trout—even trout that resumed feeding shortly after being stung by a hatch-matching pupa—and larger wire nymphs can induce nonfeeding trout to strike. Flashy wire nymphs can sink quickly to drift close to the snout of large visible trout holding in wait, or you can use the simple pattern to bring fish out of hiding when you're fishing the water.

While they are most deadly when used as midges, wire nymphs are also effective imitations of larger insects. These nymph patterns, tied with an abdomen of wire spiraled tightly around the hook shank, with a head of herl or tuft of fur, should be in every fly-fisher's fly box.

Even small patterns tied with copper or gold wire to represent chironomids quickly slice through the surface film with minimal disturbance, and their shine attracts reluctant trout. For midging, diminutive wire patterns suggesting larvae and pupae are deadly. I use #16–24 patterns in various ways to imitate unhatched midges successfully.

During hatches, when trout rise to pupae just under the water's

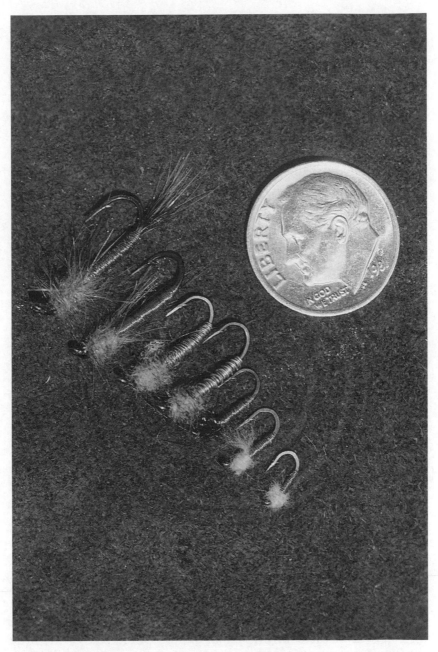

Wire nymphs, a favorite of mine, are small but deadly. (Photo taken by John Randolph; reproduced with permission)

surface, a wire pattern can take those difficult fish that refuse a matching imitation. Under these conditions, I usually grease the leader to within a few inches of the fly so the pattern drifts inches under the surface. With greased tippet, a fly tied with one layer of wire hangs from its fur head in the surface tension to lure trout that are sipping insects in the film. The pupa's posture and shine are deadly at the surface.

When chironomids are adrift, large trout frequently look for the tiny naturals near the source of hatches and in funneling currents that carry large numbers of the insects. The rippling current sliding along instream vegetation and weed-bed edges offers an abundance of unhatched midges, and large trout often feed secretively on these numerous vulnerable insects. A heavier wire nymph, presented in the mass of concentrated naturals, can take large trout even during times of surface activity. Nymphing beneath a hatch or to likely waters near sources of hatches is as effective with a small, shiny, sunken midge as it is during other hatches of larger stream-born flies.

When trout aren't visibly feeding, screening the current may reveal numerous drifting larvae. If it does, try a wire nymph for an effective presentation to trout lies both shallow and deep. I've taken trout by slowly drifting a #16 wire nymph (tied on a heavy, short-shank hook) 4 feet beneath a greased leader.

I often start with a wire nymph when I see a good trout lurking on a shallow flat or along the stream edge. Such a trout may be looking for a particular food item, but often it will take a small wire nymph drifted to its snout. A visible trout can take a little nymph without giving any signs that it has taken, and I've hooked trout simply by tightening the line when the nymph should be at the fish's snout. Remember that a trout can take and spit out a small, hard fly quickly, so look for the white of its mouth or the turn of its head or a mere nod, and strike to that movement. I do so even when using a strike indicator. A half-inch piece of hollowed fly line works well as a floating indicator, because it doesn't interfere with presentation of a light tippet and will signal an imperceptible take of the little wet pattern.

The popular Brassy is a nymph made of copper wire and a fur

head. A wire nymph's shine is eye-catching, and herl or a tuft of fur for the head of the fly can closely match the color of the natural insects in your waters. When a trout has seen enough of one fly type to resist taking it or when emerging insects abound, adding a wisp of hair at the throat and a low wing pad creates a more detailed impression of the pupa. I use a fine wisp of the same fur used for the head of the fly, and the undulating, soft fur can make the difference.

Although copper and gold are the most common colors for wire nymphs, red, silver, and other colors of wire also work well. Once a hovering brown trout feeding steadily on emerging cream midge pupae wouldn't take my dark copper pattern with a cream fur head and a wisp—a pattern that worked well earlier in the same feeding slot. So I switched to a gold-bodied fly with the same fur dressing, and although the trout was aware of my presence, it continued to feed on midges while I changed flies. Momentarily, the brown snapped in the new gold-bodied pupa. Hatches of cream midges appear often along this shallow, rippling run, and in mid- and late season they are the main emergence that lures trout to hold in the open and feed on the #22 pupae.

When I tied a copper nymph using a head of dark muskrat with flared, natural brownish guard hairs (porcupine-type image), the copper nymph took on new significance. The pattern, tied on a hook one size larger than the winged adult, became deadly on days when caddises hatched. Its shine resembles the sparkling, gaseous bubble associated with the caddis pupae. It worked well as a searching fly, one that seduced trout on the lookout for a natural, particularly in swifter runs and the heads of pools—those areas where trout are accustomed to taking caddis larvae and pupae.

During late-spring hatches of predominately #16 and #18 caddises, with a few #14s also emerging, a copper nymph tied on #16 and occasionally on #14, 2X-long hooks can provide remarkable angling. One morning during my first outing to a particular meadow stream, when trout seemed to have stopped feeding after an outstanding couple of hours with fur nymphs, I knotted a #12, 2X-long copper nymph with a dark fur head and flared guard hairs onto my tippet and began catching fish. Soon I gave my partner one of the flies, and he joined in on the renewed action. The larger copper nymph drifted deeply through the stream's swift gravel and stony runs and pools, bringing nice trout out of the stones to feed vigorously.

A larger wire nymph is not just an outlandish fly to stir trout. The success of any fly has its roots in entomology. I learned later the same day that larger caddises were on the menu. I'm reminded of a friend who said he caught a lunker brown in New Zealand on a #8 copper nymph. Various sizable copper nymphs have since given me large trout.

Wire nymphs generally are regarded as patterns for riffle water because they produce well over gravelly and rocky bottoms. But they're also deadly when patiently dredged along the bottom in gentle flows. Presenting a large copper nymph on a slow drift along the bottom and then drawing the rod slowly back in sidearm fashion, to creep it, at times attracts large trout.

A nymph with a reddish cast, such as a copper wire nymph, is deadly under a shady sky or in low-light conditions, and large copper nymphs are productive in murky water, even in turbidity that would seem to require a pattern that "moves" more water to alert the trout's vibration-detecting senses. In dark water or near the bottom of deep water, a copper wire nymph can be eye-catching. For such conditions, I often use a larger copper nymph with a tail of red squirrel.

Wire nymphs also work well when cast across and down and then swung across stream, but usually I just drift them or dredge the bottom with them. The flies also make handy dropper patterns; they are "sinkers" that catch trout.

The Deadly Hare's Ear Scud

SOME YEARS AGO I tied a Scud based on the designs of some popular shrimp flies. The pattern gave the trout something new, and it resembled other morsels, especially the caddis larvae and pupae common in virtually all trout streams. This simplified and easy-to-tie Hare's Ear Scud has helped me catch large trout from spring holes and ponds, environments teeming with freshwater shrimp and other crustaceans. The Hare's Ear Scud is as deadly today on the waters I fish regularly as it was when I began fishing it, and the fly is a great searching pattern for prospecting new waters.

Over the past five years I've shared the versatile Hare's Ear Scud with new and old friends I have met along spring creeks and limestone streams. The consensus among those fishermen is that the Hare's Ear Scud helps them take larger trout, often on their initial use of the fly. Some of the fishermen had been using other shellbacked patterns for years; others were novices who began catching trout when they used the Hare's Ear Scud.

The fly is tied of one material, the stiff guard hairs and fur of an English hare's mask (the rabbit face). The fur is the ingredient for perhaps the best-known of our universally productive nymph patterns, the various hare's ear nymphs. A hare's ear nymph from one fly tier may not be the same fly you purchase from another tier, but the fur from a hare's mask—its texture, translucence, and colors (ranging from grays to tans to creams, with hints of pink and yel-

251

My Hare's Ear Scud

low)—has long been accepted as a key ingredient of killing nymph patterns. I merely tie the Hare's Ear Scud in the silhouette of a freshwater shrimp.

The fly works particularly well when presented beneath a floating strike indicator. When you cast up-current in a swift riffling run, set the indicator up to 1½ times the depth of the crevices you are fishing so that the Scud drifts freely through the crevices. Naturals wash from their moorings on vegetation and from nooks and crannies on the stream bottom, and trout feed actively in these food lanes of the stream.

Hanging a Scud vertically beneath a float presents the fly in a tantalizing way. This balanced "rig" is especially effective on large trout lurking near the bottom in deep currents and in slow water. Even with a weighted Scud, adding a small split-shot (or several split-shot to distribute weight) to the tippet 6–8 inches above the fly often helps ballast the drift. With the proper weight on the tippet, a floating indicator enhances the natural drift by subtly slowing the

Scud's pace. The hanging Scud almost magically takes trout that ignore other patterns and presentations.

Of course, the indicator can be set on the leader to present the Scud at various depths, and the fly is most effective when presented to the feeding level of the trout. When naturals are adrift in the current, trout may feed a bit higher in the stream. Presenting a Scud from middepth to as shallow as 12–18 inches below the floating indicator can drift the fly over trout looking up for drifting morsels.

Hare's Ear Scuds often work well during insect hatches, too. Trout that rise to the surface during a hatch frequently take several emerging aquatic insects for each fly sipped from the surface. Other trout, especially large ones, dine solely on the emerging naturals under the surface, ignoring the flies on the surface. A Hare's Ear Scud, tied the size of the aquatic hatches or one size larger, has proved so effective that I often use a Scud to catch trout during a hatch.

Tied lightly weighted, with four or five turns of light wire on the rear of the hook, a buoyant Scud hanging from a floating indicator or a greased leader will drift effectively in an ascending slant. Lightly weighted Scuds can also be fished just subsurface or floating when the fly is dry or when it is tied loosely so that air bubbles form in the fibers. I carry various sizes and weights of Hare's Ear Scuds, and I use the one that can best be presented at the trout's feeding level—bottom to top.

Hare's Ear Scuds in #8 to wee #18 match the usual range of sizes common in a stream. Sampling of naturals is always enlightening in order to learn not only the sizes of naturals that are present but also their colorations. Shades of tans and grays can be matched with natural hare's ear, while dyed hare's masks of olives, yellows, or oranges are among colors notably common in matching artificials to the hues of the natural.

The Hare's Ear Scud can work best when it is fished tightly to instream moss beds and other vegetation. The naturals are abundant in the stream's "spinach," and trout hold along the weed edges to feed on them.

I prefer a neatly tied "fresh" Scud. But if I tie the pattern with the natural tips of the stiff guard hairs for the tail and legs and soft fur for the body, it doesn't lose its form, and with use it develops that "bugginess" attributed to fur nymphs that become deadlier the more you use them. The Hare's Ear Scud is a hardy fly that keeps on taking trout.

The All-Marabou Leech

AS I HEFTED the trophy trout, the glistening, wet, dark All-Marabou Leech hanging from its jaw shone starkly real. Its smooth marabou form on the long-shank hook appeared to be inseparable from the trailing marabou tail. More important, *in* the water this thin fly of one texture drifts (or swims) seductively, in willowy fashion, and is so "natural" that trout often take it presented dead still on the bottom. That 4¼-pound brown took a #8, 3X-long Leech presented on 6X tippet and was landed on a 2-ounce fly rod.

Even in such a moderately large size, this weighted, sleek fly casts nicely and is easily fished on light tackle. I often choose to wield a sensitive rod not only for the sport but also because a sensitive rod better handles a light tippet that readily sinks a fly to wary trout. A gossamer tippet gives the ultimate presentation, especially for line-wary browns in slow water, and the Leech is deadly when fished as an easily captured prey. I've taken big trout deep in a limestoner on a 2-weight outfit not just as a challenge but for the consistent effectiveness I enjoy with light tackle.

The All-Marabou Leech gives the highest hooking percentage of any wet I've ever used, even with a light outfit and tippet. That's impressive also because any long, marabou-tailed fly as a rule can bring short hits and bumps from trout. Yet in the years I've been fishing this Leech on #8 and smaller hooks with a variety of presentations, the short takes have been few. However, "strikes" to this fly,

My All-Marabou Leech

especially in slower water, are often deceptively gentle, belying the size of the trout. A trout takes its trim, meaty silhouette as surely as it would take a natural, an attribute of a "soft" wet pattern.

High hooking percentage is also a result of presentation. Most of the presentations I use mimic a leech that is easily captured. When the fly is figuratively spoon-fed to the fish, the trout tastes the morsel rather than instantly spitting it.

Not only is the no-hackle form a realistic leech, but also undulating marabou filaments on the body suggest other lifelike morsels. The fly is impressionistic of other natural foods, especially aquatic nymphs and larvae. Small Leeches are notably nymphlike in their appeal. Fred Arbona related from scuba diving that "nymphs of mayflies, caddis, stone flies, and others are actually lively, hairy little creatures that, when active, closely resemble undulating minileeches."

The trout I mentioned earlier was taken from a larger pool on a small stream that isn't a postcard scene for the fly-fisher. Much ideal water for this lure is not always pretty or pristine, and the naturals are common in sluggish current and edges where sediment sifts and settles. Silty waters with threads of current paths over clean bottom provide feeding lanes where trout lurk for drifting naturals. Big trout hunker in the comfortable eddying edges and are largely cannibalistic, but a leech is a comparatively easy meal.

Drifting the Leech and rolling it along the bottom are the most consistently productive methods in my angling. While I've become somewhat pool-oriented with this fly, a Leech remains fetching in shallowing edges and also on flats and glides usually in moderately slow current.

In shallow water or deep, the Leech appears to be natural when presented with the following delivery: Cast well upstream of slack or still water "targets" that are behind or aside welling incoming currents. Wary trout under a placid or slow current may detect any line or leader movement on or in the water that interrupts the fly's natural drift, so let the fly course naturally and settle on bottom. Leave it motionless up to minutes. Then, crawl it a few inches to a stop; a deadly direction is broadside across current, but that's not mandatory. The short crawl attracts a trout cruising along bottom or one that has been eyeing the motionless fly. Then swim the Leech along bottom, finally ascending it in an undulating, snaky swim toward the surface. Sizable trout can take a Leech at any time, from dead still on bottom to the time it laps the surface.

A Leech is an exceptional fly in murky water and at anytime to stir lethargic or recently fished trout. Numerous times one has given me action when fishing behind other anglers using nymphs. Whether a stream has become murky because of natural occurrences or from anglers or cattle, leeches are often stirred up from the bottom and are adrift in the stream. Dark Leeches work especially well in discolored water and along a dark bottom. A dark Leech has also given me larger trout at night; often the take occurs just as the fly is lifted upward in the water.

Light tackle also is effective on those bright days in low, clear water when trout hold deeply. When the stream seems fishless, this can be a sign that larger trout have taken up feeding stations on bottom. We often think in terms of light line and small flies for such conditions, but the time-proven adage "big fly, big trout" has given me results with the Leech.

Most of my larger trout have taken a natural drift or a fly on bottom, yet a swimming Leech can attract other fish. Here are two distinct ways to swim a Leech effectively: First, with the fly on bottom, jig it upward and let it fall, using quick upward flips of the rod tip. Second, swim the Leech steadily with a side-to-side motion of the rod tip while stripping in line to a rod tip positioned horizontally or lower to the water.

In sampling real leeches, you'll find varieties in coloration. In sluggish waters having some silty bottom, wading anglers must sometimes remove leeches from legs or waders; they are common also in stream areas with a hard bottom, particularly below soft-bottom pools and glides. You can also see them snaking easily along slack stream edges, and of course leeches are found in the stomachs of trout. Many naturals appear in camouflage or hues compatible with the stream bottom and water color. Black and shades of brown (light chocolate to reddish and dark brown) are universally effective flies. In crystal streams with a light bottom, I have found grayish olive leeches.

On streams I ply often, I avoid fishing this fly to the extent that the trout become wary of the imitation. When not overused, the Leech presented in an appealing manner has the effect of a knock-out punch on larger trout. This Leech is too valuable as a follow-up pattern to other wets and for times trout are on the lookout for naturals to be used randomly or indiscriminately. In this vein, it's a great fly to entice a trout that has just struck short or flinched off another wet. Even in a calm hole, for example, where trout frequently cruise bottom to feed, upon missing a fish I sometimes change to a Leech and sink it while the fish is likely to be there. Even a stung trout will take the All-Marabou Leech solidly.

Tie an assortment of these quick-to-wrap flies and tote them wherever you go. Several years ago, I took big fish in Wisconsin and Montana during a 24-hour span—thanks to my All-Marabou Leech and modern air travel. The episode began on the Root River, a Lake

Michigan tributary in southeastern Wisconsin. I caught autumn's beautiful lake-run browns and fresh steelhead using small Leeches down to #14. I fished to nightfall that cold October day, then thought about my Montana trip during the two-hour drive home. It would be good to get back to Big Sky country once again. I hurriedly packed my gear for the plane and car trip to Five Rivers Lodge near Dillon.

By late afternoon the following day, my friend John Hutchinson and I were fishing the ranch ponds. Most of our gear had been temporarily delayed by the airlines, but I luckily had the same vest I had worn the day before. Inside were the small Leeches that had so enticed the Lake Michigan salmonids. Casting parallel to the banks, I caught Montana trout after Montana trout into the western twilight, oblivious to the Rocky Mountain chill. I had come a long way with light tackle since I first waded Montana waters.

Previous Publication Credits
Topical Index

Previous Publication Credits

Mighty Mini-Rod (*Fly Fisherman*, Oct. 1970; also adapted from "Fine Points of
 Fishing: The Short Fly Rod," *Fishing World*, Dec. 1978)
Advanced 2-Weight Tactics for Larger Trout (*Orvis News*, Apr. 1991)
Same Trout Again! (*Scientific Anglers Fly Fishing Quarterly*, fall 1990)
Small Wets for Big Bass (adapted from "Little Flies for Largemouths," *Scientific
 Anglers Fly-Rodding for Bass*, 1981)
Match the Hatch for Bluegills ("Fly Fishing for Panfish," *Scientific Anglers Fly
 Fishing for Panfish*, 1981)
Skamania: Late Summer's Glory (Aqua-Field's *Fly Fishing Quarterly*, fall 1997)
Bountiful Spring Creeks (*Field & Stream*, May 1984; also adapted from "Mini
 Spring Creeks," *Fly Fisherman*, July/Aug. 1979)
Low-Water Camouflage (adapted from *Scientific Anglers Fly Fishing Quarterly*,
 summer 1991)
Fly-Fishing the Wind (*Fly Fisherman*, Apr. 1978)
Fishing the Edges Dry (*Scientific Anglers Fly Fishing Quarterly*, summer 1990)
Terrestrial Strategies (*Fly Fisherman's How to Catch Trout*, 1985)
Grasshoppers Only (adapted from "Bank on Hoppers," *Western Outdoors*, Aug.
 1971; and from "Gems of 'Hopper Fishing," *Field & Stream*, Aug. 1982)
Fish Soft: Hair Bugs and Drys for Top-Water Bass (adapted from "Soft Flies,"
 Scientific Anglers Fly Rodding for Bass, 1980; and from *Scientific Anglers Hair
 Bugs and Dries for Topwater Bass*, 1983)
Nymphing under the Hatch (adapted from *Fishing World*, Mar.–Apr. 1978)
Sight Nymphing (adapted from *Scientific Anglers Fly Fishing Quarterly*, winter 1973)
Short-Line Nymphing (adapted from *Fly Fisherman's How to Catch Trout*, 1985)
Nymphing during the Slack Hours (adapted from "Small Streams—Big Browns,"
 Scientific Anglers Fly Fishing for Trout, 1987)
Light-Tackle Streamers (adapted from *Scientific Anglers Fly Fishing Quarterly*,
 spring 1992)
Drop the Bomb Accurately for Larger Steelhead and Salmon (adapted from
 Scientific Anglers Fly Fishing Quarterly, spring 1991)

Early-Morning Eye Opener (adapted from *Fly Fisherman*, June–July 1973)
Mayfly Emergers (adapted from *Scientific Anglers Fly Fishing for Trout*, 1984)
The Duns of Autumn (adapted from *Fly Fisherman*, Dec. 1985)
Small Stream Caddis Bonanza (adapted from *Scientific Anglers Fly Fishing
    Quarterly*, winter 1992)
More on Caddis Drys—the No-Hackle (*Fly Fisherman*, Feb. 1993)
The Unknown Fly That Turns On Trout (*Fawcett's Fishing Journal*, 1976)
Midges: Tiny Dynamite for Trout (*Scientific Anglers Fly Fishing Handbook*, 1982)
Wire Nymphs (*Fly Fisherman*, Dec. 1988)
The Deadly Hare's Ear Scud (*Fly Fisherman*, May 1991)
The All-Marabou Leech (adapted from *Fly Fisherman's Fly Tying*, 1988)

Topical Index

CASTS

beating winds: casting under the wind, 91; fish concentrating on insects in surface film, 239, 240; for fish feeding on Hoppers, 118; fishing lee areas, 96, 97

casting across cover: from bank, 83; for drift and hang of fly, 109; for drift with dry fly, 207; across obstruction to skate fly, 105; to simulate falling insect, 112

curve casts: combination casts (illustrated), 106, 107, 108; current-formed for dry-fly presentation, 219; full curve, 87; right-angle curve to set up broadside retrieve, 60; to set up broadside skimming dry fly, 200; to set up quick sink with wet fly, 177; shallow curve for broadside presentation and fully looped curves, 106; short hook in tippet, 80; slight full-line curve for nymphing, 143; variety needed for new presentations on same pool, 219

hidden casts under and around a fish's window of vision: angled cast for short drift, 87; angler's low profile, 86, 87; fishing edges of the window, 87; need for longer cast to deep-holding fish, 87

long casts with weighted fly: technique, 31; triangulation, 167

reach casts: backhand, 88; directional, short reach to sail fly over obstruction, 105, 106

sidearm: flick cast, 83; hidden presentation, 78; to present dry fly beneath a bank, 104; to skip dry fly beneath over-hang, 105

LIGHT RODS

fish-parrying techniques: angling rod to keep tippet away from fish's jaw, and near end of fight, 30 (photograph); anticipating fish foray, 32; canting rod, 95, 102 (photograph); to free fish in a snag, 27; high horizontal rod against running fish, 27; pointing rod down the line 208; slack-lining, 25

hooking methods: for bulging fish, 137; with emerger just below surface, 240; line pull, 141; for nymphing, 155; opposite bowed line, 60, 150; side arm, 30, 31; slip strike, 160

landing larger fish: beaching, 40, 60, 95; jaw-lifting bass, 45; tailing grasp, 40

light-rod performance: balancing reel, line-weight choice, 20, 21; with

light-rod performance (*cont.*)
  braided leader, 18, 30; cushion
  against light tippet, 30; mechanical
  advantage against fish, 32, 33; sensitivity for wet-fly presentation, 255;
  streamside advantage of longer rod,
  tippet strength to break rod, 19; for
  warier trout, 43
reviving and releasing fish, 40, 41
short-rod performance: accuracy,
  tight-loop presentation, 25, 26; basic
  casting technique, 23, 24; direct
  control of fish, 16, 27; low casting
  plane, 78, 79; more space for cast
  configurations, 224; relaxed rod
  grip, 26; variety of water types, 16

ON-WATER TECHNIQUES
awash dry fly, the: with caddis, 218,
  228; drowning cricket, 89; with Hopper, 115, 118; on still water, 45; with
  Trico spinner, 193
brief action with caddis dry: matching
  the pace, 228; nudge, 216; "snapping" the water, 220; twitch, 228
broadside wet-fly presentation: direct
  swing, 62, 63; double-swing with
  streamer, 163, 164; to feeding level,
  140; imparting action to a swinging
  fly, 164; through murky shallows,
  180; in odd spots, 166; quick nymphing, 139; shallow sweep, 31; short
  swing, 139; swimming along bottom, 160; upward retrieve in slower
  water, 62; wriggly swim, 62
caddis on a natural drift: amid frenzied
  caddis activity, 222, 224; with no-
  hackles, 227; with realistic dry, 218
fishing a streamer upstream: drift and
  swim technique, 165, 166; jigging,
  59
fishing one-handed, 147
fly-first presentation: curl-in nymphing, 148, 150; dry fly downstream on
  swift water, 235, 236; importance of,
  80; presenting dry fly tail-first down-

stream, 80; triggering successively
  feeding fish, 98, 99
full delivery with wets: adapted to
  river-run salmonids, 176, 177; with
  streamer or nymph, 164, 165
hand-twist retrieve, 46
hanging a wet fly downstream: with
  marabou, 179; preceding upstream
  retrieve, 176, 177; with streamer,
  163
high-rod techniques with sunken flies:
  in back-swinging eddy, 156; clothes-
  line technique, 147, 172; for shallow
  presentation, 175
presenting dry fly immediately after
  fish feeds: with caddis, 220; with
  cricket, 89
simulating kicking terrestrials: matching kicks of specific insects, 113;
  twitched and double-twitched dry
  fly, 89; using sound to stir fish and in
  murky waters, 114, 115
skimming the dry fly: with caddis, 220;
  with cranefly pattern, 100, 101;
  current-induced with midge, 241,
  242; imitating an injured baitfish,
  127
slow-water nymphing: low rod, 157,
  158; upstream method, 155
still-fished dry fly: with bass bugs, 125,
  129; with brief pause on current buf-
  fered by cover, 107, 108; on calm water, 50, 51; with cricket on sluggish
  current, 89; with no-hackle mayfly,
  208; on stream eddy, 108, 109
still wet on bottom: with leech, 255;
  for river-run salmonids, 178, 179; in
  slack-water edges, 157
sudden impact with dry fly: bouncing
  fly off bank, 104; with caddis, 220;
  to cruising fish, 129; how to tilt cast
  for, 104; to match fall of specific
  terrestrial insects, 113; with stone
  fly, 232; using weight-forward line,
  77
suspending a wet fly: with backswim-

mer in micro-habitat, 84; in current under floating indicator on loose line, 61; gentle takes, 174; with indicator or greased leader for sight-fishing, 144; with mayfly emergers, 197; with midges, 240; for nymphing under a hatch, 137; piece of fly line doubling as both floating and sunken indicator, 148; with scuds, 252, 253; short-line nymphing, 147; with sow bug, 115; in still water, 51, 52; with sunken terrestrial imitations, 113; with wire nymphs, 248

top-water retrieves using rod action and line-stripping: bouncing dry along current, 101; the leisurely jogged offering, 125; rapidly swimming retrieve, broadside to current, 63; on still water, 126; varying the retrieve, 128, 129

upstream nymphing with upward draw of rod: to drift caddis pupa, 212; for natural drift and sensing light take, 148; to set up slack-line presentation, 156; to twitch up caddis pupa, 224